Watching Sarah Rise

Watching Sarah Rise

A Journey of Thriving with Autism

Jennifer Celeste Briggs

Foreword by Samahria Lyte Kaufman

SHE WRITES PRESS

Published 2025
Printed in the United States of America
Print ISBN: 978-1-64742-824-2
E-ISBN: 978-1-64742-825-9
Library of Congress Control Number: 2024917242

For information, address:
She Writes Press
1569 Solano Ave #546
Berkeley, CA 94707

Interior Design by Kiran Spees

She Writes Press is a division of SparkPoint Studio, LLC.

Dedicated to my daughters.

Some people are so much sunshine to the square inch.

—Walt Whitman

I love you so much to the square inch.

—Sarah Wellington

Foreword

WHAT CAN YOU SAY about a woman who dared to believe in her daughter on the autism spectrum when others saw only limitations? What can you say about a woman who dared to take a road less traveled to help her daughter thrive?

Here's what you say about Jenny Briggs, the mother of Sarah and the author of *Watching Sarah Rise: A Journey of Thriving with Autism*: she is brave, daring, passionate, and persistent! I honor her love and deep caring for Sarah while giving all of herself during this journey that has led to Sarah's rising.

Who am I to comment and share with you, dear reader, about the uniqueness of Jenny's and Sarah's inspiring journeys? My name is Samahria Lyte Kaufman, and with my husband, Barry Neil "Bears" Kaufman, I created an unconventional, intensely respectful, and loving methodology called The Son-Rise Program® to help families and parents transform themselves and their children on the autism spectrum.

When I was thirty years old, I gave birth to my third child, Raun. Within the first months of his life, it was clear that our son was different. At the age of two, he was diagnosed as severely autistic, with an IQ under thirty, and we were told he would never be able to talk and develop normally. The suggestion from professionals was that Bears and I focus on and be happy with our two daughters and that we consider placing our son in an institutional, residential facility. When we saw the harsh, adversarial methods being used with children in the facility to try changing them, we realized that we would never subject Raun to the behavioral techniques that professionals and educators used at that time. Instead, we created our program based on an attitude of deep respect and love for him and all aspects of his autism. We had no expectations. We would take it one day at a time. We would be open to all that was Raun!

So I began our program with Raun in a quiet, nondistracting universe—our family bathroom—working twelve hours per day, seven days a week. At first, I had no idea what to do, but Bears and I had three deep convictions:

Though others saw limits for our son, we knew nobody could predict the future. We would not be scared by what professionals told us would not be possible.

We decided Raun was always doing the best he could in trying to take care of himself—and that included his strange, repetitious behaviors, like rocking his body and flipping his hands, which professionals told us that we should stop him from doing.

We committed to joining his world; we would do what he did so we could understand him more and show our love and acceptance of him. We wouldn't move against him. We wouldn't be adversarial. We would engage him in his unique universe. Perhaps, with such love and acceptance, he would one day be inspired to join us and take steps out of his world—and into ours. And that is exactly what Raun eventually did.

Our lives were consumed and enhanced by this beautiful journey and by those who volunteered to learn and be a part of Raun's universe. Our intense program continued for three and a half years. Against all expectations from the professional community, Raun grew into a highly social, very verbal young man, bearing no signs of his original challenge with autism. He graduated from an Ivy League university; wrote his own book, *Autism Breakthrough: The Groundbreaking Method That Has Helped Families All Over the World*; owns his own business; teaches families and professionals to help children on the autism spectrum with their challenges; and travels the world doing seminars and podcasts. He is also joyfully married.

Bears wrote a book about our journey with Raun called *Son-Rise: The Miracle Continues*. An award-winning NBC movie was then made about our adventure called *Son-Rise: A Miracle of Love*.

After the completion of Raun's program, Bears and I created the Option Institute® International Learning and Training Center, which offers transformational programs for adults with challenges in their lives—covering such areas as relationships, parenting, women's issues, past traumas, health, and happiness. We also founded the Autism Treatment Center of America®, where we and our staff have taught the Son-Rise Program for over forty years to parents and professionals. As of this writing, over forty-five thousand people worldwide have come to our campus to learn how to help themselves and their children. Several million people have been touched by our teaching through our books and outreach programs worldwide. One of those people is Jenny Briggs.

For me, Jenny is a very special person. I have known her for twenty-five years through courses, dialogues, and her training at the Autism Treatment Center of America. Using that training, she ran her own Son-Rise Program for Sarah. Jenny's dedication abounds as she shows up, trying one thing after another, no matter what, to discover the depths and gifts of having a child that's different. I celebrate her.

She climbed her own personal mountain, and you will be inspired to join her in that beautiful and imperfect journey. Jenny writes this memoir from the heart, which makes this book even more special. Sarah grows and changes in the most remarkable ways, as does Jenny.

This book will also be a heartfelt journey for you, dear reader; it offers you the opportunity to grow and change yourself in the most wonderful ways.

Samahria Lyte Kaufman is the cofounder and cocreator of the Autism Treatment Center of America, The Son-Rise Program, and the Option Institute International Learning and Training Center.

Introduction

SARAH IS A FEISTY, stubborn, creative, kind, funny, snuggly, determined individual with a chromosomal difference when compared to neurotypical people.

Sarah's chromosomal blueprint resulted in delays in all areas of development, such as learning to pick her head up when doing tummy time, eating solid food, reaching for toys, rolling over, sitting, crawling, walking, and talking. We had no idea if or when she would meet these developmental milestones. By six months, we knew Sarah was different from her peers. We saw what they were able to do that she could not, but we didn't receive a diagnosis until she was one year old.

Her genetic diagnosis frequently comes with behaviors associated with autism, which is the case for Sarah. Autism has a wide range of how it presents in people. Eye contact can be fleeting or not what people expect from a social interaction. Social cues may go unheeded. There can be a strong interest in one subject to the exclusion of all other subjects. Behavior can be controlling, exclusive, and repetitive. This book is about the beginning of Sarah's story of growing and learning beyond expectations, conveyed through my experiences as her parent.

I am Sarah's mom. I am blessed to have Sarah as my daughter, and I am just as feisty, stubborn, and snuggly as she is. In college, I became certified to teach English literature before deciding that it was not for me. Instead, I found my calling as a massage therapist and as an

Alexander Technique teacher, both in private practice and teaching at a massage school. The Alexander Technique is a simple yet deeply nuanced approach to living more comfortably. Sometimes, it is labeled as bodywork, and people associate it with posture, but really, it is about how you think about how you move, exist, and interface with your world. It is about noticing your habits so you can consciously make changes if the habits no longer serve you. There are so many tiny choices we make without knowing we are making them, and each impacts how comfortable we are at any given moment. The Alexander Technique is aimed at helping a person be more efficient and at ease in any situation. It meets a person where they are in a loving and supportive way to help them become their best self. This is similar to the Son-Rise Program.

The Son-Rise Program is an approach taught by the Autism Treatment Center of America (ATCA) that lovingly and impactfully connects with people with autism. ATCA teaches parents to develop programs for their children, often with dedicated focus rooms and teams of volunteers found and trained by the parents. ATCA supplies information and techniques to help foster connection, language, eye contact, and interactive attention span through one-on-one, child-led play. Parents run programs based on what works for their lives and timing, ranging from two hours to forty or more hours per week. It can be an intense undertaking but can have an enormous impact.

Running a full-time Son-Rise Program was probably the most important and meaningful thing I have ever done in my life. This book is a journey through the incredible life-changing experience of running a Son-Rise Program for Sarah. My husband, Carl, and I decided to call our program Sarah-Rise to honor the program as well as our daughter. As you will see in the following pages, my parenting was never what I would deem perfect, but it didn't need to be.

That is what I hope you gain from journeying with us—the understanding that you do not have to be perfect to make significant changes that impact you and your loved ones. There is help to be had. There was support for parenting Sarah, beyond my wildest dreams, once I was ready to dive into the training and ask for volunteers. There are no guarantees, but there is an abundance of hope that hard situations can become easier, that language can be on the horizon even if no words are currently forthcoming, and that anything seemingly impossible could, in fact, be a little bit possible.

I wrote this book because I want to share our story, the mundane and the miraculous. Maybe our experience will bring hope or help to others. Maybe other parents will read of our successes and struggles and recognize themselves. Maybe someone will be inspired to learn more about The Son-Rise Program. Maybe hearts that are hurting and longing will hurt a little less.

I want to share how completely fallible and imperfect I am to show you that you can be that way and still run a kick-ass program for your child. You can still show your overflowing love in abundance even if you have days when you think you might get a divorce if you were married to your child.

I want you to feel that you can trust yourself. Even when something feels daunting, if you decide it is the thing to do and you embrace that with your heart and soul, then you can make it happen, and the help will follow. You can trust yourself if something feels like it would be too much or not the right fit. You don't have to do it all, and you don't have to be someone other than who you are.

My husband and I have had a profound journey with Sarah, in large part due to our decision to run Sarah-Rise. I have seen the goodness of humanity in the way people show up for Sarah, for me, and for our whole family. I marvel that I can be the recipient of so much goodness. The most inspiring, loving, creative people came into our lives, some of them staying with us for so many years that they are akin to family. It astounds me and touches my heart every time I think about it. Without Sarah being who and how she is, I don't think I would have had my heart warmed and opened in such a way. I stretched myself in ways I could not have previously imagined. Sarah-Rise is the best and most helpful thing I ever did for Sarah, for our family, and for myself. If I could go back in time and change anything, it would be to start my Son-Rise Program training sooner.

I also want to share the general picture of our experience and Sarah's path with various challenges, as well as the specific stories born from my weekly updates, which I have been writing since Sarah was almost five. I started these updates when I started in the Sarah-Rise room. I've learned that my words have been helpful to others; they've told me they felt less alone with their emotions and struggles after reading because I gave voice so honestly to my own. The updates preserve my memories and experiences in real-time, so what follows is not rose-tinted by memory but is essentially as raw as when I lived it the first time. My writing can serve as a window for you to see the reality of our playtimes, how phenomenal our progress was, and how exhausting and draining parenting can be, especially parenting a child with special needs. I prefer the use of "special needs" over "disability," though I know others prefer the reverse. I do not see that there is anything wrong with Sarah; there is no "dis" about her, but I do believe she needs extra help and support, which is precisely what "special needs" indicates for me.

Autism and genetic diagnoses span such a continuum that our story can't be used as a blueprint. Every journey will be different. There is no guarantee that The Son-Rise Program will bring changes in language or easy social interaction for every participant, although that has happened for many families. But I hope our story can touch your heart, soften judgments you may have about yourself, and help you see your situation with new eyes. Maybe it can help you see a diagnosis with new acceptance and give you renewed determination. I don't believe that any prognosis is set in stone.

I would be remiss if I did not acknowledge that there is controversy around autism and whether it is respectful or appropriate to consider it a condition that should be treated. The most important truth for me is that I want to give Sarah as much support as possible to flourish and thrive as her best self. I want her to know how deeply she is loved. The Son-Rise Program helped me communicate that love in a way that empowered Sarah and everyone who was blessed to be part of the program.

I have no idea how much Sarah will learn or what new capabilities she will achieve. She doesn't need to change at all for her to be an important, beloved part of society. She already gives love, brings joy, and has meaningful connections with people. Isn't that what most of us want anyway?

This book is focused on Sarah, so other family members do not get nearly the same spotlight, and I ask you to forgive the omission of many wonderful details, especially about Sarah's sister, Amy. Amy is the best sister for Sarah that I could ever imagine or create in my dreams. She has been an excellent model for helping Sarah to play. Amy is neurotypical, and there is no diagnosis to explain what a snuggly, kind, gentle, creative, funny, energetic ball of wonderfulness she is.

Carl is my loving, kind, smart, funny, patient, curious, and thoughtful husband. He is often a cool cucumber surrounded by one, two, or three hot peppers. Carl and I work extremely well as a team, and we delight in each other's presence and mind. Our senses of humor are aligned so that I often feel like he tickles my brain. He can help me laugh even when things feel awful. He will also sit with me and listen to my tears without offering suggestions, a gift that I requested early in our relationship. While I was the one to lead the Sarah-Rise venture, I could not have done it without his enthusiastic support.

There are many volunteers, specialists, sitters, and family members who have been, and continue to be, extremely important parts of our journey. It has certainly taken a village to get to where we are now. To those who read my weekly updates and asked when I would write a book . . . here it is.

1

The Beginning

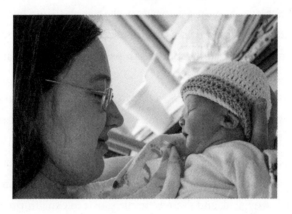

SARAH'S ENTRANCE INTO THIS world was slightly fraught, my motherhood plans going awry at the earliest opportunity. I intended to give birth without medication. As it turned out, my psyche wasn't up for handling that. I went into labor naturally, but I had preeclampsia and needed magnesium. Things weren't progressing, so the next step was Pitocin. At that point, I asked for an epidural, knowing that I couldn't remain my same self if I didn't have help. Sarah's heart rate wasn't responding well when I pushed, and soon, I found myself on my hands and knees, breathing into an oxygen respirator. Suddenly, I wasn't so confident about giving birth to a live baby, and things started feeling surreal. How was this me in this moment worrying about my baby?

Within about a minute of things not going well, a special team was in my room with forceps. My midwife stayed by my side to help calm me. I trusted him, which helped me handle all of what transpired to get Sarah out of me, forceps, specialists, and all. Sarah was born quickly and, though tiny, seemed to be in good health.

I, on the other hand, felt like I had been hit by a truck. Due to the magnesium given for preeclampsia, I wasn't allowed to be alone with Sarah for the first twenty-four hours, as my body was still under careful surveillance. I practically couldn't be alone with myself since I was confined to the bed. Carl changed Sarah's tiny diapers and gave her sponge baths for her teeny-tiny peanut self. The first two hats the hospital gave her were too big. The clothing we had for her was gigantic. Nothing fit until a friend gave us some preemie clothing. Sarah wasn't early enough to warrant the usual preemie classification since she arrived at thirty-eight weeks, but she was a mere five pounds, five ounces.

Once we were finally at home, I questioned my sanity at having sent my mom and stepdad back to their home across the state. What was I thinking? Every aspect of existence now seemed monumentally difficult. Sitting, standing, using the bathroom, nursing, waking at all hours—how was I supposed to do this? I remember feeling more tired than I had ever felt in my entire life. One time, as I held a crying Sarah, I had a horrifying moment of looking at the corner of the dresser and thinking that if I just whapped her head against it, then my life could go back to normal, and I could sleep. The thought was just a thought. But that gives you a sense of how exhausted I was. The idea of laundry or trash was overwhelming. Carl took care of everything like that, but it was hard to let go of managing our small world in some way. Luckily, we had many friends who brought us meals, all of them having survived being new parents and thus understanding the great need for food to magically appear.

Sarah was so tiny, and my milk wasn't coming in immediately, so the concerned pediatricians gave me a thin tube to tape to the side of my breast when she nursed so that we could supplement my milk with formula. That worked well enough until my milk came in, but it was a full team effort that required Carl's help, pillows, and a visit from La Leche League. My neck was achingly uncomfortable from craning to see what I was doing and attempting to get Sarah positioned just right.

At six weeks old, Sarah was doing weird, twitchy things that turned out to be seizures. We didn't know what was going on, but in my head, I bellowed to the universe, *No! We will not be having infantile spasms!* I knew that those were no good at all. Into the hospital we went for a forty-eight-hour EEG in a shared room with a small uncomfortable chair-bed to share with Carl. The seizures didn't happen at all while we were at the hospital and then, blessedly, only happened a couple more times at home after the hospital stay.

After six months, we knew Sarah was different from her peers, these miraculous peers who would roll and grab for toys. How did they do that? We started down the road of tests. A CT scan and an MRI to look for hydrocephalus (liquid on the brain) or anything else amiss, a basic-level genetic test, and a lot of blood work ordered by the neurologist. In the end, the full microarray blood test ordered by the neurologist yielded results and answers.

When he finished telling me the diagnosis over the phone, the neurologist said, "Have a good day." I'm sure he didn't know what else to say. I felt like the floor was being sucked into a black hole underneath me and as if everything was spinning at the same time. Yet, here in this newly spinning, bottomless world, I still had to function and care for my baby.

Special Children, Challenged Parents by Robert Naseef explains that parents of children with disabilities go through the grieving process. It can be challenging because you still are caring for this person with their disability while you process the grief of them not being who you thought they would be. As I see it, your life as planned gets turned on its head, and you must function upside down, pretending that you are right side up. You are grieving and trying to pretend that you are not. I remember walking home from my neighborhood's main street, and as my feet traversed the familiar sidewalk, I was stunned by the realization that I had a child with special needs. *Me! Jenny Briggs! What? This is not, not, not how it is supposed to go. This happens to other people. Not to me.*

We met with genetics specialists who told us what other specialists to see. We needed to take Sarah to a cardiologist because sometimes people with her diagnosis have heart problems. She needed an ultrasound to make sure her kidneys were in the right place. Her thyroid, eyes, and hearing should be checked annually. Luckily, her organs were in the right place, and all systems were in working order.

The geneticists also suggested that we *not* search online for information except to review a couple of recommended sites. While I did take Sarah to the extra appointments, I did not listen about not looking online. Or maybe I did, and the information that I didn't want to know was on the recommended sites. I don't remember. What I do remember is feeling like maybe I should kill myself. I haven't ever been one to lean in that direction or even contemplate it much. And I still wasn't, compared to how I know some people struggle. But reading about how kids with her diagnosis often don't learn to walk, talk, use the toilet, or feed themselves was one of the bleakest, darkest moments for me. Here, we had this diagnosis with a possibly bitterly difficult prognosis but no real information about our specific case. Having a diagnosis helped me feel less guilty about Sarah's situation, though, realizing that it wasn't anything I did or didn't do during my pregnancy.

While we struggled during her first year to help Sarah learn to roll over, sit, crawl, stand, walk, talk, reach for toys, and any other skills that come so easily to those with a full set of chromosomes, the biggest challenge we faced was getting her to eat enough. All went relatively well until she was six months old, and then, as my milk supply unexpectedly dwindled and she wasn't interested in solid foods, she stopped gaining weight. At nine months old, she was diagnosed with "failure to thrive," and we had a nutritionist come to the house, first weekly and then every two weeks, to weigh Sarah. I ran from my child needing a feeding tube like my life depended on it. Many kids have feeding tubes, and it is a great help to them and their parents. But to me, a tube felt like giving up or admitting to a disability. I was concerned that if she got a tube, then she wouldn't have any incentive to learn to eat more by mouth.

In the hopes of avoiding a feeding tube, I scoured the grocery aisles for the highest-calorie foods regardless of nutritional value. We added powdered fat to her food. I fed her oil straight up and butter pats. She could have ice cream anytime she wanted. She could basically have anything she wanted anytime as long as she would eat. I tracked calories, measuring what was left from her super-duper high-calorie "juice" and "milk," fortified drinks that barely resembled those words. I counted every Goldfish or hot dog bite. I would sing and dance and put on a one-woman show to entertain Sarah and get her to eat. I would walk and walk and walk with her in the stroller because she would eat better then. I would drive around and around and around because she would often eat in the car. Anything. I would do anything.

There were many moments when I felt desperate and despairing about her eating. I cried, cursed, and screamed in the kitchen. There were also many moments when I felt desperate and despairing about her ever learning to roll over, crawl, or walk. It all seemed so impossible. The desperation and struggle were present for much of her first few years, from around six months through age four. Certainly, there were also many wonderful, easy moments and times of ecstatic celebration when she rolled over, crawled, and walked. The eating gradually became easier and better, but it was so gradual that there wasn't one definitive moment when we declared that we had crested the hill we were climbing. It was more that there were daily celebrations when she happened to eat well and easily.

When she was perhaps seven months old, I remember lying on the rug with her as she did tummy time, something she hated with a vengeance I didn't know was possible. Instead of lifting her head to strengthen her neck muscles, she would push her forehead into the rug, beet red with rage. But every once in a while, she would be motivated to want a thing. One particular afternoon, she wanted my copy of Herbert Kohl's *36 Children*, with its distinctive black cover and white writing. She scooched toward it the teeniest bit, and it was a victory coupled with the despair of how impossibly difficult this seemed.

Though I had a supportive husband, friends, and family, I was so lonely. There were so many hours that it was only Sarah and me. While the diagnosis may have absolved my guilt at her condition, I certainly still felt responsible for her progress or lack thereof. The physical therapist, occupational therapist, and speech-language pathologist came weekly and left me with suggestions and homework—and many hours in which to feel inadequate.

My friends with babies the same age as Sarah were kind, and we had playdates, but they were coming with these perfect overachiever babies because their kids happened to get the full deck dealt to them, whereas my kid was missing a few cards. Sometimes, this was all fine, and sometimes, it broke my heart. Sometimes, I secretly yearned for a new baby to be born to a friend and for that new baby to be like Sarah in some way because then I would be less alone.

When Sarah was a year old, she could sit on her own. At eighteen months, she started crawling. By the time she was almost three, she could walk on her own. She was playing with toys. She was even eating a bit more easily. She was not talking, but she could use sign language for many things, and we made a board with pictures of food so she could indicate her preferences.

When Sarah was three and a half, we found out that Carl's cousin was pregnant with her second child. Carl and his cousin are close in age and were close companions through their childhoods and college, and her pregnancy reinforced our desire to offer the same opportunity of companionship to our offspring. Though we had already been thinking about having another child, I had previously said I wanted Sarah walking, talking, and eating well before we made a move for more. Since she was eating enough (even if not healthily) and she was walking, we decided to go for it.

Amy was born on my birthday in March. Sarah had just turned four.

Within those first four years, we tried many different therapies for Sarah to help with many different challenges. We did occupational therapy, physical therapy, and speech therapy. We tried feeding therapy, horseback riding therapy, water therapy, conductive education, massage, Reiki, acupuncture done on me with the hope of impacting Sarah, and the Anat Baniel Method, which is gentle bodywork aimed at waking up and creating new neural pathways. I worked with a nutritionist.

Sarah received weekly speech sessions with Gregory. Gregory was a speech therapist we paid for out of pocket because he came to the house, even after Sarah aged out of Early Intervention, and had a wonderful way of basing his interactions on Sarah's interests. The first time he came to meet Sarah, she was three. He talked and signed at the same time, and whenever Sarah made a sign or an attempt at spoken language, he said, "I hear you." It warmed my heart, and he has been working with Sarah ever since.

We made sure our house had climbing apparatuses and a variety of toys to help with fine and gross motor skills, which was a way of allowing occupational and physical therapy development to continue through play at home. We consulted with an adviser for Gut and Psychology Syndrome (GAPS) to guide us when we tried that dietary regimen to help Sarah's digestion. We worked with a naturopath to help with Sarah's overall health, and we were advised on neurodevelopment. We followed the How to Teach Your Baby to Read program, which worked beautifully. We tried the related How to Teach Your Baby Math program, which didn't work at all for Sarah.

Through everything we tried, it was The Son-Rise Program that garnered the most impactful, long-lasting changes and created a framework for other therapies to be successful.

2

The Son-Rise Program

"We do not put limits on the possibilities for your child."
—Autism Treatment Center of America

I HAD KNOWN ABOUT The Son-Rise Program since I was in college, getting ready to be an English-literature major and majorly stressing about doing well, fitting in, finding a forever romance, and the other challenges that go along with becoming a more independent adult. My mom and stepfather gave me a gift of books by Barry Neil Kaufman (aka "Bears"). One book was *Son-Rise: The Miracle Continues,* and the other was *Happiness Is a Choice.* They thought these might help me because I struggled at times with my own levels of happiness. Kaufman's approach is an empowering one, explaining that our beliefs influence our feelings. Using the Option Process® Dialogue, Barry Neil Kaufman and Samahria Lyte Kaufman (the original Son-Rise Program parents and the founders of the Option Institute and Autism Treatment Center of America) guide people lovingly and non-judgmentally to question their behaviors so as to uncover any hidden beliefs that may be unhelpful. I found this mightily intriguing at nineteen. Just recently, a friend pointed out how unusual my interest had been given the amount of goth culture and misery poker surrounding us at college. (Misery poker is where everyone shares what they have to deal with as if trying to one-up the others on how bad they have it.)

The summer after my sophomore year at Swarthmore College, I

attended an eight-week course at the Option Institute called "Living the Dream," which was taught by the same people who run ATCA. It was a wonderful eight weeks where I learned a lot about myself. I also put pressure on myself to be happy because I somehow twisted the message from the Option Institute and began telling myself that I should be happy all the time. That isn't their message. In fact, they have no *shoulds*. But I desperately wanted to be happy *all* the time and thus, conversely, made myself rather miserable at times, giving myself no wiggle room to just be me. I'm still really glad that I took the course, and after some time and tears, I was able to apply what I learned about beliefs and choice while being gentler to myself when I had feelings other than happiness. The course also enabled me to spend a lot of time with the original Son-Rise Program parents. I knew that they were trailblazing, loving, inspiring people who had helped bring about incredible changes for many families. In the world of parents who decide to run Son-Rise Programs, Bears and Samahria are celebrities. I was so deeply moved by the Son-Rise story when I was in college that I sort of wished I would eventually have a child with autism so I could run such a life-changing program.

While I knew that The Son-Rise Program was used at least once to help a child with severe feeding issues, by the time I was struggling with Sarah's delays and feeding issues, I was reticent to try The Son-Rise Program. I didn't think it was the thing for Sarah, or, if I'm even more honest, I didn't think I could do it for Sarah. I knew from my college days that The Son-Rise Program would be a huge undertaking, which was hard to contemplate when each day felt like a giant hurdle that I was unsure I'd be able to clear. I was daunted, overwhelmed, and not ready to turn to this resource that was essentially sitting in my back pocket. But by the time Sarah turned four and was still not talking and not reliably making eye contact, I reconsidered.

Sarah had some moments where she was doing repetitive behaviors and seemed to be unreachable, as if in her own world, and I thought that maybe The Son-Rise Program could help. I started with a free consultation call with the Autism Treatment Center of America to discuss my situation. I explained Sarah and our life, and the family consultant encouraged me to make plans to attend the training. He explained that after I had completed the training, I could design a program that worked for my family.

ATCA does offer intensive programs where a family brings their child to ATCA, receives training and feedback, observes The Son-Rise Program staff playing with their child, and receives help to unpack their own belief baggage that may be a hindrance to their goals. However, the consultant encouraged me to do the training and start my own program before considering an Intensive because it was important to see that I could make a difference on my own. In all honesty, I originally spoke with Carl about The Son-Rise Program by saying, "Maybe I should just take Sarah up for a weeklong Intensive and let the ATCA people fix her and her eating struggles." I was desperate for anything to get Sarah enough nutrition to support whatever she needed for language to develop, but after my phone consultation, I realized it was not going to be a quick fix. Sitting on the couch with Carl the evening after my phone call, I hiked up my emotional bootstraps and started making plans to attend the training course in person.

Bears and Samahria initially developed The Son-Rise Program to help their son Raun. Raun was on the autism spectrum and was intensely in his own world. Instead of stopping his repetitive behaviors—as so many therapies sought to do—Bears and Samahria decided to join Raun in his behaviors. They wanted to understand him and make sure he knew he was loved. They used his isms (exclusive, repetitive behaviors) as a way to build a bridge of connection. (Many people refer to such behaviors as "stims," while ATCA refers to them as "isms," as do I.) One way to understand The Son-Rise Program approach to connection is as follows: If I am watching my favorite TV show and you come over and tell me I should come watch your show instead, I will probably ignore you. But if you sit and watch my show and love it too, then I will be more apt to trust your recommendation of what to watch next—your show.

Samahria and her team of volunteers spent twelve hours a day, seven days a week, in a distraction-free room playing one-on-one with Raun. She and Bears developed innovative ways of connecting with Raun and building upon that connection to help him process the world more easily. He eventually was able to engage completely and easily with others and became the global director for the Autism Treatment Center of America, where they teach people to run Son-Rise Programs of their own. What follows is my specific path with the Son-Rise Program I ran for Sarah.

Carl and I talked about all that would be involved with my going away for a week for the training and to set up a program. First, I wasn't going to bring Sarah with me. The Son-Rise Program Start-Up is just for grown-ups. I had never been apart from Sarah for so long, which was a big deal, and it would be a big deal to come home and set up a program, too. Carl worked a very full-time job and often traveled for work, and while I had his support in all of this, it was going to be me at the helm.

The first step was the training.

Since Amy was only five months old and still nursing, I couldn't be apart from her for a week. My mom, known as Mom-Mom, came with me to Sheffield, Massachusetts, to help care for Amy while I attended class. Carl's sister Sonia, who lived in Seattle, flew to our home in Pittsburgh to help Carl with Sarah. It was a team effort, as everything has been since that very first week I was away. My mom, Amy, and I stayed at a bed-and-breakfast a few minutes away from ATCA and the Option Institute campus where the training took place. The three of us ate lunch and dinner on campus, but I attended class by myself.

Over the next two years, I attended two more weeklong training courses. They were easier than the first course because Amy was older, and I didn't need to nurse her on my breaks. I rented a house for the three of us twenty minutes away. My mom and Amy had adventures during the days, and Amy and I reconnected for snuggles and play in the evenings.

You may be wondering why I brought Amy and not Sarah to my trainings. Amy was fairly easy to care for, as she always has been and continues to be. Not that she doesn't have her challenging moments, but Sarah was and is more challenging. I wanted to be able to focus fully on learning to support Sarah without the stress of parenting her. It also would have been difficult for my mom to care for both kids in spaces that weren't our own home and were without other supports. The weeks of training turned out to be wonderful bonding times for my mom and Amy, as well as a good opportunity for Carl to fill my shoes regarding Sarah and have more focused time with her. It also allowed Carl's sister, Sonia, and Sarah to have lots of one-on-one time together before we even knew how much of a role Sonia would come to play in our future program.

On the first day of training, I hugged and kissed Amy and my mom, left them in a small, slightly awkward sitting room, and headed over to the building where the training would take place. It was a new building that hadn't been there when I attended the Living the Dream program in college. While the campus was familiar, everything also felt new, and I was a little nervous as well as excited. I entered a large room filled with BackJacks (aka floor chairs), blankets, tissue boxes, and many parents seated with their notebooks and ready attention.

We listened to various teachers, including Bears and Samahria Kaufman, Kate Wilde, and William and Bryn Hogan. Kate had been part of ATCA for many years. She was one of the primary teachers during my time there and has since written multiple books about Son-Rise Program strategies. Bryn is Raun's sister and participated in his program. She and her husband, William, also ran a program for their adopted daughter. Their daughter had autism, and the program helped her develop fluent language and an easy comfort with neurotypical interaction. Everyone who spoke during the training was inspiring, and I learned many specific techniques that seemed simple and obvious once stated yet were not things I had thought of on my own.

Throughout the week, the facilitators made space for us to share our feelings and our experiences thus far parenting our kids as we explored what worked and what didn't. I hadn't realized I was carrying a ton of emotional bricks around with me until I dropped them during that first training week. So much guilt and responsibility fell from my soul.

I had been feeling guilty for Sarah's condition, as if it were my fault, even though logic said it was just a fluke of a chromosomal abnormality. I thought that *if only* I had been different in some way when trying to get pregnant, or *if only* I had worked with Sarah more in the first few years, then she wouldn't have faced the challenges she did. Being in a room with so many other parents who were struggling with similar challenges, and being with teachers who held no such judgment toward me, was freeing. I left the week filled with passion, determination, and drive beyond what I had had before.

The idea of running my own Son-Rise Program felt overwhelming but also completely doable and attainable. I could run a program. I could make time to be with Sarah in this way. Every night, when I talked with my mom and when I called Carl to share about our days, we discussed the changes I would soon be making in our life to make a program possible. I brainstormed about what childcare I could arrange on a regular daily or weekly basis to allow me time to do The Son-Rise Program. We also talked about how some of the big plans for a dedicated room would have to wait until more aspects of our life were ready.

As soon as I returned with my new Son-Rise Program knowledge, things changed. I gave Sarah more space and time, but I also asked much more of her. I started interacting with Sarah differently. I requested more in terms of language, and I waited for her response with more time, encouragement, and belief in her ability than I had previously given her. I celebrated her attempts hugely. She was already able to make each individual sound for the letters of the alphabet, but I rarely asked her to combine them. Usually, I would jump into action at the slightest verbal output, but now I was much slower to respond physically. I gave her my immediate and encouraging attention, but I didn't leap to do her bidding as soon as I guessed what that bidding was. I made her work a little harder.

One afternoon I was home with the girls and Sarah started saying, "Mmm," and making the sign for "milk."

She was asking for a milkshake, so I asked her if she could say the whole word. I waited with delight in my eyes and bated breath.

"Mmm . . . kkk . . . sh . . . kkk."

"Oh my goodness! Yes!"

I could not contain myself. *Yes, I will get you a milkshake, you amazing individual!*

Our world started shifting with the milkshake moment, and it didn't stop there. With only a few dedicated moments a day, Carl and I saw changes. This was exciting because I didn't yet feel like I had a program up and running *at all*. I was still in the preprogram planning phase, so our bits of Son-Rise Program time were really just small adjustments to our lifestyle. When Sarah wanted to walk up and down our front steps, I joined her and walked up and down our front steps, too. In the past, I would have stayed put and observed—to make sure she was safe. Now, I was enjoying the moment of connection with her and the game that those steps could be. I made sure she could see my face easily when I was talking. I gave her more time to respond and believed more in her possibilities.

Carl and I decided to call our future program Sarah-Rise. We were excited to eventually get things up and running with more focused hours in a day but, at this moment, nothing was officially in place except for changes in my mindset. I wasn't ready to establish our program more fully because we were in the process of moving to a new house. We knew right away which room would be the Sarah-Rise room. A small bedroom with magenta walls was the corner room at the top of the stairs, with windows on two walls. It had a closet with one shelf. In this room, we could have dedicated one-on-one time with Sarah to help her with language, eye contact, connection, and playing games. The Sarah-Rise room would enhance everyone's ability to focus because we wouldn't have distractions.

The move itself felt exciting and overwhelming. Thankfully, Sonia flew to our aid again—to help with the packing, the moving, the unpacking, and the childcare. I remember thinking her presence was vital as I stared at the rooms piled from floor to ceiling with boxes. After much of the unpacking was done and we were moved in enough, I started doing half an hour a day of Sarah-Rise time in the Sarah-Rise room. There was intentionally very little in the room. We had a scrap of carpet from our old house, a plastic kid-sized table, and a few toys on the closet shelf. We didn't want toys or books that Sarah could reach. We wanted her to communicate with us in some way about what she wanted from the shelf. We didn't have pictures on the walls because we wanted to be the most interesting thing in the room.

For my first few sessions, we played with containers of Play-Doh. Sarah loved opening and closing lids, so that is what we did together. As we opened and closed our Play-Doh containers, I waited for Sarah's attention to come to me freely. When it did, I held the Play-Doh next to my face and commented on it. Having it next to my face made it easy for her to look at the item and at me at the same time, and it encouraged her to look at my mouth. If she could watch my mouth as I said words, then that would make it more feasible to learn to say the words herself. We had one container with soft dough and one container with hard dough, so the first words I focused on teaching her were "soft" and "hard."

I was slightly intimidated about the idea of doing this real time in the real room, which was different from the small lifestyle changes I had been making—asking for more language and waiting for it or joining her for walking up and down the front steps. This room felt sacred. Here, I felt like I didn't know what I was doing, and I also knew exactly what I was doing. There was a magical, soft, quiet quality to being in there with Sarah. I could be with her and focus on connection, love, and teaching. There was no pile of mail or stack of dishes beckoning to me, and I knew that Amy was cared for and occupied. I could be 100 percent present with Sarah with our simple guidelines to follow.

Keeping it simple was as much to help her as it was to help me. I wasn't aiming to teach her the entire English language. I was aiming to get her closer to saying one or two words a little bit more clearly and fully than she had done before. As "soft" and "hard" became easier for Sarah to say, I also worked on her clarity with "Amy," instead of her usual "Mm-eh-ee," and with saying the names of colors—she often liked pretending our white tissues were many different colors, and she delighted in correcting me if I picked one up and said the wrong color.

Once Sonia went back to Seattle, I lost my daily hours in the room with Sarah, which I had squeezed in during the time Carl was at work, around mealtimes, snack times, groceries, nursing Amy, seeing clients, continuing to unpack and settle in, and painting the upstairs bathroom. The bathroom was painted by the time Sonia left, but the rest of the daily household and childcare needs of laundry, dishes, book reading, generally occupying two little ones, vacuuming, food preparation, and diaper changes for both kids were still part of my daily experience. By the time Carl got home at the end of his workday, it was time for dinner and the kids' bedtimes. I knew I needed assistance during the regular workday hours to get Sarah-Rise off the ground, and I was entirely overwhelmed with how to begin.

"Do one small thing at a time," I told myself. My dad often reminded me of a line from a poem that reads, "Leg over leg, the dog went to Dover." This was our family motto for just doing the next step and trusting that enough of these small steps will add up to the journey.

The first thing I did was get out my binder of materials and notes from The Son-Rise Program Start-Up. Since Sarah attended preschool for a few hours each morning, that gave me time in the mornings when I didn't see clients to attend to household needs. One morning, when Sarah was at preschool and Amy was napping, I reread all my training materials and notes. ATCA provided suggestions about how to find volunteers. That was one small step I could do. I could send an email to my friends here in Pittsburgh and those who might know people in Pittsburgh, asking for help. Along with this adorable photo of Sarah to grab peoples' attention, I sent the following email:

Hello all,

As you know, our spunky, sunshiny daughter Sarah is not quite like other kids. This summer, I learned how to run a Son-Rise Program with her. We are calling it Sarah-Rise. It is an intensive one-on-one home-based therapy program where we work in a distraction-free room with Sarah, encouraging increased eye contact, language, and social connection through play and following her lead. It is an extremely loving and accepting therapy that has had amazing results with some kids. While we have no idea how far Sarah will go with this, the exciting part is how limitless our goals and desires for her can be. We can want everything for her but need nothing from her to continue loving her with all our hearts. We want you to know about this new part of our lives, and we are hoping that you or someone you know may be able to help us with it.

The Son-Rise Program is based on the work of Bears and Samahria Kaufman whose son, Raun, was severely and supposedly unreachably autistic in 1974. They were told there was no hope, but they decided they wanted Raun to know how much they loved him. Samahria began working with Raun in a small room, joining his repetitive behaviors, and celebrating each tiny flicker of his acknowledging that she was with him. They spent years working twelve hours a day, seven days a week with him. He emerged from his autism completely. This approach has been used to help many other children emerge completely from autism and other challenges. I have personally spoken to parents whose children were extremely challenged in varying ways and now are thriving, typical kids. As I said, I don't know if this will be Sarah's story, too, but it doesn't hurt to try! We are already seeing improvement and growth, and we are enjoying our connection with her, which is the most important part. To learn more, you can go to http://www.autismtreatmentcenter.org/.

There is a book by Barry Neil Kaufman (aka Bears) called Son-Rise: The Miracle Continues.

We are looking for volunteers to be part of Sarah's team. If you are interested in being in the playroom, we are looking for a commitment of four to six hours a week for six months. This will include two two-hour sessions in the playroom each week plus training, feedback for how to increase your effectiveness, and a two-hour monthly meeting with all team members. We are looking for loving, nonjudgmental, energetic people who are open to learning new ways of interacting with Sarah.

We are also looking for volunteers to watch Amy while I go into the playroom with Sarah. Ideally, two to four hours a week for six months would be a lovely commitment, but an hour a week is also extremely helpful.

Reasons why it is awesome to be a volunteer in the playroom: For the time you are in the room, you drop all baggage and judgments and joyously connect and play, stretching your creative self. You practice being energetically encouraging and happy no matter what. In fact, this is the way to be most effective. The Option Process (the basis for The Son-Rise Program approach, explained in the training provided) helps you sift through any beliefs or baggage that might be getting in your way. So, by helping Sarah grow and change, you also grow and change, possibly becoming happier in all of your life, but at least for the time you are playing with Sarah.

If you think this is a lovely idea and want to help but volunteering doesn't make sense in your busy life, then please just cheer us on. All support is most welcome. Cooking us an occasional dinner is also quite helpful, allowing me more time to focus on Sarah rather than on food prep. :)

If you are interested, please get in touch, and I will provide more information and we can decide if this is the right fit for you. If you know anyone who might be interested, please feel free to share this with them and give them my contact information. Some of you already know what we are up to and are a part of Sarah's team in other ways; I send this to you because you are a part of the team, and I want you to know how we are proceeding (and maybe you know someone who will love to participate).

Generally, we are seeking afternoon and early evening participation (1:30–3:30, 5–7 ish).

Thanks! I hope you are all well and thriving.

Jenny

3

Sarah-Rise Volunteers

People usually just call me Sarah. But when I am in the Son-Rise room, I am called Sarah C. When I am called Sarah C., I am exhausted from playing so hard. I am asked to read the same book over and over again. I am told to "move back" when I am being annoying. I am used as a human ladder to climb upon and reach the toy shelf. I am a construction worker, creating cribs and castles out of blocks. I am a bus driver, a cook, a cat, an airplane, a storyteller, and a preschool teacher. I am a tent pole. I am a blender. I am an observer. I am a student learning about patience, fun, and creativity. When I am called Sarah C., I am loved by a little girl named Sarah and I am my most joyful. Being called Sarah C. has shown me all the amazing things that I can be, and I will forever cherish that lesson. And it's all because of a little girl named Sarah, whom I will love forever.

—Sarah Ceurvorst, volunteer

PEOPLE OFTEN ASK ME how I found my volunteers. I started with that email and expanded from there. Some people offered meals, others were ready to leap into being with Sarah or hanging out with Amy, and some wrote, applauding our efforts and wishing us well. Every response—and there were all kinds—mattered to us. Here is a sample of the responses I received.

Sonia wrote:

ME, me, me, meee!!! I want to help! Quick, have Carl invent a teleportation device so I can be there anytime you need me. Or a cheaper way for me to fly there. :) You are doing a wonderful job. This is a great email, and I'm so proud of you. I know it can be tough to ask for help. Keep it up! Yay, Team Sarah-Rise!

In hindsight, Sonia's response is notable. I had no idea when I sent my email that later, she would become such an integral part of our program. I included family near and far in case people had Pittsburgh connections and so they knew what we were doing.

Erika, one of my best friends, who lives in Europe, wrote:

This sounds like a really beautiful way to go—and a way that can only benefit Sarah. I wish I was there to help and volunteer (I would love to), but I can't see any feasible way of doing it. If I can help in any way, please let me know. You guys are so loving and supportive and are building such a strong supportive family in all of this. It really is beautiful. Keep up the good living!!

My fellow massage therapist and friend, Kara, wrote:

I loved your email—how it showed your commitment and love for Sarah and how you unabashedly asked a village to help. I can be on the dinner team for now and can bring something once a month.

Please let me know if there are particular weekdays where a dinner drop would be most helpful.

My mother-in-law, living in the Midwest, wrote:

Wow. Beautiful photo, well-written letter. I'm a little too far away to volunteer but lean to the west-northwest anytime you need a cheer, and you'll hear us!

Laura, who did become a volunteer, wrote:

I would love to be part of your plans. I have time freed starting in the middle of January. My life goals have always included selfless service to all, and I can't think of a better way to honor that than playing with Sarah or creating time for you to do the same. The only experience I can offer is my endless patience.

My friend Karen, who was part of the inspiration to share my family updates with a wider audience as she wanted to follow our journey, wrote:

I have been keeping you guys in my thoughts and prayers. I hope all is well. She is very lucky to have such a committed mother and father who would undertake such an extensive project. Keep me posted on how things are going.

One friend forwarded my message to their friend, who, though well-meaning, didn't have the space to trust me with my own decisions for my own child. My friend's friend knew of some children who had autism who had been helped tremendously by Applied Behavior Analysis (ABA). Although she raved about it, I had heard of a range of experiences with ABA, some positive and some less so. I'm sure it matters who is facilitating the children, how they were trained, and how well they mesh with the children. I knew that many Son-Rise Program families turned to Son-Rise after having a negative or unhelpful experience with ABA. When we spoke, she continued raving about how much the kids changed thanks to ABA. I'm glad it worked so well for them! I know the same can be said of many who go through Son-Rise Programs. It wasn't the pitting of ABA against The Son-Rise Program that bothered me; it was the fact that this person who didn't even know me or Sarah wanted to save me from making a mistake. She must have missed the positive details in my email about how Raun and other kids had flourished. Or, she missed my determination and joy to proceed as I had planned.

My plan was not open for discussion. I share this experience to point out that everyone may not be on board with the intention to run a Son-Rise Program. I wasn't deterred in the slightest. It probably helped that the resistance came from a stranger and not from a family member. I know some people persevere against resistance from friends, family, and sometimes spouses, and I'm glad I didn't have such challenges. Volunteers came from various sources of connection. Some were my friends, and some were acquaintances of neighbors or students of Alexander Technique colleagues. Everyone brought with them their own unique gifts and what made sense in their lives as a way to contribute to Sarah-Rise. Some played with Sarah, some played with Amy, some brought food, and all of it mattered.

Every volunteer was welcomed and trained in the same manner. We started with short bits of time in the Sarah-Rise room, where I explained the basic principles of The Son-Rise Program and some techniques for playing effectively. I wanted volunteers to show enthusiasm regardless of how successful Sarah was at whatever she'd just attempted.

If you were my volunteer for the Sarah-Rise room, I would explain that one of the most important things to understand is how to "join" Sarah when she isms. "Joining" is a Son-Rise Program term that describes a certain way of being with someone when they are isming. It means getting your own identical or similar toy or engaging in a similar activity, without intruding on the person's space. You seek to emulate them, but you aren't simply copying them. You are really doing the activity, too, and letting yourself become immersed in it. You, too, are enjoying it fully. The difference is that you are attentive to any flickers of eye contact or acknowledgment of your presence, ready to respond if and when those occur.

Regarding Sarah, if she is really into sticking plastic candles between her toes, you join her. Sit a few feet away from Sarah and take a few plastic candles or crayons and stick them between your toes. You want to position yourself in her line of vision, so she is able to look from her toes and candles to you. Make it easy for her to see you, but do not request or require her to look at you. Be silent. Have fun with your own toes and candles! If she looks at what you are doing, then you can change it up a bit. You could put two candles together between a set of toes or put the candles between your fingers! If Sarah looks at your face, then you could hold a candle next to your face while you say "candle" with delight in your eyes. You can explicitly thank her for looking at you or give a thumbs-up or point your fingers toward your eyes in celebration. If she is still attending to what you are doing, then you could begin putting the candles in the pretend cakes that come with the candles and sing "Happy Birthday." This addition or variation to the activity would be called "building" in Son-Rise Program terminology. If Sarah is engaging with you then you are no longer joining; you are building and inviting further engagement. Add something new only if she is looking directly at you. If she seems to lose interest in you, do not be deterred or feel you did anything wrong! Go back to joining with those candles in your toes. If she never looks at you at all, that is still okay! It is a gift to give her the time, space, and opportunity to interact. She gets to decide what to do with that gift. What is important is that you are presenting it.

Whatever the play or the joining is, it is important that you position yourself so that Sarah can easily look into your eyes and face but without crowding her. Since she is often sitting, to make it easy for her to look at you, you might have to lie on your belly propped up on your elbows. Or sit a few feet away from her.

I observed volunteers remotely by watching the live-stream footage from a wireless video camera we installed in the room, and then I gave them feedback. Before the camera, volunteers would verbally describe their time, and I would base my feedback on what they said, but I found it helpful to see things firsthand. A volunteer's first time at the house would involve two fifteen-minute sessions, and I would give feedback after each session. The next time would be two half-hour sessions. Then they would work their way up to doing two hours in the room at a time. Usually, this worked beautifully, and volunteers were up and running for their two-hour sessions in a matter of a week or two. Occasionally, someone thought this would work for them, but after one or two sessions, realized it was not a good match for their schedule or it was not what they thought it would be, and that was okay, too.

After each session, volunteers spent some time writing a few sentences about what they did, what worked well, and any questions that they had. We had team meetings once a month with all of the volunteers to help us focus as a team for Sarah and to brainstorm new ways of playfully helping her. There was never a set number of volunteers. It fluctuated based on our needs and the lives of those participating in Sarah-Rise with us.

One of my first volunteers was Julia. Her mom worked with one of our new neighbors. Our neighbor mentioned that Julia had some experience with kids with autism and might be interested in babysitting. I had other ideas! Julia and I connected, and she came to meet Sarah. We started right away, and I described The Son-Rise Program and introduced her to the basics of how to play effectively— just as I describe above. Julia began her first session with Sarah that day, and after fifteen minutes of play with Sarah, Julia and I spoke about how it went. I offered suggestions, and Julia and Sarah played some more. Julia was enthusiastically on board with joining our program as much as her college schedule allowed.

My friend Kara brought us dinner once a month, as her email had promised. She also did Reiki with Sarah, but Sarah often wanted to play with Kara rather than just receive the good energy. My friend Diane became a regular companion for Amy, as did my friend Jennifer and her young daughter. Our friend and previous next-door neighbor Cara offered to watch Amy, along with her own young daughter, on Thursday evenings when I saw clients, which allowed Carl to have Sarah-Rise time. My friend Sarah B. brought her vibrant, energetic enthusiasm as a Sarah-Rise team member. Laura, a fellow Alexander Technique teacher, brought her quiet, present enthusiasm and "endless patience" to us for four hours per week. She played with Sarah for two hours and took care of Amy for the other two. Marilyn, another Alexander Technique teacher, played with Sarah on many weekends for a couple of hours.

Gregory was happy to be part of our Sarah-Rise team. As Sarah's speech therapist, I considered him a paid volunteer, but he was open to my feedback in a way that I expect not all specialists might be. Then again, the reason we liked him so much was because he had already connected with Sarah in a way that was deeply respectful, responsive, and playful. In response to our creation of Sarah-Rise he wrote:

The beauty of programs like Son-Rise is that they impact not only "the child" but, ideally, the systems within and around the child . . . so they help us to modify our communication and interaction styles.

These programs recognize that a child exists in a web of communities and relationships and if we want to see real, authentic change . . . we must impact the web to the extent possible.

A couple of months after my initial volunteer-seeking email, I contacted the Friendship Circle, an organization that matches neurotypical teens with kids with special needs. Usually, the play is normal play, but I explained that I wanted someone open to my input and training. The Friendship Circle said they had one teen that was not yet matched with anyone. Noah's mom brought him over to meet Sarah, and he began volunteering twice a week for an hour each time. He often biked over to our house, and Sarah loved his pants and shorts. Fashion aficionado that she is, Sarah has a penchant for plaid, corduroy, stripes, dots, athletic gear, logos, and clothes with holes, seams, or notable buttons. Noah had corduroy and was open to the training. He and Sarah often played with Play-Doh together, making countless pretend food items and milkshakes. Noah commented on how helpful he found the team meetings to be, giving him more focused insight for how he wanted to be in the room with Sarah. After many months of working with Sarah, Noah gave a presentation to his high school class about The Son-Rise Program and Sarah-Rise. Maiti, his classmate, was so moved by the presentation that she joined our team.

I also forwarded my initial email to an Alexander Technique teacher who worked with the drama department of Carnegie Mellon and to a friend who worked with theater students at the University of Pittsburgh, asking that these two friends forward my email to their students. I wanted volunteers who were comfortable being silly and playful. I don't know how many students received my forwarded email, but I only got one response, and that one response turned into a hub for other volunteers. Adrian wrote:

Hey Jenny,

How are you? I read an email about the Sarah-Rise program, and as I am here during the summer, I would love to help out. I'm graduating from CMU as a drama student, so I like playing—I also play the guitar.

Let me know if this is a possibility. Thanks much!

Adrian enthusiastically told his friends about what he was doing, and thus, Shephaly and Katya joined our team, too. Adrian, however, needed a summer job, and I wanted more hours in the Sarah-Rise room, so he became a paid volunteer, clocking three two-hour sessions a week with Sarah plus time with Amy while I was with Sarah. When the summer ended, I was heartbroken to see him go. Whenever his smiling face appeared at my door, I felt like life was better. I had so much help, but I still felt up to my eyeballs in things to do. Adrian's energetic, sunny presence allowed me to offload a bit of what was on my plate, because when he arrived, I got to stop juggling two kids and could focus on one.

I would be spending time with Amy, and I could hear giggles from Sarah in the Sarah-Rise room with Adrian. He would tip over with her, following her lead of tugging on his suspenders. He would sing about the moon hitting your eye like a big pizza pie, and I'd hear Sarah crack up and try singing it, too. Sarah was in good, playful, creative, and respectful hands. When Adrian spent time with Amy, I could completely focus on being with Sarah in the playroom and enjoyed the satisfaction of accumulating more hours of Sarah-Rise. But, as Adrian had said from the beginning, he was moving and had other adventures on the horizon.

Sarah C. (quoted at the beginning of this chapter) was a friend of Adrian's and knew how central he had been to our program for those few summer months. She contacted me in the hopes of filling some of the gap when he left. She bonded with Sarah instantly, as I saw from just the tiniest bits of interaction. When I showed her the Sarah-Rise room during our initial meeting, I could tell she understood everything I explained and was ready to dive in headfirst. Sarah C. became a regular volunteer, coming twice a week, at times a paid volunteer coming thrice a week, and eventually, a beloved babysitter, too. The year she went to Thailand, a few years into our program, I was heartbroken again, faced with how much her presence in our lives lightened a load I rarely realized I carried. When she returned from Thailand, she returned once a week to the Sarah-Rise room and has since evolved with us all.

While I generally sought people who could commit to at least two, or ideally four, hours per week, at the beginning, I was flexible about accepting what help was offered to us. I think this worked well for our family and, in hindsight, I wish I had been this flexible the whole time. After a year or so, I felt some internal pressure to require four hours per week—because four hours was what ATCA strongly suggested. When I talked with some other parents during one of the post-Start-Up training sessions, they said I should require four hours and not settle for less and that it would really improve my program. I wish I had listened to myself and not to them.

Sheri, my massage office suitemate and friend, was a wonderful volunteer who had extended love and joy toward Sarah from the earliest days of Sarah's babyhood. I remember how it broke my heart to tell Sheri when we had a diagnosis to explain Sarah's delays. Sheri had shown such love and acceptance that I hoped maybe she hadn't noticed that Sarah wasn't a typical kid. But, of course, she had noticed, and she listened to my teary admission with kindness but not surprise, and her love for Sarah never wavered or diminished. Sheri was only able to volunteer for two hours a week, so when I somehow got it in my head that I had to require four hours per week, it no longer worked for Sheri to participate. One of my biggest regrets is that I gave up my flexibility and thus lost a wonderful team member. Sheri has continued cheering us on, though, and her love for Sarah continued its unwavering course.

As soon as I began my official time in our official Sarah-Rise room, I started writing weekly updates to a small handful of family members. The emails were brief, and I enjoyed writing them. It made everything seem more real. As the weeks passed and more friends like Karen asked about how our program was going or how Sarah was doing, I decided that the best way to answer was to share my updates more widely. I added our Sarah-Rise team members to the recipient list because I thought they would also enjoy reading about Sarah's progress and some of what happened in play sessions that weren't their own. Gregory suggested that I turn the updates into a blog, believing my words could be helpful to other parents. It took months, but I began a blog where I shared the same content as I sent out in my weekly emails. I don't get a ton of people replying to my emails or commenting on the blog, but I do get a few readers every month who say that my words have helped them in some way in their own life. Some of these readers are parents of kids with special needs, and it means so much to me that maybe my journey can help others. Over the years, that recipient list grew to include lots more family, many more friends, some Son-Rise Program parents, and parents of kids with the same medical diagnosis as Sarah. My friend Priscilla, who is the reason I became an Alexander Technique teacher, read my weekly missives to her friend Mary. One day, Mary called me because she wanted to be a part of what we were doing. She became Amy's treasured friend, coming weekly for many years.

Volunteers came and went over the years. Students moved away or became inundated with their own coursework. Some people could only fulfill my requested six-month commitment. Extended family members spent time in the room when they visited or focused time in their own homes when we visited them. Lastly, I found a handful of volunteers through ASD Climber, a website designed to match Son-Rise Program families with potential volunteers.

The number of Sarah-Rise volunteers and the hours of our program over the years could be plotted on a wiggly-lined bell curve. We started small in terms of hours and helpers, then grew to having many helpers and many hours, then few helpers but many hours, and then fewer helpers and fewer hours. What I see in hindsight is that it was an ever-changing river that I navigated to the best of my ability, all along making new boats for each leg of the journey. Just when I thought I had things arranged in some semblance of stability, life would change for at least one volunteer. Just when I thought that if only everyone did two sessions per week, then our program would be the most impactful it could be, it became apparent that two sessions wasn't feasible for most volunteers. Just as I ran from needing a feeding tube for Sarah, I was running toward Sarah-Rise hours with the thought that if I did *enough,* then everything would be okay.

Yes, I know that most of my words of celebration and delight in Sarah show everything was already okay, but there was an undercurrent of concerned hope that fueled my determination to run this program for her.

By the end of the first calendar year, just a couple of months into anything official in the room, I spent at least half an hour in the Sarah-Rise room every day. I wasn't ready to increase my own time beyond that until we were more settled in our new house, which happened as we rounded the bend into January. At that point, because I had volunteers to be with Amy, I was able to increase my time to an hour or two per session, with at least one session most weekdays. On weekends, Carl and I traded which child we were with, so each of us had some time with Sarah in the Sarah-Rise room. Sarah's language capability exploded immediately. It felt like I was observing a cartoon snowball picking up animals along the way as it careened down the mountain— Sarah's language was the snowball, and the new words the animals. It was intoxicating progress, and I looked forward to each session I had with Sarah, knowing that each day we would be adding vocabulary and clarity to her spoken repertoire.

4

Getting in the Room

THE ROOM STAYED MOSTLY and intentionally bare for the duration of the program. The goal behind the Sarah-Rise room was to omit the distractions that so often pepper the walls of traditional classrooms or kids' bedrooms. We replaced the small carpet remnant with an off-white area rug to make the whole floor more hospitable to our knees and rears. We had a mirror so that we could make eye contact through the mirror even if we were both facing the same direction. There was a big blue bouncy ball, a small plastic table, an easel, and a small potty, since we were hoping to help Sarah with toilet training. Even though the bathroom was directly across the hall, having a potty in the Sarah-Rise room meant we didn't have to leave the room during our session and that she could get to it almost instantly.

The toys on the closet shelf expanded over the months from a few containers of Play-Doh to include Eric Carle animal cards, matching squares with pictures of candy, fish-shaped cards for playing Go Fish, wooden blocks, stickers, crayons, paper, magnet sticks, musical shaker eggs and a tambourine, a handful of books, and two silk scarves. One scarf had stars, planets, and moons printed on a blue background. The other looked like a rainbow with changing colors throughout. Sarah has always loved visual patterns and fabrics, and she loved these scarves. She liked having them draped over her head or spread out in front of her on the floor so she could touch them with her hands.

With our imagination, there was no limit to the possibilities for play. If Sarah wanted something and we didn't have it, we drew it or made it using what we had. Anything could be anything. Scarves could be placemats, tablecloths, food, visual wind, rainbows, stars, dresses, pants, socks, telephones, or enormous tissues. The main thing was that the toys were relatively simple and did not involve technology. Technology is too distracting, and it is impossible to compete with it for attention, even if you do your best to join. The toys and games were a vehicle for personal connection and language practice, and they were a reason for making eye contact.

Sometimes, we talked and didn't even need toys. Sarah loved talking about a moment when I bumped my head on the wall. When she communicated enough in her way that I knew her intent, I responded.

"Me?"

"Yuh-oo."

Sometimes, she initiated bumping our heads with the large blue bouncy ball, practicing her best attempt at "bump" or "head," which started as "buh" and "hh-d." She also liked sitting on the ball. It was wobbly, so I liked to stabilize her, but Sarah preferred to be independent and told me to "Lll-eh-tuh goh."

Her language grew daily in the Sarah-Rise room. When we played with the candy-themed matching squares, she attempted to say "lollipop" when that card came up: "la-l-pa." Our play with the Eric Carle cards often was tied to singing, and she would say "ss" for sing and then "La la la!" with increasing glee.

I repeated or built on whatever she chose to do in the room, adding tone, loudness, or new sound. There were times when she cued me with which sound to do next. To hear her sounds and witness her earnest attempts at more language was all so exciting. Each day, over the course of the first year, she became more prolific with her single-letter sounds and attempts at telling stories about whoever bumped their head or how she bumped her knee on the sidewalk.

I remember the day Sarah said "done" and "nose" flawlessly, as clearly and perfectly as you or I would. Such a progression from her usual "dun-ah" and "n-zz!" We witnessed an increased number of the full words she said, in part because we prompted her to do so more frequently, and because she was getting more comfortable expressing herself verbally. She strung three words together more often, such as "buh heda wa-ll," which meant "bump head wall." I began thinking I just needed to hit my head on whatever thing we wanted her to learn to say next!

I often added new toys to the room and retired those that didn't garner much interest. I wanted to keep the options fresh and interesting for all involved. One such addition was a spinning egg chair. Sarah liked to play in it with the chair visor pulled all the way down, so she was fully enclosed. She pressed her hands into the visor, and I tickled them or gave her a high ten. If a hand snuck out into the air, I gave it kisses.

With Sarah about to turn five, she and I were getting into the flow of our Sarah-Rise program. Carl, too. Not only did he spend time in the room with Sarah—some evenings and on the weekends—he implemented the Son-Rise Program ideas into his lifestyle. We both did. For instance, if Sarah was absorbed in pressing her fingers on a bedsheet, then we might sit next to her and press on the sheet. This wasn't necessarily part of an official Sarah-Rise session, but it was a moment in our lives when we took time to be with her in that way.

I was honored by how open my volunteers were to what I had to say and how eager they were to bring their love and attention to Sarah. When I hosted my first team meeting, a babysitter stayed with the girls while four volunteers, Carl, and I met in the Sarah-Rise room. We sat in a circle on the floor, taking turns sharing the moments where we connected well with Sarah. We talked about our goals of helping her with the clarity of her words and with her eye contact. I emphasized that if she could watch our faces as we spoke, if we exaggerated how we formed a word, if we celebrated her every attempt at language, if we believed fully that she could learn to speak, then that was the best way to help her. In that first meeting, and in all the meetings since, I appreciated the support and thoughtfulness of the others. It was so important to have people besides Carl and me thinking about Sarah, thinking about how to add nuances to the games we offered, and the ways we interacted. Allowing this outpouring of love to enter our home and to accept such a gift was humbling.

Later that month, to my delight, Sarah had many full words and partial words. This was in contrast to the five partial or full words she had when I did my initial Son-Rise training, words that included "Mom" and "mo-re" but that have been lost to memory as I was not yet writing my updates. After a couple of months of Sarah-Rise, Sarah could say 122 words, partially or fully, including "pink," "stroller," "chicken," and "bunny."

She had so many words!

How did we get to this point?

We made it fun, and we kept it simple. Sarah's baby doll wore pajamas, and I coached enthusiastically, like a cheerleader coaxing the crowd, "Pa! Ja! Ma!" Sarah repeated after each sound, looking at me, and giggling. We went through rounds of three to four practices before she told me she was done. Later that day, we returned to the room to practice more. "Pa! Ja! Ma!" That night, when it was time to get her own pj's on, she said "pa-ja-ma," with very minimal pauses between the sounds. Fun and simple.

One day, there was a moment when I was slightly mad at Sarah. She said, "La la," very angrily, instead of using the words I now knew she could say.

"I don't know what 'la la' means!" I said, just as angrily. "Tell me something!"

There was a pause.

"Ah vv," she said sweetly.

"Ah vv" means "I love." She sometimes added "eeoo" to her "ah vv" for "I love you." "Ah vv eeoo." How could I stay mad in the face of an "I love you"?

Soon, Sarah was saying so many new things so frequently that it was almost silly to share her new words with Carl—because of course she'd said something new! She did that every day! How deliciously lovely it was to be at this point, laughing with delight at each new word our newly verbal five-year-old said.

Five months into our program, Sarah's words were notably more fluid. She liked talking about how we would ride or fly on a plane together to see Grandma and Grandpa. This sounded sort of like "wad on p-ain to-ge-ahr. G-ma, G-pa." She also talked about her other grandparents: "Ma-ma, Pa-pa back h-m," which meant that Mom-Mom and Pop-Pop drove back home after their visit. Her connection to her grandparents seemed to be growing as our program progressed. Once, when Mom-Mom called, I put the phone to Sarah's ear. Sarah listened intently and smiled as Mom-Mom reminded her of their playtime around saying, "Mac and . . . *cheese*!" The conversation continued, and when Mom-Mom said that if she were still at our house, she "would give Sarah kisses," Sarah turned toward the phone and gave two kisses! It was such a sweet moment of connection and love.

It can be hard to imagine what it was like to have to teach your kid each tiny bit of every single thing. Amy got things so easily, and I took that for granted, even as I fully appreciated that I didn't have to work hard to teach her to walk or talk.

Sarah did not get things easily. We taught her *everything* in minute detail again and again and again. Sarah was certainly the final person putting things together, and she was remarkable in how she persevered to learn *everything*. She persevered without much frustration over how much she had to practice everything. We all persevered with her. *We taught a person to speak.* We taught a person—who did not easily know how to hear the music of language or know how to produce it on her own—to talk to us! Our Sarah-Rise team did an amazing thing, which we continued to marvel about and celebrate during our team meetings.

Part of what made our sessions successful were the games we created and played. Games were what made practicing words and expanding Sarah's interactive attention span easier for all of us. A game Sarah and I both loved was Typewriter Kisses, which I created, though I'm sure I wasn't the first to do so. I kissed the length of her arm and then said, "Ding," and then I started at the beginning again. After a couple of passes, I paused, and she said, "Ding." We repeated the kisses, pauses, and dings many times. Whenever we had any game or kind of connection, I would repeat it as many times as Sarah was willing to repeat it, with as many slight changes and builds as she would allow.

I loved the game Chicky Boom. This is not surprising given that I loved Sarah's books with "chick" as part of the title. There was *Chicky Chicky Chook Chook* by Cathy MacLennan, *Chicka Chicka ABC* by Bill Martin Jr. and John Archambault, and *Boom Chicka Rock* by John Archambault. Admittedly, I find the word "chicken" inherently funny.

Years ago, when I had a job that included cleaning a chicken coop, I would laugh to tears if I accidentally said it was time to "cheen the clicken choop." At another job, I had the nickname Chicken Lips, which started as a joke and stuck but was always used affectionately. Anyway, to me, the game Chicky Boom had personality spilling right out of it.

It is a very simple and wonderful game. There is a wooden balancing board that goes atop a rounded block, and on the board, you balance wooden hay bales, wagon wheels, and chickens (of course!). When Sarah asked for the game, I would get it off the shelf and start dancing and singing, "Chicky boom, chicky boom, chick-chick-chicky boom." This song came up throughout our time playing the game. I would balance the pieces, and then Sarah would knock over my chickies.

"You boomed my chickies!" I'd shriek, tumbling onto my back. "Who boomed my chickies? You boomed my chickies! Oh no!"

Sarah would giggle and keep knocking over all the wagons and hay bales—and every one of my chickies.

Anytime I could get her laughing was a great time for learning, connecting, and expanding her interactive attention span. What I loved most about playing Chicky Boom with Sarah was that I didn't have to make any effort to pretend to enjoy it. That came naturally.

Who doesn't like booming chickies?

When Sarah was a baby and then a toddler, I watched her peers vastly outpace her in terms of development. I was frustrated when I read baby books suggesting what to do with your child, when my situation was clearly not what they were writing about. It was as if all of us parents had been given kits of furniture to assemble that came with instructions for building a desk. Everyone else's desks were coming along beautifully, but try as I might, my desk was not looking like a desk. I had instructions for a desk, but my pieces would never build a desk.

With Sarah-Rise, I could now see that we were building a book-case. No wonder I couldn't assemble a desk! Having a desk was never an option, but oh what a beautiful bookcase. With instructions from ATCA for assembling the bookcase, and people to help me build one, this task was no longer so impossible or daunting or frustrating.

My "desk" instructions suggested that Sarah was on track to attend kindergarten at a public school in the fall of her fifth year. She had been attending preschool at a public school since she turned three because that was the way for her to continue receiving Early Intervention—her occupational therapy, physical therapy, and speech therapy paid for by the public school system. Carl and I agreed that Sarah was now getting more from the Sarah-Rise sessions than she was from her preschool and her OT, PT, and school speech therapy. We wanted to focus as much time on Sarah-Rise as possible. Kindergarten would be five full days of school per week, and that seemed like too much if we wanted to keep going with Sarah-Rise. Decisions about schooling usually need to be made in January or February for the following school year, so four months into our Sarah-Rise program, Carl and I decided against sending Sarah to kindergarten and opted to keep her home full-time.

At that time, she was attending public preschool Monday through Friday, from 9:15 a.m. to 11:45 a.m. Two mornings a week when she was in preschool, my sitter Caitlin came to be with Amy while I went to see one client. In the mornings, when I didn't see clients, Amy and I went to the library for their program with songs for babies, or we did errands before getting Sarah from school. After school, the three of us went home and had lunch. This left the afternoon open for volunteers and Sarah-Rise time.

The hope for the next school year, when Sarah would be at home full-time, was that our Sarah-Rise time could expand into the morning hours.

5

Outreaches, Training, and Dialogues

With Bears and Samahria during my Son-Rise Program training

THERE WERE SO MANY people available to support my Sarah-Rise program. When I first began our program, I called my friend Joanna, who had been my roommate when I attended the eight-week Living the Dream course at the Option Institute. She had gone on to train at ATCA, working with kids who attended the intensive programs and training families to run Son-Rise Programs. By the time I did my training, she had moved on to other life adventures, but I still wanted to tell her what I was doing. She suggested I contact her friend Megan Simpson, who had also trained extensively at ATCA.

In April, six months into our program, we had our first Outreach with Megan. An Outreach is when a specialist comes to your house and observes you in your actual habitat, plays in your

Son-Rise room with your kid, and gives you and your volunteers feedback.

Our Outreach with Megan was helpful beyond measure. It was instructive watching her work with Sarah. She was relaxed in the room and respectful of Sarah, letting her do what she needed to do when isming. The moment Sarah was reachable and interested, Megan was full-on energy, fun, and engaging in play. She interacted with the underlying assumption that Sarah could play games and would want to. Megan played with Sarah as if Sarah were a typical kid, but she gave her extra time and encouragement. She trusted that Sarah would enjoy things that any kid might enjoy, bringing in more imaginative play and more games than we had been doing. I had been waiting for Sarah to show me more signs that she was ready for games at levels beyond Chicky Boom. Now, by observing Megan, I understood that I should model how to play any given game, and that I should not expect Sarah to participate in a big way. We were teaching Sarah how to play games as simply as we could to make them seem fun and like something she could do.

Megan observed me playing with Sarah in the same way I observed the volunteers. She then gave me feedback, pointing out the moments when I could give Sarah more time or when I could run with a game a little longer. Some of the volunteers were able to come for short Sarah-Rise sessions to receive Megan's feedback too, and others had time to observe Megan's time with Sarah. Everyone found this first outreach visit informative and helpful.

Megan came later that summer for a second Outreach, and I cannot stress enough how impactful that visit was. I was so close to Sarah and to our Sarah Rise program that there were things I couldn't see. I had no idea how much Sarah had progressed between April and July! Sarah had a longer interactive attention span and better eye contact. Sarah ismed less and talked more. As part of the second Outreach, we had a team meeting facilitated by Megan, where we added new goals, such as helping Sarah participate in games with rules and taking turns. Megan was an artist of play, and she helped us become better artists, too.

ATCA specialists like Megan offer consultations and Option Process dialogues to help people and families navigate challenging situations and all the feelings that complicate the challenges. Dialogues are official Option Institute and ATCA sessions that people can book with various trained facilitators. You describe something with which you are struggling, and they ask questions to help you find your own answers about your beliefs that maybe are invisible to you but are holding you back. Dialogues help you come to your own realizations and clarity about how you want to move forward or think about your given situation. I benefited greatly from many dialogues with Bears, Samahria, Megan, and William.

William Hogan was a beloved teacher at ATCA, and I always found my time with him to be illuminating, allowing me space to see where I held my desires so tightly that I left no wiggle room for others to be themselves. He was able to ask me why I felt annoyed, in a moment when annoyance felt like my only option, in such a way that I cracked up laughing at myself because his phrasing and tone made it seem like I had a million possibilities for how to respond. "Why, when Sarah didn't want to get dressed when you wanted her to, did you feel annoyed?" he queried kindly, with his British accent adding to the light delivery of the question. He clearly wasn't judging me, but by asking the question he was suggesting that maybe I had another choice. So why did I choose annoyance? I didn't always have an answer for why, and I didn't always find a different path, but he assisted me with loosening my emotional tightness so I could laugh and thus think a little more clearly. The questions broke the tension I had accumulated when I felt like I had no choice. Here he was opening doors of options by asking why I had chosen the only door I saw.

After our second Outreach, it was clear that Sarah was progressing with language and games, but we still had the challenge of potty training. When I tried the usual recommended routes—bare bottom or undies—it led to many puddles and upsets. Then I got tense, trying to guess when to grab Sarah and put her on top of the toilet or portable potty. My tension did not help anything, so I scheduled a phone consultation with William about Sarah's resistance to the potty.

William gently guided me to the blindingly obvious realization that I did not in fact have control over Sarah and her potty use. *Huh!* Certainly, I could coax or force her to sit, but it was Sarah who made anything happen. The same was true of her eating. I could offer lots of options, but Sarah was the person doing the eating. And that was what we wanted! We wanted Sarah to control what she was doing. William encouraged a new potty plan.

I could suggest potty use, even bring Sarah to the potty if she was willing, but if she said no, then I respected it instantly and maybe even theatrically. "No potty!" I said as I dramatically closed the bathroom door, to reinforce for her that she had control. I also added in more play around her potty use when she did sit, and I sang various songs, substituting words about the potty or toilet. To the tune of "Rubber Duckie," I sang, "Little potty, you're the one . . . you make bathroom time so much fun." My favorite song was to the tune of "sign your name across my heart, I want you to be my baby." My version, with dancing and great gusto, was "pee your name across my potty, I want you to pee in the potty." If nothing else, Sarah liked my dance moves.

We added potty use as one of our official goals in the Sarah-Rise room, working toilets into play whenever possible. For instance, when it was time for the Lego people to be put away, they used the toy potty first. When we played with Sarah's baby doll, she pooped or peed in the toy potty. When we played with ribbons, sometimes they were awards for best potty pooper. When we played with zip, button, and snap boards, I explained how sometimes we had to undo our buttons or snaps or unzip our pants when we used the potty. This didn't lead to any actual pooping on the potty, but pee progress was happening! As with all things we wanted Sarah to do or learn, I reminded myself that this was something I *wanted* for her, not something I *needed* in order to love her and delight in her.

By becoming more relaxed and playful around potty use, and by honoring Sarah's control of the situation, she progressed notably. She was pee-potty-proficient within the span of a month. It was an incredible achievement, but it took a long time, a lot of patience, broad creativity, and possibly a trip to California.

Carl, Sarah, Amy, and I flew to California to hang out with a group of college friends for a week at a rental house. For Sarah, the travel itself and the novel bathrooms seemed to help everything click into place. By this point we often had her wearing a pair of cloth undies with a pull-up diaper over top, and in California she had dry undies time and time again. I continued to regale our friends with details of what a potty rock star she was. To our friends' credit, they cheered us on and never seemed weary of my dry reports.

That October, I attended my second training course, which was called The Son-Rise Program Maximum Impact. My mom and Amy came along, but this time they were in a rental house. They had their days to do whatever they liked, and I saw them in the mornings and the evenings.

That training course was one of the best weeks of my life. It was as life-changing as The Son-Rise Program Start-Up. I learned new ways of thinking about Sarah and how to help her. I was able to let go of more layers of guilt about being responsible for Sarah's challenges. I felt empowered and excited about moving forward in our program. The people who run ATCA are some of the most deeply loving, masterfully insightful, and thoughtful people I have ever encountered. Not only did I learn about how to run an even-more-effective Sarah-Rise program, but I also considered how I wanted to live my life in general.

That week I was happier and freer to envision a more expansive life than I'd previously thought I could live.

I clarified my purpose and my goals for Sarah. My renewed goal with Sarah-Rise was for Sarah to thrive and flourish to the best of her ability. I would do this by loving her completely and unconditionally. I would look at any place within myself that got stuck with loving any part of her. I knew these had been my goals and intentions from the beginning, but it helped to refresh them. Whether it is with The Son-Rise Program or the Alexander Technique, to this day I find myself saying, "Oh! I just have to . . . ," and then I state the foundation of the technique or approach as if I'd just learned it. For instance, with Sarah-Rise, I often come back to, "Oh, I can just love her and let her be herself while giving her my enthusiastic loving presence!" With the Alexander Technique, I often come back to, "Oh, it's all about keeping my neck free and easy!"

During the training, I also reconnected with the concept of bound-aries. I could still set boundaries in my life with Sarah so it wasn't a five-year-old running the house, but I could do so without anger. Sarah could desperately want to do a certain activity, but that didn't mean I had to say yes at that time. I was allowed to have my own space to do what I wanted to do in a given moment. She could really want to watch a TV show and she could yell and scream about it, but I could still say no. She could really want to wear a certain item of clothing, but I could calmly say no if it really needed to be washed or if the desired item was Amy's. I didn't have to fear her upsets, nor did I have to squash them. Her upsets could coexist with my taking care of the things I felt needed attention or limits.

If I felt angry or sad or hopeless, then I could ask myself if I was acting on a belief that I didn't want to believe anymore. For example, if Sarah was not figuring out a puzzle and I felt upset, I could ask, *Why am I upset?* If I realized I was upset because I believed that if she didn't figure out the puzzle in that moment then she would never get it and therefore I'd failed as her mother, I could ask, *Is that true?* Hmm, perhaps not getting the puzzle in that moment didn't signify anything about the next moment, and it didn't actually reflect on me as a mother. Sarah not figuring out the puzzle meant she was having trouble *in that moment.*

Once, I had an Option Process Dialogue with Bears about my feeling sad that maybe Sarah would never be a typical child.

"Why, if you don't get what you want, would that be so painful?" Bears asked me.

This was a very freeing question. I didn't know my full answer, but the question pointed out that there was a choice. Maybe I could say, "I wanted a typical child. She isn't. Oh. Okay. I can still have an awesome life. It doesn't have to be painful or mean that I am somehow a bad person. It just means I didn't get what I'd thought I wanted."

While I was away at the training program, Sonia flew to Pittsburgh to help Carl take care of Sarah and facilitate the volunteers and their usual Sarah-Rise sessions. Carl wrote about his experience:

Since Jenny and Amy were away this week for more Sarah-Rise training, I got to have some quality Sarah & Dad time earlier this week, and then my sister Sonia arrived Tuesday to help out. When I mentioned that it was just me and my daughter to another engineer at the company we're working with right now, he said, "So, ice cream for breakfast and Legos all day, huh?" It was pretty funny to very truthfully answer yes, since it was literally what we had done the day before.

Hanging out with Sarah is really fun these days. We can have real conversations, make jokes, laugh about things, and she often genuinely impresses me with something new. At the same time, a full day with Sarah is long and my patience with certain requests definitely decreases as the day goes on (as does her tolerance of my saying no to those requests). As with most endeavors, living a day in another's shoes gives new respect and understanding.

As a parent, I think there are many tensions that play out in our interactions with our children, and one that I thought about this week is impatience vs. laziness. I'm sure there are other words with more positive connotations that could work just as well, but these are the ones I was thinking about, so I'll keep them.

There are a number of things that need to get done every single day with Sarah (often multiple times): getting dressed, brushing teeth, going to the potty, etc. Many times, I am impatient during these events, especially if we have a time deadline, and then I can give up quickly and do many parts of these tasks for her if she is not responding to my requests. But I am also lazy and would really rather not put her pants on for her. This week I decided to really embrace the lazy side and just reject the impatient side. I wanted Sarah to do everything, and I was prepared to wait.

So, Sarah got dressed almost all by herself every day this past week. I still guided and encouraged (sometimes a lot) each step, but I didn't do anything for her. This made a really big difference and I feel like she responded to it really well. A common management problem is to delegate responsibility without delegating authority, and I realized that I was doing something similar with Sarah. I was requesting that she do these things, but then I wasn't letting her do them the way she wanted or on her timeline.

This was an area where it was really helpful to have Jenny at the training because she would tell me about what she was learning when we chatted each evening, and then I could apply it right away. One of the things they worked on was being creative and persistent with requests and working on expanding the time that it feels okay to continue making the same request (it is amazing how small this is by default—20 seconds feels very long when I feel like I am being ignored). So, the next morning I was much more creative in how I asked Sarah to put her pants on. The result was that we both had more fun, I had no need for being impatient, and I got to enjoy my laziness.

Another place that switched for me this week was a re-realization that Sarah is extremely capable of learning many things, but she often needs more practice. Jenny and I had been saying recently that it would really improve our quality of life and open up new family activity options if Sarah could stay next to us when we went places instead of running off. So, this week I decided to practice this.

Sarah and I went to a few stores (without having anything that absolutely needed to get done at those places) and beforehand we talked a lot about how important it was that she stay next to me and not run away. Then at the store, I tried to continually talk about this and praise her when she was doing it and talk with her right there when she started straying away. And the whole experience felt really different and hopeful for me. At some point she still ran away so then we left the store and I talked about why we left, but she stayed with me much more during that trip than I had realized she could without me physically holding her hand, pulling her back, etc. Practice is important for everything, and these skills are no different. Sarah will get there—she just needs practice.

In early November, I went to my final training program, which was called The Son-Rise Program New Frontiers. Sonia helped Carl, and my mom came with Amy and me to Massachusetts. The classes covered the perfect mix of topics; they helped me change my attitude and also gave concrete specifics for how to improve my techniques in the playroom. I got a better understanding of how to build on Sarah's isms. To "build" is to add one small thing to what is already happening. For example, if Sarah and I were making balls out of Play-Doh, then I could build on the activity by forming a worm or an oval. Similarly, if we were having a tea party and pretending to drink from our cups,

I could add to that by pretending that the tea had grown cold and needed to be reheated. I also learned how to create games, how to initiate games, how to request things of Sarah more effectively, how to think creatively about props, and how to use Sarah's motivations to help her reach her goals.

Carl and Sarah also had learning experiences. In his words:

Sarah can now put toothpaste on her toothbrush, which means that she can do all parts of getting ready for bed all by herself, and she usually does each step all by herself with some gentle encouragement to string the steps together. She has also been getting faster at putting on her clothes in the morning and more independent as well (some mornings at least). This had the added benefit of meaning that Sarah and I could sleep in a little later in the morning, with Jenny and Amy out for the week. I've been continuing to practice giving Sarah more space and time in the Sarah-Rise room during semi-exclusive behaviors (or especially when she says "Move back"), and really waiting for a strong green light of steady eye contact with some words or something else that really feels like she is ready to engage. This has felt good to honor where Sarah is, and it seems like we have better connections afterward when I really am patient and wait until she is fully ready. Patience is good.

The training made it easy to think that I had figured out parenting and happiness forever and that I would never lose it because it all seemed so simple. But that was when I was mostly on my own as an independent adult without the varying challenges that Sarah can present. Back at home, I was helping Sarah get dressed one morning and was feeling quite angry and impatient with her. I was frustrated with myself for not being perfectly happy and patient. Despite my new training and inspiration, I was still getting upset in the day-to-day moments. I left Sarah's room and went to talk to Carl, who reminded me that I could make a decision. I could hide Amy's sweatpants that Sarah desperately wanted to wear, and then Sarah could have her reaction.

Such wisdom!

Once I quit resisting Sarah's screaming, stuffing the sweatpants in the back of a closet without her seeing, it quickly stopped. I then playfully encouraged Sarah to get dressed, which she did rapidly.

The key was to remember this process of reassessing my response the next time I made a decision and Sarah yelled about it. The reevaluation of the situation instantly shifted my attitude. At least in the moment described above, I stopped judging my decision as bad based on Sarah's reaction. I often took the screams of my children to mean that I'd made a bad decision. Then I got frustrated and told myself that I was stupid or should have done something different. Remembering that I could stand by my decision and allow for screaming without doubting myself helped immensely.

6

Play

CERTAIN ACTIVITIES MADE QUITE an impression on Sarah. One day I was in the family room with Amy, and I brought out a big wooden sea-themed shape puzzle by the brand Melissa & Doug, where each shape had a corresponding cut-out hole. The puzzle had three sea creatures with large wooden handles that made them easy to grasp. Sarah took the crab piece and threw it across the room. In the past I would have taken this as a rejection. Now, understanding how to include her behavior with my overall goal of increasing her interactive attention span, I responded enthusiastically: "The crab went far!"

She went over to it and moved it farther, so I said, "The crab is going far away."

Our puzzle play consisted of Sarah moving the crab and saying, "Cab go fahr," while I made distressed faces, pretended to wipe away tears, and called, "Crab, come back!" Crab never did receive Sarah's help to come back, but she did spend a tiny bit of time getting the fish and the turtle pieces in the board. She was most interested in my mock distress.

Just as my line about the crab going far made an impression on Sarah and she repeated it, other ideas also made an impression on her, and she liked to say certain phrases often. We called them Sarah's Rules to Live By:

Don't fall in the hole.

Don't get bubbles in your eyes.

Don't bump your head on the table.

Don't fall down the stairs.

After any of these statements, she might say, "Oush piece ice hrt lot go hobital" (Ouch piece ice hurt lot go hospital).

I was grateful for how much Sarah was willing to practice words. Even two years into Sarah-Rise, she didn't tire of the repetition or our corrections. In contrast, Amy resisted any correction to her pronunciation. Sarah found words funny. Or maybe it was my face and voice when I said certain words. Once, she asked for markers, and we practiced saying "markers" for a good five minutes before I got the markers. I only got one perfect rendition of the word from her, but we were laughing and connected and enjoying our time of practicing together.

Sarah was five and a half when she drew her first picture. This was the summer when we had Adrian, Noah, Gregory, Laura, Sheri, Katya, Sarah B., Julia, and Marilyn playing with Sarah. Our first Sarah-Rise summer. One day she didn't have any volunteers coming to visit despite the size of our team, and she was pining for Noah, our teen volunteer that I'd found via the Friendship Circle. It hadn't been long since his last visit, but the poignancy with which Sarah might miss someone didn't depend on how long it had been or how long she had to wait to see them. She wanted to see him *now!*

To help Sarah move through her upset, I suggested we write a letter to Noah. After we wrote the letter, I gave her a blank piece of paper and pencil. I didn't say anything or do anything except pay attention. Writing to Noah seemed to satiate her desire to connect with him, and so she moved on to a different activity. She began to draw some arcs and scribbles, followed by lots of dots and short hash marks.

"Wain," she said.

"Are you drawing rain?" I asked.

"Aya," (yes), she said.

"Are the scribbles clouds?"

"Sigh," she replied; this was Sarah's word for "sky."

What was remarkable about her creation was that it was the first time she conveyed that she was putting on paper a vision that she had in her head.

Sarah loved her volunteers; her whole being radiating joy upon their arrival. She would immediately head for the stairs, starting to play even before reaching the Sarah-Rise room. She went through a phase of being extra attached to Noah, as you can surmise from her pining for him the day she drew her first picture. In fact, when she did see him next, she spontaneously gave him a real hug, not a chin-press on the head or a shorts-isming hug (pressing on someone's shorts because of liking the fabric), but a *real* hug. It was rare for her to show such quintessential physical affection, even though she clearly was attached emotionally to her volunteers.

The day after she drew the picture, Sarah's speech therapist, Gregory, arrived for his Sarah-Rise session. When he came in, Sarah looked up at him and said "ha" (hi) before he said anything to her. Then she headed upstairs and told him, "Come up," waiting for him part of the way up the stairs before dashing off with glee for the Sarah-Rise room.

This moment was notable because we had been working on Sarah being able to issue greetings and farewells at appropriate moments, and here she was verbally greeting him and inviting him to join her.

Another volunteer that Sarah enjoyed was Adrian. She frequently referenced Adrian's suspenders and the game they played with them. The game was that she would pull his suspenders while he leaned over, causing her to tip back while he made an *aaah* sound. Sarah loved his suspenders so much that a different volunteer gave her a kid-sized pair as a gift. She still wears them to this day when she plays dress-up in an old pair of my jean shorts.

Sarah also loved saying that something went down the wrong tube, and we said it whenever someone coughed after taking a drink. One day when Gregory was here, he built upon this idea without even knowing he was doing so. Amy was drinking and then coughed. Gregory said, "Something went down the wrong pipe!" Sarah clearly understood him and was tickled by this choice of "pipe" compared to her usual "tube."

I made a conscious choice not to dumb down my speaking for Sarah. Certainly, there were times to be simple, such as when we were teaching her to say a word, but there were many other times when I purposely smarted up my speaking and used big words, weird words, and nerdy words. I so much appreciated when other people also expected that she could understand a varied vocabulary.

Sarah's newest phrase was "come in," said when she wanted a certain person to arrive. One evening as I was putting her to bed, we were talking about the glowing star stickers on her ceiling and about how there was no moon sticker on the ceiling.

"Moon, come in."

Sarah was taking her language this next step further into spontaneous new sentences and sentiments.

The more time I spent in the Sarah-Rise room, the easier it was for me to spend time there, inviting Sarah's growth while following her lead for the path toward that growth. The hours seemed to pass more quickly because I was more comfortable with my role and how to advance toward our Sarah-Rise goals. I began to comprehend and appreciate the concept of joining more fully. Joining was called for when Sarah was exclusive and not easily connecting with us. That was when we would do the same thing she was doing a few feet away. I would do my own play with part of her chosen toy or use something similar, but sometimes I had a different goal in mind and wasn't as present with the joining as I could have been. When I joined with no other motive than to truly do what she was doing and to enjoy it, that was when she would shift and start paying attention to what I was doing. Sometimes she would shift immediately, and other times I would join her for half an hour, opening and closing lids on containers, for example, before she was ready to include me.

When I wasn't joining, I was building by adding on to what we were doing. Some days builds worked, and Sarah would incorporate them in her play. Some days she didn't add to what she was doing, but I considered that the build worked if she continued watching me. If I tried to build on what we were doing and she went back to something that didn't include attention to me in any way, then I joined her. I was following her lead. I was constantly issuing the invitation to connect with me just by being in the room. If she was receptive to watching me, that was still a way to add to her repertoire of awareness and ability. The more Sarah looked at us, the more she learned.

I had been working with Sarah on the alphabet song for months, pausing more often for her to fill in more letters. After ten months of Sarah-Rise, she was singing the whole alphabet by herself with minimal help. At the end of one Sarah-Rise session, I said it was time to clean up and then sing our ABCs. As I was putting the Play-Doh containers back on the shelf, I realized that she had started singing it.

I celebrated her hugely and then requested that we sing it together. I waited for her to start and then I sang with her. Prior to this moment, we'd always taken turns singing, but this time she allowed me to sing with her and she kept going. This was a first! We sang a song together! Clearly our collective playtime was paying off.

7

Help

Our program is in a bit of flux at the moment as we bid farewell to some of our volunteers and begin scheduling some new ones. Julia is about to return to college and Katya will be studying abroad for the semester. Adrian is about to move to NYC. Shephaly just started. Noah's time slots will shift with the start of school. I have one new person to schedule for her first time and two potentials that I have yet to meet. Flux is not my favorite thing to deal with. In general, I like things decided yesterday. I think I've relaxed about schedules a bit, but I am also eager to get everything settled for the coming year. Once I have my volunteer schedule settled, I will see what other help I need to arrange to meet my goals and keep our life running as smoothly as possible. One step at a time.

—Sarah-Rise Update, 8/20/2012

AS THE SUMMER CAME to a close, I realized I would need more assistance if I was going to take our Sarah-Rise program to the next level of hours and impact. Adrian was gone, so I didn't have someone coming weekly for several sessions with Sarah and to watch Amy. Noah could no longer come multiple mornings a week because high school was starting for the year. He was able to come on Sundays, which was still incredibly helpful, but I wanted to keep going full bore Monday through Friday. The reality was that I no longer had enough people, and I was struggling to keep up with laundry, dishes, groceries, and general parenting alongside managing volunteers and getting what Sarah-Rise time I could. What I really wanted was a second self to share the load. Sarah was thriving, so I knew she was up for continuing with a large number of hours in the Sarah-Rise room. The question was how to support both of us in a way that would truly lighten my load rather than adding several more volunteers to train and observe.

I wanted a full-time helper who could assist me with the minutia of the daily household requirements, help me get consistent hours in the room with Sarah while they watched Amy, do hours in the Sarah-Rise room with Sarah, and allow me to observe my volunteers and give them feedback without my simultaneous need to attend to one or two children.

The more Carl and I talked about how to find the best helper for me, the more we talked about Sonia.

Sonia had already been this kind of helper for me when she assisted us with moving into our new house. She was adept at being with Sarah in the playroom, having done Sarah-Rise time when she was here after our move and while I was away for my training courses. She was easily comfortable with both girls, their level of ability, and how I was parenting them. She was skilled with helping our life run smoothly overall, as had already been proven experientially multiple times. Whenever we were together for any family gathering, Sonia would magically swoop in to help me. Sonia had a way of making everything seem less daunting. It was more than having an extra pair of hands. It was the extra pair of hands that were attached to such an observant, intuitive, energetic person. I could breathe more easily when Sonia was around.

Sonia was the most phenomenal option we could dream of, but there was one slight hitch: she lived in Seattle. However, since we knew she was looking for a new job, Carl and I proposed the idea to her anyway. We offered her a full-time job with us for a year, working forty hours per week as my assistant. We had financial backing from my maternal uncle and aunt. I know not all families have such bounty, and I am grateful that we had the support to pursue our dreams for Sarah-Rise without concern about the cost. This support was offered without my even asking, simply because my uncle and aunt wanted to help our family. With a husband and cats in her Seattle home, Sonia had a lot to think about before responding to our offer.

After time to consider all the life changes this would entail, Sonia said yes to our proposal. We understood that she couldn't start immediately. It would take time to make all the arrangements needed to move her belongings to an apartment in Pittsburgh and drive cross-country with her cats. She and her husband would temporarily be in a long-distance relationship. I searched for possible apartments with gusto. The idea that she was coming to be my official helper was liberating and exhilarating. Sonia and I would be able to get even more hours of Sarah-Rise time per week than my current volunteers and I were getting. Maybe my house wouldn't be a constant mess. I'd have a friend and coworker by my side for so much of the day, helping me navigate parenting stresses, frequently hungry young people, and never-ending piles of laundry and dishes—or, if she was not by my side, she'd effectively be allowing me to be in two places at once. The idea of being able to do errands or have someone else do errands while I stayed home to focus on the program was extremely appealing.

As it was, when I went almost anywhere, I took both girls with me, especially since Sarah wasn't in school anymore. In theory, I could do errands with Amy when a volunteer was with Sarah, and sometimes I did, but I was also needed at home to observe each volunteer remotely for fifteen to thirty minutes, making notes for when we spoke after every session, giving feedback and further training. This was an important part of the program that required time, thoughtfulness, and presence. Having Sonia around to help with the kids would help me focus more on the volunteers and my feedback, which felt good given how much focus my volunteers were giving to Sarah.

Going grocery shopping was always a bit of an unknown venture. Either child could have a meltdown or be too restless. I often chose stores that had big shopping carts with the play car at the front, complete with a steering wheel that made the child think they were driving. Our local food co-op does not have such carts, but it is only five minutes away and has items that I can't get elsewhere. It was necessary to make it to the co-op at least every week or two. While I was eager to have Sonia's help for errands, I noticed that shopping on my own with the girls provided me with some real-life moments to notice Sarah-Rise progress.

One day, at the co-op, I experienced a miracle of Sarah's listening and self-restraint. Normally, I had Sarah in the cart while she clamored to be done shopping so she could enjoy playing with the automated door. If I had her out of the cart, she compulsively ran to play with the door, so I had to keep a firm hold on her hand. This time I let her stand, without restraints, on the standing board of Amy's stroller. The three of us did a fast shopping trip and got everything we needed. As we were checking out, I told Sarah to stay with me until I was done paying, and then I would let her play with the door. She did it! She was mere feet from the door, chomping at the bit, but she restrained herself and waited until I said she could play. All went beautifully until I told her it was time to leave. She tried to get away from me so fast that she nearly collided with the corner of the bagging area of the checkout counter. Still, I counted this as an achievement—for both of us. It was important that I was willing to let her play. If I had stuck to saying no, then she wouldn't have waited because she would have been so desperate to get in any door play. It was important that she could listen to my rules, wait patiently, and uphold her part of the arrangement. Though this outing was an achievement for both of us, grocery shopping would still be easier with Sonia to watch the kids at home or to get the groceries while I was with the kids. Or one of us could each handle one child whether at home or at a store.

A couple of months after Sonia moved to Pittsburgh, I felt like I was managing a small business. Our days were packed with things that aimed to provide an uncluttered space and an unhurried pace for Sarah, especially in the Sarah-Rise room.

Our house was a social hub of volunteers coming and going, exchanging warm greetings at shift changes. The air was often filled with delicious aromas as we began making more homemade healthy food. The atmosphere of love and support felt healthy, too. We had so many people in our life providing good attention to Sarah and Amy, and having Sonia around allowed me to give good attention to processing my own thoughts. Sonia was a thoughtful listener and a creative planner, making it easier to navigate each day as smoothly as possible.

While our days were packed full, the two of us successfully created an *unpressured* cooker for Sarah by designing a life that gave her many opportunities to learn and grow but with no pressure to do anything she wasn't ready to do.

With Sonia in a full-time, forty-hour-per-week capacity, that still left time for me to be on my own with the girls, playing, doing errands, or merely trying to survive if everyone needed something or was upset simultaneously. I often had a volunteer for Sarah or Amy come in the late afternoon or early evening after Sonia was done for the day, and I either did a final Sarah-Rise session with Sarah, played with Amy, cooked dinner, or did some cleaning around the house. It wasn't until later in the evening that Carl would get home.

His job as a robotics engineer was flexible but also demanding. He often worked long days with variable end times. Even if he thought he could be home by seven o'clock for dinner, a meeting could run long, and he'd be later than expected. This variability was challenging for me, but the years of full-time Sarah-Rise in many ways were easier for me than the pre-Sarah-Rise years, in terms of how much I needed Carl to be at home in a timely fashion. The days were filled with people and with help, and for that reason I didn't feel lonely, and I didn't struggle as much with Carl's erratic work responsibilities as I did before Sarah-Rise.

I loved being at home with the Sarah-Rise program in full tilt, and I also very much valued my time in my office with clients or my teaching hours at the massage school. It was then that I got to use a different part of my brain. It was centering and replenishing to work quietly in my dimly lit office with relaxing music playing, listening with my hands and heart for what my clients needed. Whenever I thought I should give up my paid work to focus more on Sarah-Rise, I reminded myself how much I needed the centering of my paid work to help me be my best self at home.

If contemplating running such a program yourself feels overwhelming, remember that each family designs the program that works for them and what supports they have. The number of supports can grow in ways you may not expect. You get to think about what makes sense for your life, taking it one step at a time. Even small changes can make a difference. In general, people like to help others, so don't be afraid to ask. Time and again I am reminded of how much it meant to our volunteers to be part of Sarah-Rise.

8

Halloween

Halloween . . . ah . . . another opportunity for me to reflect upon why I get so attached to things going MY way and get upset when they don't. Sigh. We let Sarah lie down for twenty minutes before attempting costumes. She didn't sleep but I think giving her a break was good. She had been trying to nap and I was out of my SR mindset of allowing it and into my Halloween mindset that it was time to get dressed! This is why it can be helpful to have two parents. Carl suggested giving her the break, reminding me that it was our desire (not Sarah's) to do trick-or-treating. Why is it sometimes so hard to remember that the most important thing is having a loving relationship between myself and my family—rather than getting out the door in costumes by a certain time? With all of these places where I lose my happy equilibrium, I am reminding myself that the first step is accepting and acknowledging where I am and then I can change from there. I often try to skip the acknowledging and accepting and that sometimes works but not always.

—Sarah-Rise Update, 11/4/2012

SONIA MOVED TO PITTSBURGH just in time to help with Halloween, but to prepare for that holiday, Carl and I had to take the girls on a very important errand. Sarah needed a Halloween costume, even though Halloween had never been something that held her interest. Amy was going to wear one of Sarah's old costumes, so we didn't need something new for her. When Sarah was very young, we put her in costumes. She allowed it but perhaps only because she had no understanding of what was happening. As she grew older, she participated in trick-or-treating with some coaching about what to do. She often wanted to put already-collected candy from her basket into the basket of the hander-outer. Or she wanted to go into their house. Mainly she liked playing with pencils and didn't give a fig about the candy, which was fine by me.

We went out as a family to get Sarah a costume, looking at every option in Sarah's size. She rejected all of them. My pre-Sarah-Rise self would have picked something anyway and forced her into it later, but this year we left without a costume. I was grumpy and disappointed, believing I had wasted our time. All I could think about was how she would never be into Halloween and how much I wished she would be. For me, Sarah being interested in Halloween in a neurotypical way was a marker of progress toward passing as "normal." I acknowledged that thought while wishing I didn't have it, knowing that fundamentally there was no "normal" that we needed to attain and no "passing" that anyone ever needed to do. Halloween was also a treasured memory and experience from my own childhood, and I wanted her to have the same delight in it that I remembered having.

Later that night, Carl pointed out that it was really great to have done the trip to the store because Sarah considered the costumes and made a definite choice that she didn't want one. Making such a present and thoughtful decision could be deemed progress, a sign of understanding about this whole Halloween business.

That evening I realized two things: one, it is okay if Sarah never is into Halloween (not all kids are); and two, maybe she will be next year (if she isn't, refer to realization one.)

On Halloween night, Sonia handed out candy while Carl and I navigated trick-or-treating. Sarah decided at the last minute that she did want to dress up and join Amy, Carl, and me. She went as a Pittsburgh

Steeler, wearing her 86 Hines Ward jersey with smudges drawn under her eyes to match what many athletes do. Amy went as Tigger.

The night went smoothly overall, with just the tiniest hiccup of forgetting to feed the children enough real food before their foraging adventures. Sarah even completed her trick-or-treating without trying to go inside *everyone's* houses—just a few of them! She and Amy were a bit hangry by the time they got home for their macaroni and cheese dinner, hastily made by Sonia. Despite my earlier worries and grumps, I actually did get my wish of a traditional Halloween experience.

9

What Worked?

What worked?

Pausing and waiting! I was quieter today than I usually am and Sarah often filled the silence with her own thoughts and words.

Playing "ribbon fireworks." She liked the game of putting all of the ribbons on her head and so she put them all on`my head too so I could join in the fun.

—Sarah C., session note, 10/12/2012

What worked?

Today Sarah initiated "lump in the bed," as usual loving to be rolled around under the covers, then when I commented that the lump was giggling, delightedly revealing the identity of the lump, always to my huge surprise.

Thoughts?

It is very exciting to see that language is now a very usable tool for Sarah—there has been a huge explosion of language since the summer, even since early Sept. She continues to astonish! Her presence and eye contact and ease continue to expand visibly and wonderfully.

—Mom-Mom, session note, 10/20/2012

What worked?

Every once in a while I pretended the ribbons were stuck to my eyes, ear, nose, arm, or head and I needed her help to pull them off. This brought great eye contact and a sly smile from Sarah, like she knew I was being cheesy pretending they were stuck.

—Sarah B., session note, 10/23/2012

What worked?

Having something as my goal of a game or activity to share helps give me a focus for when I have an opportunity. Being really present with joining (not worrying about what to do next) helps me have fresh energy when I do get an opening and then it doesn't feel hard to build because I am so present and playful. Joining's not waiting. Joining is playing.

Thoughts?

Just because S tells me to stop singing or move back doesn't mean I shouldn't have tried. When I judge myself then I lose presence and joy and love of S.

—Jenny, session note, 10/25/2012

Thoughts?

Wow! From the very start, her eye contact and speaking was incredible. By backing off from initiating everything on my part, Sarah has taken the lead and really started offering impressive verbal communication.

—Sarah C., session note, 10/29/2012

What worked?

Squeaky, loud, unexpected noises, people falling over.
Celebrating giggles with tickles.
Having Sarah draw a card, one at a time, from me (fish). When

Sarah started to grab more than one or with her other hand, asking her "What are you going to do with the one in your hand?" had her refocus and finish putting the first fish in the box.

—Laura S., session note, 10/30/2012

What worked?
Having long conversations and working on practicing certain words. We talked about people and their shoes, hats, noses, and hair. We also built Lego towers and then broke them over and over again.

—Sonia, session note, 11/01/2012

What worked?
We had fun in the dark. We tried doing Follow the Leader and it sort of worked. She really liked walking in a circle in the dark. I don't think she really got the idea of "leader" or "follow" but, hopefully, this planted the seeds and it was fun.

—Carl, session note, 11/01/2012

What worked?
Waiting longer to get a stronger green light.
Smaller builds.
Backing off if build doesn't take.

Thoughts?
Jenny's recent comments on build vs. introduce were really very helpful.

Being more patient for Sarah to get really ready led to better interactions.

—Carl, session note, 11/16/2012

What worked?

Acting as if I have no idea where something she asks for is is always fun for her.

Thoughts?

It was very exciting for her when she blew up the balloon and I noticed she wanted to return to that activity numerous times throughout the hour. Probably obvious, but I think she greatly enjoys accomplishing a task she has been working on for a while. I think this idea will give me new ideas of things to work on with her throughout all my time volunteering here.

—Noah, session note, 12/2/2012

IN THE EARLY DAYS of our program, it was an accomplishment for me to do twenty minutes in the Sarah-Rise room. That amount of time was never to be sneezed at because it was infinitely more than nothing, but the more hours I clocked in the room, usually in two-hour increments, the easier it felt to be there, and the more I felt empowered to do even more. Sarah was used to doing multiple two-hour sessions per day. One year into our program, our team of volunteers included Gregory, Noah, Sarah B., Sarah C., Shephaly, Marilyn, Sheri, and Laura in addition to Sonia, Carl, and me. That was a lot of input and a lot of hours!

When a volunteer came and I was home, I greeted them and got them settled with Sarah in the Sarah-Rise room. I made sure the wireless video camera was running and that my laptop was streaming the footage. Once they had been playing for a bit, I sat at my desk with a notebook open to a blank page with a line drawn down the middle. I watched for about fifteen minutes before writing anything down. To the left of the line, I wrote notes about specific moments that I observed. To the right, I wrote down suggestions for how to respond in the future in a similar situation or what worked well. Sometimes, I'd observe again toward the end of their time and take more notes. When the session was over, Sonia or I took the volunteer the binder full of blank pages where they could write down some notes of their own about the session—what worked, what they did, and any questions or thoughts. If we had another volunteer coming in immediately, then the first volunteer stepped out of the Sarah-Rise room to write their notes. If not, then Sonia took Sarah downstairs, maybe for a snack or play in the family room, while the volunteer wrote their post-session notes in the Sarah-Rise room. Afterward, I gave them my observations and feedback and talked about how they felt about their time.

I observed every volunteer at least once per week, always more frequently in the beginning training phases. I observed Sonia and Carl too, and I had Sonia observe me and give me feedback. Sonia, at my request, had attended The Son-Rise Program Start-Up training course soon after she started working for us. We arranged for the time and funding to do so, knowing it would help her be an even stronger part of our program. When needed, Sonia observed and gave feedback to the volunteers in my stead, but most often that was my role.

In December, I decided to do a three-hour session with Sarah. I had never done such a long one before, and it went surprisingly well. Usually after two hours I was ready to be done and use my attention in other ways. In contrast, Sarah was content to spend two hours with one volunteer and immediately embark on two hours with the next. This was probably because she got to take care of herself in whatever way she needed, as we were there to follow her lead. Sarah was existing in an extremely supportive environment completely designed around what she needed and wanted, while I was in her world aiming to bring my best, most flexible, enthusiastic, creative, and present self, which took a lot of energy.

For my three-hour session, Sarah and I started with the book

Press Here by Hervé Tullet. My reading involved her pressing dots while I made beeping noises. She loved this. The book also has other instructions such as to shake it or tap five times on a dot. She did both, including counting to five with some prompts to keep going.

Then we did three activities in a row, and I was impressed by her level of participation, imagination, and attention with each. First, it was drawing dots on the whiteboard to beep (like the book), and, at some point, I drew an umbrella. Sarah then told me that the umbrella had stripes, so I added stripes. Next, I drew clouds.

"Daw wain," (draw rain) she said.

We both drew rain.

I drew a stick figure with a smiley face.

"Hi!" she said, spontaneously.

She was excitedly waving at it.

I asked her who it was, and she said, "Mom."

I asked her to add hair, and she did.

We then practiced drawing smiley faces in general. Sarah was sort of like a young Picasso, in terms of where parts went, and her noses were gigantic, which might be how they seemed to her in real life and why she liked them so much. When I thought she was finished drawing faces, she asked for sunglasses. It didn't occur to me that she might have wanted to draw sunglasses. I went straight to the dress-up bin to find an actual pair of sunglasses—and brought out the whole bin. While she played with the sunglasses, I put on necklaces and scarves, telling her that we were dressing up to go to a party. I helped her into my jean shorts with suspenders, a scarf, and an old pair of my heels.

As we got up to walk to the party, I inwardly thought, *Crap! What now? I didn't expect this to work!* I had expected her to lose interest and ism with something that I would then join or that she would request a new activity, so I had no plan about what would happen next at the party.

I improvised by inviting her to dance, but she said, "No dancin."

So I started singing. She said there was no singing. I got out a small dry-erase board and started writing down her party exemptions: no dancing, no singing, no drinking (except water), no eating (except "some cake"), no tickling, no kissing, no hugging, and no tapping. I suggested there could be tea at the party, and I brought out the Tea Party game. In the past she would ism a lot with the tablecloth, pressing on it with her hands while her jaw opened and closed—content in a world made up of the tablecloth and herself. This time she ismed for maybe a minute, and only twice. We took turns with the game's spinner, and she was attentive to the pieces I gave her. She watched me pretend to drink tea, and when she got a teacup, she pretended to drink tea. Then, after observing me, she pretended to add milk and sugar to her tea.

This was all so exciting! She had such flexibility and attention for so many activities with me in a row. She was connected to me and responding to my suggestions in some way for almost the entire three hours. This was unprecedented and showed me that maybe my previous expectations were imposing limits on what was possible.

Our next two-hour playtime in the Sarah-Rise room started with the Tea Party game. When Sarah requested it, I asked if we were going to have the party in the sand or snow. She said snow, so then I pretended that everything was cold. She liked the idea of cold cake and repeated it several times. When she turned her attention to the holes in the jean shorts that I was wearing over my pants, as per her request, I started saying we could fix the holes with parts of the tea party.

I sang, "There's a hole in my jean shorts, dear Sarah . . ." to the tune of "There's a Hole in My Bucket" and then added a new verse about each item of the tea party fixing the hole.

Sarah mentioned going to a party at Dad's work, which we had done a few weeks ago, and I said that she had eaten cookies and a roll at the party. She then said that she was all done with her roll, so I said, "All done with the roll!" with great emphasis, which she enjoyed. She put herself across my lap and said, "No roll." I pretended to taste her, confirming that she was not a roll. I then continued pretending to eat her while guessing which item of food she might be. We deduced that she was a juice box that, when squeezed, would spill juice all over, necessitating mopping up with the tea party tablecloth. She reinitiated the squeeze game several times by saying "skeeze," all while sitting on my lap. This was such a fun playtime between the two of us with many moments of shared laughter. While joining involved physical space between Sarah and whomever was joining her, when she was open to interaction then she loved being close, accepting snuggles, tickles, and squeezes, as evidenced here in her juice-box moment.

She next asked for Play-Doh and our play became semi-exclusive. I joined her by opening and closing the containers, sitting a couple of feet away from her so we could easily see each other. I believe that after stretching herself to interact with me for a long time she needed to regroup with some isming. I found it relaxing, too. It was a nice way to be together, recharging the way we might if alone. We were being alone together. It's not that I ever chafed at the concept of joining, but as our program progressed, I reached new levels of comfort with it, understanding the value of it more than I did at the beginning, when I was doing it because that is what I was trained to do. I could use the moments of joining as a way of centering myself in addition to offering a loving presence to Sarah.

Aside from my one extra-long session, we all continued with our usual one- or two-hour time slots. Carl and the Sarah-Rise team members enjoyed wonderful connections with Sarah too, as they had from the beginning. She was growing ever more capable of communicating and participating, and as a result everyone's play became more nuanced.

Our first full year of Sarah-Rise was filled with an abundance of different sources of love and creativity provided by the people who spent time in the Sarah-Rise room with her. At the time we had three

Sarahs! We had volunteers Sarah B. and Sarah C., plus our Sarah. Sarah B. played with balloons and created Bob the Balloon, who ate prunes under the blanket tent. Sarah C. found a Mr. Potato Head tent that had Velcro for the face pieces and two doors. It was a perfect toy that capitalized on Sarah's love of doors, tents, and Mr. Potato Head. Sonia had a conversation with Sarah where they whispered about whispering. Carl made a contraption out of the play tool kit and the ribbons that he and Sarah determined was a swing for her leg. Gregory played with the blanket tent that was often erected in the Sarah-Rise room as per Sarah's request. He fell out of the tent and then gave a big "Hello!" when he reentered the tent. Sarah picked up on this play departure and arrival, adding some of her own greetings and invitations for him to come back into the tent.

Sarah was flourishing, and I knew from the team meetings that the volunteers valued their time in the room for their own growth and learning as much as for Sarah's. It helped them be more present in the rest of their lives to have their dedicated two or four hours per week with Sarah. They learned to trust their creativity and joyfully witnessed Sarah's progress. They knew they were making a difference.

10

Changing the Menu

WHEN SARAH WAS LESS than a year old, she was diagnosed with failure to thrive. Every month in which Sarah didn't gain enough weight, our first GI doctor gave us a one-month grace period before we would need to consider a feeding tube. I kept that tube at bay by working my rear off, stressing about it constantly, and having an Early Intervention nutritionist come to the house every two weeks to weigh Sarah and help me brainstorm high-calorie food options and feeding strategies. My obsession with Sarah's eating was driven by a fear of the feeding tube and an intense determination to avoid it.

Many kids have feeding tubes, and they are a great help for the kids and their parents. But to me, at the time, a feeding tube represented giving up or worse. It meant admitting to even more of a disability than we already faced. I was scared that if Sarah had a feeding tube she would lose any incentive to eat more by mouth, so I tracked calories meticulously and conjured up all kinds of ways to squeeze in two and a half more calories from one more Goldfish cracker.

Over the years, the struggle to get Sarah to eat eased. She began to eat more and to eat regularly. When we began Sarah-Rise, her diet was based on whatever she wanted to eat whenever she would eat it. This meant ice cream for breakfast or butter pats and Andes Mints for lunch if that was what she wanted. That was fine by me, because Sarah was four and we had successfully avoided a feeding tube. Did it matter that her diet wasn't exactly healthy? I asked myself this question often, doubting my choices given our other struggles.

Sarah was chronically constipated, holding everything in until she was asleep, when her willpower couldn't hold it in anymore. This meant rough nights for all of us—dark, tired hours filled with midnight clothing and bedding changes. Amy miraculously slept through everything, even the lights being turned on and her sister screaming. Sarah, who also wanted to be asleep, would scream through her clothing changes and while she waited for us to switch her bedsheets, and sometimes even more when she wanted to continue wearing the specific pajamas that were so recently soiled. I imagine the chilly wet wipes to clean her previously warm bum were also not the loveliest experience, adding to the reason for her vocal protest.

We were ready to help Sarah with potty training for bowel movements, but if it was so uncomfortable for her to go that she would hold it in at all costs, Carl and I knew this was going to be a difficult task.

Some of my friends who were also Son-Rise Program parents had tried the GAPS diet with their children. GAPS stands for Gut and Psychology Syndrome. The diet is a protocol to heal a leaky gut, which is when toxins that are normally blocked by the intestinal wall pass through the wall and into the rest of the body. We decided to try it.

Sarah had just turned six, Sonia was fully integrated as an

indispensable part of the Sarah-Rise program, and we felt that we could tackle the challenge presented by a massive overhaul of the way Sarah and the rest of our family ate. Sonia and I read *Gut and Psychology Syndrome* by Natasha Campbell-McBride, self-medicating with chocolate after each chapter that showed us in great detail the deprivation we were about to experience in the coming months.

Before our GAPS journey began in earnest, Sarah needed pre-GAPS blood work. I told her ahead of time about what would happen, and we went through the scenario several times. I didn't have any books or toys with me, so luckily, the wait at the hospital was short. Sarah loved the chairs in the waiting room and the big chair for the blood draw. While the nurse was getting things ready, I explained to Sarah again about how it would go faster if she could stay still when they had the needle in her. The nurse overheard me.

"It is usually best not to tell kids ahead of time what is going to happen," she said.

"Oh! I've found just the opposite to be true for Sarah," I said. "She has special needs, and it seems to be helpful if I tell her repeatedly about exactly what is going to happen."

The nurse then stepped out to get an assistant, which was required since Sarah was so young. When she returned she said, "I wouldn't have known she had special needs if you hadn't said anything."

While such a comment was music to my ears, I can reflect now that such a statement could be made and heard without any connotation, positive or negative. It just is what it is. So even though I was wanting Sarah to pass as neurotypical and may sometimes still dream of a life with such seemingly increased ease, "passing" is not something I covet.

Sarah stayed still in my lap, watching the whole process. She cried but didn't fight it. Both nurses were very impressed.

"Fun budwok," Sarah said when we got home.

"The blood work was fun?"

"Aya."

Sarah often now answered with "yes" or "yeah," but sometimes our beloved "aya," still made an appearance.

Now we were ready to begin a gradual transition of how the family ate. I explained everything to Sarah and Amy, detailing how their eating would change and why. There was very little protest or upset from anyone. Sonia and I practiced some of the recipes for the GAPS intro, such as chicken soup in the slow cooker, with the chicken cooked much longer than I usually would cook it and with specific things added like garlic and apple cider vinegar. I got a GAPS cookbook called *Internal Bliss* by International Nutrition, Inc., and made delicious cowboy stew and sunflower cake. I stopped rebuying anything that would not fit within the GAPS framework, which meant that I no longer purchased cereal, crackers, bread, chocolate, cookies, or dairy products. The plan was to make everything we ate from scratch.

Within two weeks of phasing old foods out and new foods in, Sarah was already eating things I never thought she would. I stopped buying fruit leather, but now she loved prunes. She drank chicken stock. She ate lima bean hummus. The early days with Sarah and eating had been so hard that I was perpetually living in a terrified, tight space about her eating and maintaining weight, but with GAPS it was exciting to see that it was possible to make changes and that Sarah would in fact still eat.

The GAPS protocol starts with eliminating nearly all foods, save meat and cooked vegetables, and then gradually adding foods back into your diet. The intro level begins with chicken soup and chicken stock only, then gradually builds by adding foods such as homemade lactose-free yogurt, fresh vegetable juice, and eggs, up to what is known as full GAPS. Full GAPS, the most lenient level, includes fruit, nuts, and honey, but it is still grain-free, gluten-free, lactose-free, and refined-sugar-free. We were not quite ready to start the GAPS intro with Sarah, but I continued to move the whole family toward full GAPS.

I felt healthier and less tired than usual, even when I hadn't gotten much sleep. I also noticed that when I ate overly processed foods, like Peppermint Patties or Goldfish, within about fifteen minutes I felt sluggish and tired—and I wanted more! *Hmmm.* Very enlightening to discover, and slightly disappointing, too. GAPS showed me that the very thing I thought was helping me was hindering me.

As a family, we were still eating a small amount of grain, sugar, and dairy, but less and less each day. I made cow-milk yogurt because homemade yogurt, cooked for twenty-four hours to remove the lactose, was GAPS approved, and we had carrots fermenting in the cabinet. Dilly carrots and other fermented foods were highly recommended under GAPS as they helped populate the intestines with probiotics. Sarah was eating a wider variety of foods and her weight was steady. She asked for stock and for homemade juice. We all snacked on dehydrated apple and zucchini slices. Both girls were eating a range of new foods. They loved raw sprouted pumpkin seeds and chicken soup.

Sonia had her own apartment, where she was free to eat a non-GAPS diet, but she ate what foods we had in the house when she was with us. Carl has always been a flexible and adventurous eater, so he didn't balk at the changes either. Maybe, like Sonia, it helped that he could eat outside of the GAPS parameters when he was at work.

After a month of gradually shifting our diet, we were ready for Sarah to begin the introductory level of GAPS. The intro involves a day of just chicken soup and then you gradually add in other easily digestible foods such as cooked egg yolk, a spoonful of lactose-free yogurt, and ground-beef stew. On day one, Sarah ate chicken soup all day without a problem. My mom was visiting to help give snuggles and attention. She made up a song about it. It went like this: "Cold chicken, hot chicken, chicken stock . . . bok, bok, bok-bok, bok, bok-bok, bok, bok."

Mom-Mom also initiated calls on her napkin phone, and the girls immediately picked up on their napkin phones. Sometimes, I connected on my oven mitt phone. I thought we were going to sail through the whole process. Ha! While many people can have chicken soup all day and not experience a healing crisis, for someone whose gut is compromised in some way, a healing crisis will probably occur. That means they are going to feel sick.

On the second morning of the GAPS intro, Sarah threw up but otherwise seemed mostly okay. She didn't want chicken soup but did have two cups of broth, a bit of probiotic, and some sauerkraut juice. That was it, which left her increasingly lethargic, as was expected.

On day three, she only ate some avocado and drank some water. She was a tired, listless, napping, getting-carried-everywhere lump. She threw up again at the end of the day.

She'd lost two and a half pounds since we started the intro, and her knees looked oh so knobby. I was inwardly panicking a little bit but was outwardly being enthusiastically calm about the whole thing. I had heard from other parents that this phase was normal, so that helped quell my fears to a manageable level.

On day four, GAPS permitted a teaspoon of yogurt but no more because we wanted to see if she had an unfavorable reaction to dairy. The practitioner guiding us through this said she could have more yogurt since the teaspoon seemed to have no ill effects. She proceeded to eat twelve ounces throughout the day, perking up into more of her normal self.

By days five and six, she was eating zucchini chips, frozen whipped avocado, pureed cauliflower, scrambled eggs, and squash pie (butternut squash, eggs, coconut oil). She barely touched her stock and spat out her meat, whereas in the past she often ate meat easily and drank stock easily. I assumed that she still had an association with feeling sick after eating the chicken soup. The tricky thing was that her gut wall needed animal fats, meats, and stock to heal. We started getting creative about ways to get stock into her. I added it to the squash pie and to the pureed cauliflower. It was also the basis for other stews and soups that she did find amenable.

Our main aim with GAPS was to make sure Sarah wasn't

chronically constipated, always needing a laxative, so when we started GAPS we stopped giving her any laxatives. But on day six, she was not yet pooping. I was worried that things weren't working. I was worried that we couldn't get enough animal products in her. Maybe she just needed more time. Maybe I didn't have to freak out immediately, but I am highly skilled at freaking out immediately.

Our GAPS adviser suggested giving Sarah a GAPS shake for a couple of mornings. That involved adding a raw egg yolk to freshly made carrot juice. While the thought of it turned my stomach, Sarah drank it. And then she pooped! My stress level decreased. To increase how much stock Sarah ingested, we started making milkshakes that included coconut milk, a couple of cooked veggies, and stock. Somehow the coconut milk masked the rest, and she liked the idea of drinking a milkshake through her thermos straw. After several weeks she even went back to accepting chicken soup occasionally. It took many weeks for her constipation to ease fully and for her daily holding patterns to abate.

As we progressed through the GAPS levels, adding more and more variety to Sarah's food intake, we also focused more on potty training regarding poop. Sarah would hold it in and fight her body trying release it. Carl, Sonia, and I decided to try bribery à la the typical potty-training experience. We told her that if she pooped in the potty, then one of us would put on my full-body footed pajamas. One night, Sarah B. was finishing her Sarah-Rise time, and Sarah needed to use the potty. Sarah B., Sonia, and I rooted for Sarah like a pack of rabid cheerleaders. Then we held our breath. Sarah pooped! Just a tiny bit. We went wild again! Sarah B. donned the coveted pajamas, and the three of us were ecstatic thinking we had found the magical path to potty training.

Alas, as the weeks went by, we realized that Sarah only squeezed out the tiniest bit of poop to get the pajama reward. She wasn't allowing her body to do what it needed to do. We reevaluated. Sonia and I discussed the examples provided by ATCA of how to marry your child's general interests with their time in the bathroom. We devised a new plan. I put a large stack of books in the bathroom, and every few hours, or when it seemed like Sarah had the urge to go, Sonia, Carl, or I went into the bathroom to read with her. Sometimes Sarah B., Sarah C., or Laura took on that reading role, too. The adult of the moment immediately put on Sarah's favorite plaid pajama pants of mine on top of our clothes, and we sat near her, reading books out loud. She loved the pajamas. She loved books. If anything happened in the toilet, that was great. If it didn't, that was great too because we had just spent quality time together connecting over books.

After enough successes on the potty, which took months and months, her output became more manageable, no longer something she had to resist. Finally . . . after so many years of struggle.

Some parents see behavioral changes in their kids with GAPS, but we did not. We did solve the constipation issue, and that was good enough for us. GAPS helped us enjoy a broader variety of foods, and I learned how to cook many more things than I previously knew how to cook. Sonia, Carl, and I became quite creative as we attempted to make foods that paralleled "normal" food but followed the GAPS guidelines. I ground freeze-dried peas into flour to make crackers and pizza crust. We shredded carrots to emulate cheese for the pizza. I made cookies from eggs mixed with cashew butter. I also made vanilla pudding from cashew butter.

We continued with GAPS for several months after things seemed stable, and then we gradually added non-GAPS foods, which our adviser thought made sense based on how Sarah was doing. GAPS is a protocol to heal the gut, but it is not something that people necessarily stay on forever. While I still make some of the recipes we loved, Sarah now eats a regular diet that includes dairy, grain, gluten, and refined sugar. Perhaps it is not all so healthy or homemade, but it does make our lives easier—and my mental health a bit healthier, knowing I have more leeway in what foods Sarah can eat.

11

Progress and Preschool

Wow!!! I haven't been with Sarah since Dec 2012 . . . I understood every word! And Sarah's intention. Sarah's playing the marble game is far more advanced than anything we played before. After a few minutes of it she said, "This is fun." She was fully engaged talking away about the marble and the ramp and the black piece and, and, and. She asked me to read to her as she ate with gusto. Sarah is so much more present than one month ago. Present and engaging and amazing. A month ago it was still often about the box, today she was pointing to the picture on the box and demanding that I change up the design of the marble game.

—Laura S., session note, 2/13/2013

We played with a variety of games today—Marble and ramps, "Cat in the Hat" yellow arch, world puzzle, Colorado. We also built a castle, she ate <u>lots</u> of peas, and we read the chameleon book and drew him. This is more different activities than usual, and I noticed she also strung together longer sentences: "go underneath the yellow arch," and "play with different shapes on blue duck blanket." That's pretty awesome!

—Sarah B., session note, 3/20/2013

Two years into our program, Sarah's language continued galloping apace, expanding daily in range, fluidity, and clarity. These are some of the sentences she said around this time:

"Read to me *Not a Stick*."

"Sit in the light," referencing the sunlight in the Sarah-Rise room.

"Nice in the light."

"Play with marbles in the light."

"Play with marbles on the mountain," because we had a new balance beam toy, and she liked to have us build mountains. "Mountain" was a description she provided from her own imagination.

"Play cat in the hat on the mountain."

"It's different," referring to one of my milkshake concoctions. "It's coconutty."

Since things were going so well, I decided on continuing Sarah-Rise full-time, at least through the next school year. Such a decision had to be made well in advance because most schools wanted to know their autumn roster by the preceding February. Continuing with Sarah-Rise meant thirty to forty hours of one-on-one time for Sarah each week, which was basically the equivalent number of hours as traditional school. Thankfully, I didn't have to do any homeschooling paperwork yet. The mandatory age for schooling in most of Pennsylvania was eight, and Sarah was six.

When I thought Sarah was ready to expand her range, I started setting up more interactions with larger groups of people. I signed her up to take a gymnastics class, with Sonia or me as her helper. I planned a weekly playdate with a friend who had a similar kid situation to my own, and we began considering a more traditional classroom setting again, albeit in a very part-time capacity and with preschoolers. Sarah was technically the age of kindergartners, but developmentally, she wasn't there yet.

I arranged for Sarah to visit the preschool connected with Amy's day care. Sonia would be by her side and, if it went well, then that would be an option for the upcoming school year. This would include a minimal amount of school structure without taking too much time away from Sarah-Rise. The preschool would be two days a week, from 9:00 a.m. to noon, with three- and four-year-olds. The teachers loved the idea that Sarah would come with a personal helper, and they invited Sarah to begin immediately. She and Sonia attended preschool two mornings a week starting at the end of January. This became part of our regular routine until the end of the school year in May.

As Sarah's language expanded, my confidence in her interactions grew. We started seeing all kinds of exciting moments between Sarah and our volunteers. When Sarah C. wrote the name of her cat on the whiteboard, "C-H-E-S-T-E-R," Sarah started pointing out the different letters. While we knew she knew her letters, this seemed like a different kind of interest and understanding. Sometimes, when we thought Sarah's understanding was expanding, it wasn't some overt thing that we could put our finger on. It was more like sensing a quickening in the atmosphere and feeling something with our intuition. She was delighted to learn the name of Sarah C.'s cat and to connect the letters in the word to the name. She henceforth decided that almost anything that required a name received the name Chester.

One of Sarah's favorite books was *What Color Should I Be?* by Betty Ann Schwartz. It is about a chameleon asking other animals what color it should be, becoming a new color on each page. There was a time when Sarah B. drew a blank chameleon on the board and asked Sarah what color it should be. Sarah started filling it in with different colors, confident and purposeful in her choices. Then she drew her own chameleon! If you didn't know what you were looking at, you might not guess it was a chameleon, but the intention was what mattered. Similarly, when Carl drew a pair of pants and asked Sarah to add polka dots, he felt she really understood and enjoyed the activity. We saw that Sarah was learning to stay within the lines of her own accord.

During one of my sessions with Sarah, we made a birthday card for Amy. I wrote "AMY," and Sarah watched attentively. When I asked her to draw a picture, she intently used one color, making specific marks, and then chose her next color. After I wrote Sarah's name at the bottom, she said, "wite name" and proceeded to make very specific (if totally unclear) marks on the page. I loved that her desire and purposefulness was there. Skill could come later, but the desire had to come first.

Granddad and Grammy, my dad and stepmother, visited in the spring, and Sarah gave them a warm and connected greeting. As she came down the stairs, her face brightened with delight, and then she kept repeating their names, sometimes while looking at them and sometimes while giving attention to Granddad's pants. She pointed out that his pants were light brown and that her pants were dark brown. Compared to when they last saw her, they were aware that she was talking much more and seemed to understand the world more.

The nuances of these experiences in the Sarah-Rise room with volunteers and outside with family members were showing me that we were on the right path and that my choices to expand Sarah's activities outside the Sarah-Rise room were appropriately timed. While some of these changes were possibly less quantifiable than an increased vocabulary, it was undeniable that Sarah was doing more activities with more skill and participation than she had in the past. What I especially appreciated was that these changes came easily by spending loving and playful time together.

In my field of work, within the Alexander Technique, there is a concept called "the means whereby." The idea is that if you only focus on your final goal, then you may be tense and out of alignment as you move toward that goal. But if you address the manner in which you move toward that goal, then you will achieve that goal more comfortably and successfully. I can see that through the Sarah-Rise sessions, our means whereby was to be present and attuned to connecting with Sarah. Without forcing anything, our goal of increasing her capabilities overall and her ability to connect with others was happening with comfort and success.

Come April, I gained the confidence to try another little experiment in the Sarah-Rise room. I took up much more physical space than I usually did, and I hammed up whatever we were doing more than usual.

Sarah climbed back-and-forth over castle walls made of blue plastic balance beam pieces arranged in a circle, and I joined her. As she started watching me climbing the walls, I changed how I moved a tiny bit. Sometimes I ran. Other times I jumped. She smiled. Then I got down on my knees and pretended to have a hard time crawling over the wall, asking for help, which she provided.

Next, I tried breaking the castle wall and asking for her help to reassemble it. I was melodramatic about this, yelling "Help!" with an exaggerated, panicked expression. I grabbed her sweatshirt where lapels would be if sweatshirts had lapels. Sarah was cracking up. This session felt connected, lively, and fun. While in theory that was always my goal, in practice, I didn't always feel energized or creative. Some of our times together were quite low-key, with more joining or with me reading a book to her while she ate. I did so animatedly, and we still had a good time, but the castle game felt like a home run. The time passed easily, and I was challenging Sarah to engage in more physical activity herself, which was a goal of ours. I was in the zone—aligned with myself and with Sarah.

Another way I took up more physical space in our play was when she wanted to have a snack. Usually, when Sarah wanted a snack in the Sarah-Rise room, I read a book to her, staying close so she could see the words and pictures. Now, when she chose a familiar book, I acted out the book rather than just reading it. She no longer needed to see the words and pictures because she knew the book so well, and I used the whole room as my stage while she watched me and ate her snack.

One of her favorite books at this time was *A Special Day for Mommy* by Dan Andreasen. I pretended that I was getting sticky after making a jam sandwich or doing a craft with glue. She let me do this and watched and laughed for much of the time.

I soon learned that hamming it up worked beyond the castle-walls or book-reading sessions. When she started talking about foods that she wanted but couldn't have, I grabbed her shoulders and said, "Oh no! We don't have any! Help! What are we gonna do?" She loved it. In general, she loved it when I physically moved her around as part of the play, whether scooping her up in my arms, tipping her backward, nuzzling the top of my head into her chest, or moving her hips in rhythm to a song. I just hadn't thought until now to add physicality to make a lack of a desired item into something playful. My mock distress helped her not be distressed for real.

Easter had always been rather like Halloween in terms of Sarah's understanding and participation. In our family, Easter involves baskets and egg hunts. That spring, we did an Easter egg hunt with plastic eggs, and each girl approached it differently.

Amy, who was two, immediately knew what to do and started filling her bag with all the eggs. Sarah, who was six, found an egg and opened it and closed it and opened it and closed it before putting it down. Then she found another egg to open and close repeatedly. Eventually, Amy had all the eggs, except for the one Sarah was holding. Upon realizing this, Amy changed course and put some eggs from her basket into Sarah's. I could barely contain my tears over Amy's sweetness. Next, Amy wanted to open and close eggs like her big sister, but she couldn't close them, so Carl suggested to Sarah that she help Amy close her egg. Sarah did, taking Amy's egg as her own and giving Amy one she had previously closed.

As I watched, I felt affirmed in my understanding of Sarah. All the times I'd seen neurotypical kids engaging in an activity and thought,

Sarah wouldn't do this activity, I had not been making it up. It was true. Most of the time, Sarah did something entirely different, or she did the activity in a different way. Easter morning was another opportunity for me to notice where I was stuck on how things should be a certain way. By recognizing the stuck spot as my mental pothole rather than as truth, I could open my heart to allow it to be wonderful, as it was. It was not just okay; it was really great that Sarah did things her way. I could allow Sarah's way to be perfect and also be overjoyed that Amy participated in the neurotypical way.

It was and is so transformative to have Sarah be who she is; she has helped me open my heart and let go of *shoulds*. It was and is so great to have Amy be neurotypical, filling my heart with the contented joy of a childhood parenting dream come true. Their differences are not about my parenting skills. There is no right or wrong to being neurotypical or otherwise. There may be social pressures and expectations, but the absolute value of each child is equal.

Sonia usually accompanied Sarah to preschool, but one day it worked with my schedule for me to be there. Anytime I interacted with the other children or watched them play in a group, I felt daunted. Sarah did not engage with other kids the same way most of them were interacting with one another. She watched them play, often specifically watching their feet as they ran around. Or she played alone at the sand table, absorbed in the texture of the grains. At home, I could easily join such an ism, but at school I instead saw it delineate the difference between how the other kids played and how Sarah played. As my feelings momentarily dragged in the metaphorical mud, I reminded myself that she did not need to be like the other kids.

The moment I let go of the belief that she should be like the others, I felt much better. Sure, I would love for her to play with other kids, but my priority was to love her exactly as she was. As her progress thus far had demonstrated, loving her in the moment was the means whereby we could eventually get to more playful interaction with other children.

Later that evening at dinner, Sarah was in fine form answering questions, and when Carl told her she could get forks for herself and for Amy, she responded, "No. Use the hands."

When I asked her if she had a plate or if she needed one, she answered, "Have one."

We were still a bit surprised and delighted when her language came forth easily, appropriately, and of her own creation rather than practicing a word or phrase we had just said.

As with so many things, I found myself wondering if the reason for her progress had less to do with her growing intelligence and more to do with my getting out of the way so that the intelligence and independence she had could shine forth. Maybe she didn't do some things because she knew I would do them. Maybe the biggest gift was to ask her questions and give her time to answer, and to give her the space and time to do an activity before swooping in to be "helpful" but really taking away her autonomy.

A few days later, Carl was in the Sarah-Rise room with Sarah reading *Knuffle Bunny Free* by Mo Willems. He asked Sarah about what was going on in the book. His questions included "How did Trixie feel?" and "Why?"

After each question, he waited . . . and he waited.

Inspired by our recent efforts to learn Italian and noticing how much time we needed to supply newly learned words, he waited longer for her answers than we normally did.

He waited a long time.

And she answered! Many questions. It was clear that she really was understanding. She said that Trixie was sad. When Carl asked, "Why?" she said, "Lost Knuffle bunny." Carl shared the details with me that night after the kids went to bed. We marveled at Sarah's progress and at our own need to consistently remind ourselves to give her ample time to respond to our questions or requests. I think adults tend to ask a question and wait a second or two before they prompt a child for an answer. It is as if they are playing music and expecting the flow to continue with constant quarter-note pacing when actually they should add a rest. Instead of waiting for two seconds, they need to wait ten or fifteen seconds, which can feel like an eternity.

As the year went on, we noticed Sarah progressing in her physical participation in the playroom. She did her best to copy jumping jacks, and if we built stairs from interlocking plastic planks and bricks, she readily climbed up and down. Of course, we knew Sarah could climb stairs because she did so regularly within the house, but the stairs we made in the Sarah-Rise room could have extra-big gaps or have differing heights between steps, requiring a different kind of balance and adventurousness. And now, Sarah played Twister! She didn't understand leaving her hands and feet in place, but she would take turns spinning the dial and moving her hand and foot to the correct color after I moved my appendage. Twister was both adorable and exciting.

We had been encouraging her to copy facial expressions by exaggerating our own, as ATCA suggested that copying facial expressions was a helpful developmental step, and now she was doing just that. She had an earnest sad and mad face, and you could see her glee shining from her eyes even as her mouth was downturned. She did a variety of pretend cries. I don't know what allure sadness and crying held for her, especially when hammed up for pretend play, but she loved it. We also modeled shaking our head *no* and nodding *yes*. These movements proved elusive in terms of looking natural or graceful. Even now they aren't the movements that come the most organically from her, but she does them appropriately and usefully.

Sarah was moving forward in leaps and bounds, and Carl and I were growing as parents. I was gaining more wisdom to share with the volunteers, who were also able to be more effective in how much space and time they gave Sarah to help her continue flourishing.

12

"A" Is for "Allergy"

"P" IS FOR "PECAN." "A" is for "anaphylaxis."

We learned the hard way that pecans cause Sarah to go into anaphylaxis. Previous experience had alerted us to Sarah's mild peanut and walnut allergy. She'd get a runny nose, itchy eyes, and an itchy face, which would last for thirty minutes. Otherwise, she had been eating tons of almond butter and cashew butter and had tried pistachios and macadamia nuts with no trouble at all. So one day, I thought I would add some variety to her coconut milkshake. I used pecan butter instead of almond or cashew butter. That was a mistake.

It was immediately obvious that she was allergic, because her lips started swelling and her eyes were getting a little red. Five minutes after she had her shake, she was lying down to nap, when she normally wouldn't nap. I could tell that this was more than a mild allergy. I called the pediatrician, who advised me to give her Benadryl and to call 911 if I thought she was having trouble breathing. She wasn't having hugely notable trouble, more like 2 percent of a change from her normal breathing, but her lips continued swelling, hives popped up around her mouth, and all the while she was trying to sleep.

With deep fear, thinking, *I can't believe I am in this moment worrying about the life of my child*, I scooped her up and carried her downstairs as I dialed 911. Once emergency services were on the way, I called Carl to tell him to meet us at the hospital. The fire department arrived first, followed by the paramedics. Sarah's breathing was still okay, but they wanted her to go to the ER anyway. I transferred her car seat to the ambulance, and away we went. Sonia and Amy stayed at home, explaining the situation to a cluster of concerned neighbors.

Carl beat us to the ER because he worked near the children's hospital. When we arrived, Sarah vomited half a day's worth of food and fluid all over herself and her car seat. I hadn't brought any backup clothing for her, but they put her in hospital scrubs anyway. A combination of IV fluids, Benadryl, steroids, and epinephrine helped Sarah to stabilize, but not until after she turned into an itchy mess covered in hives with puffy lips and a swollen tongue.

We'd been told that anaphylaxis can have a second flare-up, so the doctors wanted Sarah to stay and be monitored overnight. Sonia delivered clothes, some favorite toys and books for Sarah, and a phone charger, books, and snacks for me. Eventually, Carl went home to be with Amy. Sarah and I spent the night at the hospital.

The next morning, we had a surprise visit from Captain America—he was cleaning the windows outside of Sarah's room! Sarah was interested in the fact that someone was hanging outside her window but didn't know who Captain America was. Captain America helped our whole experience end on a positive note because who doesn't like having a superhero clean their window? Maybe it helped me more than it helped Sarah.

When we were finally discharged and able to return home, we had an EpiPen in tow. (EpiPens are emergency medication to be given in case of an anaphylactic reaction to something.) Now, that pen goes everywhere with Sarah.

Pecans would not cross my threshold again if I could help it, and we scheduled an appointment with an allergist to find out if Sarah had any other severe allergies. Her blood work returned no surprises, just the now-familiar culprits: pecans, walnuts, and peanuts. She was also mildly allergic to dust mites and cats, although she had always been okay with our cat as long as she didn't stick her face where there was an accumulation of fur.

Anaphylaxis aside, Sarah had many breakthroughs in the next couple of months. At preschool, she reached out during circle time and spontaneously started a tickle game with the boy next to her. Since it was the end of circle time and the kids were about to line up for handwashing and a snack, the game didn't go beyond Sarah tickling the boy while saying, "Tickle," and his tickling her back once. Still, this was unprecedented and phenomenal for her to initiate a game with another child.

While playing Twister with Sarah C., Sarah initiated including her stuffed animals Gerald and Piggie into the game. She placed them on the circles and put them near the spinner. We later learned that Sonia had been inviting Gerald and Piggie to participate in other activities with Sarah, so it was even more exciting that Sarah had expanded on the idea of her own accord.

The weekend Mom-Mom and Pop-Pop visited, Sarah went upstairs with Mom-Mom when Mom-Mom asked to see the girls' room. When they got to the room, Sarah ismed for a few moments, opening and closing her jaw and hands. Then she stopped and opened her arms wide.

"Nice room," she said.

She began walking around and pointing.

"Share bed. Share dresser."

Then she showed Mom-Mom the separate drawers that she and Amy had, and she said, "Clothes in dress-er."

Not only was her language improving, but her awareness of what was said in her periphery was expanding. This meant I had to pay more attention to my own language all the time, not just in direct interactions with Sarah. I came to this realization when Sarah repeated her first curse word, uttered by yours truly: "Fuck."

It slipped out of my mouth when I spilled some of the medicine that Sarah needed to take for a few days following the anaphylaxis.

From behind me chimed Sarah's perfect repetition of the word: "Fuck."

And then came Amy's attempt, which sounded more like "uck."

This was an excitingly typical milestone for me as a parent. I knew Sarah had been repeating tons of new words that she heard, so from her perspective this one word was no different, but it was certainly different from my perspective and meant that I needed to clean up my speech in addition to the medicine I'd spilled.

Sarah's language grew more nuanced and fluid. We were thrilled to hear so many new sentences, some of which included "Fuh-lint," our cat, who would "sleep on pill-ow in Mom's closet." Or "Daddy have buh-lack hair," which was not true but worth it for the sentence construction. She also requested to "puhlay with Mom-Mom in Sayra-Rise room . . . now."

This tremendous verbal progress paved a path to Sarah's growing interest in writing. We had bath crayons that the girls played with during bath time, and I noticed that Sarah started using them to make the marks that we knew were her letter-writing attempts, while spontaneously saying "S-A-R-A-H" as she wrote each squiggle. Each of her marks looked the same, but the fact that she could spell her name and wanted to write it astounded me.

We'd come so far from celebrating the first time she tried to say "milkshake."

At least once a day, three-year-old Amy would cry brokenheartedly about needing help. I could relate. When I felt like I should be doing more but couldn't possibly do more, I wanted to cry about needing help. In the moment of feeling helpless, Amy and I were each stuck. What we needed was someone to listen kindly and provide the space and time to get our sad out, and then we could feel clearer and more capable moving forward.

It was easier for me to trust that Amy would move through her sadness and stuck feelings than it was for me to trust the process for myself. Before trusting that it was okay to be feeling what I was feeling, I wanted to know if such acceptance would work to make things better. I had a desire to peek to see if acceptance of my feelings was the trick that would make Sarah progress faster. However, the most important belief to affirm was that it was 100 percent okay if Sarah didn't change any more or grow any more. Accepting her as she was, with no need for her to change, was crucial. This was not because such acceptance would then magically garner change in Sarah but because it would foster change in me. Acceptance would bring more peace and equilibrium in me.

Fundamentally, I had been believing that if I'd done a better job as Sarah's mom, then she would be "normal" already. As if that were the goal. But what if that wasn't the goal? What if the goal was to be fully present and loving and accepting? What if the goal was to help Sarah develop and learn for the sake of being the best Sarah she could be?

Wasn't *that* the crux of this whole business?

One of Sarah's favorite snacks was freeze-dried peas. We kept a bag in the Sarah-Rise room. That May, when Mom-Mom and Pop-Pop were visiting us, Sarah started a game centered around the fact that "Pop-Pop don't have any peas."

We all reacted in the exaggerated way she thought was fun, and so the game grew. Sarah added to the list of what Pop-Pop was missing. Poor, destitute Pop-Pop apparently had no peas, toothpaste, mirror sunglasses, ladders, stripes, fish, stairs, milkshakes, milk, pants, eggs, flossers, beds, sheets, blankets, or houses. Pop-Pop had to live in other people's houses! Mom-Mom always seemed to be better off. Only occasionally was she missing something, as the game mainly focused on Pop-Pop. Eventually, "Pop-Pop *don't* have any . . ." became "Pop-Pop *doesn't* have any . . . ," which was notable because Sarah corrected it herself without us drawing specific attention to her word choice. Even Amy voiced her own rendition of Sarah's phrases with great glee.

It was clear that Amy adored her older sister and wanted to be in on whatever verbal game we were all playing. Sarah and Amy were often around each other and usually enjoyed similar songs and games. Sarah sometimes came along for the ride as I took Amy to day care, to enjoy the connection together for a bit longer and to go on "an outing," however short. While Amy and I appreciated her company, when my timing felt tight, I was not always the most patient about Sarah's pace throughout the drop-off process. She liked taking her time, and I wanted to be speedier.

ATCA advises parents to give kids more time to answer questions than people normally give, whether the kids are neurotypical or not. I realized I could give Sarah more time to respond to my prompts, requests, and suggestions in general. I decided to experiment with this on one of our trips to Amy's day care.

Upon arrival, I prompted Sarah.

"Time to get out of the car."

Instead of re prompting two seconds later, I started counting in my head: *One, two, three* . . . I never got past fifteen seconds because Sarah got out of the car, easily! On her own.

Once we crossed the street and were outside the entrance to the day care, Sarah paused on the threshold. She liked the lines on the floor that were often present as the transition from one type of flooring to another. I verbally nudged her to go through the door. And before I nudged again, I started counting in my head: *One, two, three . . . nineteen, twenty . . .*

If I hadn't been counting internally, those twenty seconds would have felt like forever. But she did go through the door without my needing to prompt her a second time. In fact, I wonder if I needed to prompt at all to get her out of the car or go through the door. Those were familiar activities, and the situation itself was probably a sufficient prompt. Perhaps I could trust Sarah's knowledge of what to do rather than worrying about our timing. I could have patience and leave room for Sarah to be herself, for all of us to be our selves.

13

And the Crowd Went Wild

A game based on Alexander and the Terrible, Horrible, No Good, Very
Bad Day *by Judith Viorst*

ONE EVENING, WITH A sitter at home with the kids, Carl and I went
to a Pirates baseball game. We enjoyed our night out and our hot dogs
and ice cream. With a win, the Pirates would make the playoffs for
the first time in twenty years. The cheering was intense. As I listened
to the crowd of some forty thousand people cheering, sometimes for
one person, I thought about what that might feel like. What if that
cheering was for you? What if we cheered that intensely in our own
heads for our own achievements? What if each parent who helped
their child learn to speak was given a deafening standing ovation, just
like the Pirates were when they won that game?

The achievements of kids with special needs and parents of kids with special needs are no less incredible or important than a home run in baseball. For that matter, the achievement of every person to get up each day and strive for their dreams, or just to get through the day, is worthy of that degree of cheering and recognition. Instead, some of us berate ourselves. We give ourselves a hard time for falling short of our goals, rather than celebrating what we did accomplish. At least, that tends to be true for me.

I often got mad at myself when I got mad at the girls, especially if I yelled at them. Sometimes, I got grumpy about things that were miracles of achievement. It was wonderful that Sarah wasn't getting around to brushing her teeth because she was busy talking about how the sink was empty, pronouncing each word perfectly. Or because she was pretending the toothbrush was a melting Popsicle. It was wonderful that Sarah didn't keep her butt parked in her seat during breakfast because she just had to put pretend lemon juice on Carl's food. She loved it when people made sour faces, and Carl provided wonderful faces. Sarah, the girl who didn't like to eat, now helped herself to food from the freezer, the fridge, and the counter! She liked helping in the kitchen, and she wanted to participate so much that she was constantly underfoot and in my way. While I got frustrated, I reminded myself that this was actually what I wanted. I wanted her to want these things and to be so engaged and solicitous of involvement.

But I fell into the classic trap of only noticing the climb ahead instead of how far we had come—filling the roles of both anxious coach and adoring fan, cheering while also always going for more. I cheered Sarah on more fervently than I cheered for my own efforts on her behalf, all the while noticing my shortcomings—five minutes of grumpy yelling—rather than my long-term endurance runs of love, patience, creativity, and organization. Writing my weekly email updates to friends and family and receiving their cheering and support helped me recognize my own abilities. I could get back onto my emotional feet and, if not cheer wildly for myself, at least not berate myself so much for coming up short.

The summer when Sarah was six, we had an influx of new volunteers and returning volunteers. It was wonderful to welcome past volunteers who already knew what to do as soon as they got in the room. It was also exciting to have new volunteers with fresh perspectives to contribute to the playroom. When we had a team meeting, as we did every month or two, I became acutely aware of how influential we were as a team. The volunteers, Carl, Sonia, and I shared our recent moments with Sarah, and then we reviewed our goals and motivations for Sarah—all of us working together, each of us with different ideas. This team could provide a variety of play experiences for Sarah that she wouldn't get if it were just me.

In one meeting we spent the last half hour developing games, which were inspired by our craft supplies and the pictures I'd printed out of people that Sarah knew. By the end of the meeting, we had two poster-board games. One was a matching game with pairs of duplicate faces, made of the pictures of family and friends, which we stuck to the board with Velcro. Another board had a transportation theme and utilized the same Velcro faces as the matching game. We also made cut-out heads of these family and friends and stuck them onto Popsicle sticks, where we adorned them with interchangeable construction paper hair and accessories. We finished our work by hiding small construction paper snails around the room, leaving out a pile of their matching counterparts with written reminders about where the hidden match was.

Each hour of focused, loving Sarah-Rise time was such a gift, and the group meetings took that time to the next level. We had a whole group of people meeting with the sole purpose of helping another person be the best that she could be. I loved my team so much, and I was so impressed with everyone all the time. Every time I saw their glowing faces and heard their love as we talked about Sarah, I was filled to the brim with gratitude. The beauty of The Son-Rise Program was that the best way to help Sarah was for us to clear our own emotional junk and be the best version of ourselves that we could be.

Sarah C. had a session where she and Sarah played with two themes for the whole two hours. She and Sarah made milkshakes and then buses. That was phenomenal in terms of flexibility, imagination play, and interactive attention span. Sarah then determined that Sarah C. was the only one who knew how to build a bus appropriately.

While Sarah thrived on building buses and making milkshakes, jigsaw puzzles remained a huge challenge. I appreciated Gregory's work with Sarah during one session when she was playing with a puzzle. Gregory let her be. He let her fiddle with it and make mistakes and put things together wrong. That was something I didn't do, because I was so concerned with teaching her to "get it" and not wanting her to get so frustrated she would give up. I was reminded by Gregory's interaction that perhaps the best thing I could do to help her "get it" was to get out of the way and give her time. That was probably true for many things, not just puzzles. Essentially, letting Sarah puzzle things out more independently was akin to letting her go up to bat and swing at pitches, rather than arranging for a walk.

As Sarah progressed, we continued following ATCA's guidance of adding one small thing at a time as the way to build into more complex play scenarios. I didn't see this play out extensively until one week in June when Sarah and I started with a tent, and I kept adding small things to our tent scenario. We drew a campfire. Then we sang camp songs and songs about the plaid tent. We roasted hot dogs and marshmallows and ate pea donuts. Soon after, we switched to creating a bus. First, I was the driver; then we got a steering wheel and Sarah was the driver. We stopped for Play-Doh ice cream. We read a book on the bus. In both play scenarios, what I really appreciated was how we both added ideas and how I was able to incorporate some of her ideas into the original theme instead of switching to new play, as I might have done in the past. When she said to get ice cream, I made sure that was a stop on our bus ride instead of ditching the bus.

Sarah was knocking my socks off repeatedly with her learning, creativity, and spirit. When we were out of yogurt, she drove a little toy car around and told me she was driving to the yogurt maker. She started putting her plate away on the counter in the mornings without any prompting. She took a bath and said, "Bump, bump, bump . . . riding in a white tub bus." She also said, "Swim like a fish. Pop-Pop swim like a fish. Sarah Wellington swim like a fish." She played balloon baseball with me, which was a big deal to have such physical play and to stay with the theme for at least ten minutes. I called her Batter Wellington, and she wore a yellow construction helmet. She hit a balloon ball and ran around a very small baseball diamond. The crowd of one mom went wild!

At one point, when she was sitting at my desk, she said, "Do one more email. Sarah Wellington do one more email. I do one more email." It was incredibly rare for her to use "I" correctly. This was all so exciting, and I kept telling myself that if something happens once, then it can happen twice.

During a car ride, I saw Sarah put a book against the back of the seat in front of her and hold it up with her feet. *Such coordination!* And one day, Sarah made up a new word, unintentionally, as she tried to say "envelope." Her new word was "empty-lope," referring to an empty envelope. I think it should be a real word. I loved it. *Such creativity!*

There was the time when she was sitting on the toilet fully clothed after using the potty and Sonia checked on her.

"What you doing the toilet paper?" Sarah said, seeing Sonia pop in.

Since it didn't seem that Sarah was doing anything amiss, Sonia left. Sarah remained in the bathroom for several more minutes, so Sonia returned.

Sarah quipped, "What you doing the toilet paper, missy?"

This time Sonia looked more closely and found that Sarah had been unrolling the toilet paper and stuffing it in the storage rack underneath the roll. *Such sneakiness!*

As with the beginning avalanche of Sarah's language, this progress was intoxicating. Around this time, Sarah and I had the longest session of playing a board game we had ever had. We were playing Chutes and Ladders. Normally, she wanted to hop her piece around the board, but for the first time she was amenable to following my prompts to leave her piece in place or leave my piece in place and to take turns spinning. We took at least ten turns each. One of our long-term goals for Sarah was to play games the way they were meant to be played, so this felt like a home run in that department. *Such progress!*

To foster interest in board games in general, I decided to create a game based on her interests. Sarah loved *Alexander and the Terrible, Horrible, No Good, Very Bad Day* by Judith Viorst, so with suggestions from Megan during one of our consultation calls, I crafted a board game. The pieces were made from a cut-up egg carton with pictures of the characters glued on top. To play, you rolled a die and then moved through the events of Alexander's day, by either answering questions about the event or acting it out. The first person to reach Australia won.

The first time I brought out the game, Sarah and I played for forty-five minutes! She still needed a lot of coaching about when to roll and how to keep the game pieces on the board, but The Alexander and the Horrible No Good Very Bad Day Game was a success. Her favorite part was when the elevator door closed on Alexander's foot. As soon as she started trying to recite that part, she laughed so much she could barely get the words out. I felt like this time I was the one to hit a home run—and I went wild.

Expanding imagination games to prolong interactive attention span and flexibility was another goal of ours. One favorite game of

Sarah's that worked well with this goal was started by our volunteer Sarah C. The game was to pretend to eat Popsicles or ice cream. Sarah C., Carl, Sonia, Amy, and I all played this game at varying times with Sarah. We pretended they were too hard and hurt our teeth or that they were melting all over and we had to lick them quickly. We pretended to put lemon juice on them and then made sour faces. Once, Sarah and I had a small playful battle where she put salt on my Popsicle, so I put pepper and paprika on hers. She countered and won by putting garlic on mine! *Bleh.*

Even with such progress, there were at times conflicts between what Sarah wanted to do and what we wanted her to do, but we sought creative solutions so that we weren't just telling her no. Sarah loved doors and thresholds, but we did not allow play with outside doors or with the Sarah-Rise-room door during sessions because it was not something we could easily join. Doors bore the risk of injured fingers, and the back storm door that led outside was *loud.* When she wanted to play with the back door, I said no, explaining why and offering options such as blowing bubbles or playing in the sandbox. This didn't always go over well. During one of my Sarah-Rise sessions, she said she wanted to play on the sheet porch, so we made a porch out of a sheet on the floor and used blue planks to be doorways. She loved it. As she walked over a plank, I said, "Slam!" and she cracked up. It felt lovely to cater to her love of doors in some way in the Sarah-Rise room.

Crack. And it's another homer for Jenny Briggs!

On some days, I felt guilty about all the time I spent with Sarah in the Sarah-Rise room. I worried that I wasn't giving Amy enough of my time. Sonia reminded me that part of why we were doing Sarah-Rise was to allow for more of a connection between Sarah and Amy in the future, which would be a boon to both girls. When their connection was notably increasing, I felt my path affirmed. That summer, Sarah played more with Amy than she used to. We had a three-way game of catch and of ring-around-the-rosy. Twice, in response to my prompt, Sarah helped Amy up after a fall. One evening during dinner, Sarah stood up to eat her avocado Popsicle. Amy got up and sidled as close as she could to Sarah. Sarah started spinning. Amy started spinning. Carl and I cracked up at this sisterly spinning moment, so similar to a falling-in-love scene from a 1980s romantic comedy when characters might go to a park and eat ice cream and swing together.

Amy was the embodiment of acceptance, love, and delight. She was such a gift to the Sarah-Rise program. Sure, the girls fought, but that was important, too. The Sarah-Rise room specifically removed conflict so that Sarah could grow without that added challenge, but to be ready to integrate into the rest of the world, Sarah benefited from the real deal of sibling struggles. Two-year-old Amy helped Sarah with social interactions and with learning to resolve arguments, with adult assistance. Amy was without the capacity at that time to recognize that Sarah was different from neurotypical kids. For this reason, Amy asked 100 percent of Sarah during any interaction, whether fraught or peaceful.

Amy invited Sarah to play with no doubt about Sarah's ability, just a desire to play. Sometimes she didn't ask; she just began the activity. She would throw a ball at Sarah or squirt Sarah with water in the tub. Sarah loved being squirted, and she did play ball a tiny bit with Amy. When Sarah said a line from a book that she loved or described what she was doing, such as "jumping on the bed" or "sitting in the dark," Amy repeated the line with enthusiasm bursting out of every pore.

I bowed down to Amy's embodied joy. Sarah could totally rock interactions with adults, but she still needed help where other kids were concerned. Amy was the first step. She was familiar and safe, and Sarah knew her well enough that it was probably easier to take her sister in without it being overwhelming or overly exciting.

Sarah developed a confidence through Amy.

"Pay with Harry," Amy said one day, as the girls waited for our volunteer to arrive.

"Puh-lay with Sheri," Sarah said to her.

She had corrected Amy's pronunciation! They were waiting for Sheri. Amy couldn't say the "s" sound yet, so it was quite adorable when Sarah helped her. Amy also called Sonia "Honia" and referred to Sarah as "Hara," with a longer "a" sound in the middle. When she eventually figured out the "s" sound, we were all a bit sad, even though we knew it was a good thing for her to be able to speak clearly.

Sarah started preschool when she was six, two years after I completed my Son-Rise Program Start-Up. It was her fourth "first day" of preschool. When she was three, she had her initial first day, and then she continued attending preschool for some part of each academic year after that until this fourth "first day." While six was old enough to be in kindergarten, we felt that it was now best for her to be around her developmental peers in preschool.

She attended school two mornings a week from 9:00 a.m. to noon. It was the same preschool she had attended the preceding spring, in the basement of a neighborhood church. It was welcoming and flexible. Sonia went as Sarah's attendant, but she didn't need much attending this time—except when she did, and then she really did. On an easy day, Sarah would enter the classroom, move her name token to the attendance jar, hang up her coat, and begin playing. She would easily join the circle and do what the teachers suggested as the activities for the day with little prompting or redirection.

On a day when Sonia needed to be more involved, Sarah usually was more distracted by things that were interesting and had less attention for what the teachers aimed to have the kids do. On days like this, Sarah needed more prompts and redirection, and it was beyond the scope of the main teachers to keep up with that level of individual attention when they had a whole classroom of kids. Sonia could then help guide Sarah's focus and give her any specific interaction she wanted.

Sarah had always enjoyed school, and this year was no exception. I also noticed that more people understood her. While at the sand table, she said that the sand was soft, and another kid responded. Other *kids* understood her! She even drew a self-portrait when that was the assigned activity. She played with the calendar and Velcro number pieces, and because Sarah's teachers were so supportive of her, they created a Velcro alphabet board to expand on how she played with the calendar board. They also made her an extra attendance packet comprised of a single binder ring that held cards with each student's name.

Sarah's self-portrait

Her favorite thing to do at school was to pretend to be her teachers, Ms. Colleen or Ms. Michelle. After circle time, when the kids were dismissed to free play, Sarah seized the opportunity to sit in Colleen's rocking chair and do what she could to sing the weather song and the days-of-the-week song, complete with movements. Though no one besides me or Sonia was near her to witness it, we usually heard her squeak out, "Pretending to be Ms. Colleen!"

At preschool, there was snack time, so I would pack Lydia's Green Crackers made from vegetables and seeds or some homemade beef jerky. The day the other kids had vanilla pudding, I was Sarah's helper, and she made it clear to me that she wished she could have pudding, too. Sarah usually handled her food restrictions very well, and she even handled this limitation well when I told her we would make some at home. I had no clue how I would make this happen.

When I got home, I mixed a large dollop of raw cashew butter with some coconut milk. She loved it. The texture was a bit thicker than regular vanilla pudding, but she didn't mind. Since I served this creation in a glass dish, I didn't send her to school with it because I didn't want to risk the dish breaking, but it became a staple snack for her at home.

Sarah had been doing well with the GAPS diet. She was eating healthily and plentifully, gaining weight, and seemingly avoiding constipation. When I consulted with the GAPS adviser, she said we could depart from GAPS somewhat and that maybe the addition of foods such as rice and potatoes would be a good next step. GAPS is usually not intended to be a forever diet; it is a means to an end of a healthier gut. We were excited to have a wider range of things Sarah could eat. Maybe she would even benefit from the variety in terms of nutrition, and we wanted to keep adding things to support flexibility in food choices.

We went along slowly with the change, being conscious about what Sarah ate while adding non-GAPS items in small quantities, such as potatoes, sweet potatoes, brown rice, and quinoa. We found that Amy loved mashed sweet potatoes, but we discovered that Sarah was not a fan. However, if I mixed sweet potatoes with some eggs and spices, baked that mixture, and called it a pie, then Sarah would eat it. Sarah was excited to have rice again. I served it as a side with dinner, simply cooked in water with nothing added. She also ate regular mashed potatoes with a bit of soy milk added. It was exciting to see Sarah experience more variety in her diet in addition to her ever-expanding capability to play and connect with people.

This became more apparent on the next visit with Mom-Mom and Pop-Pop. When Sarah wasn't glued to Pop-Pop and his striped shirts, she and Mom-Mom spent time in the Sarah-Rise room. Mom-Mom noted Sarah's increase in verbal clarity, imaginative play, and inner calm. Sarah spontaneously told Mom-Mom "I love you," completely unprompted, for the first time. It wasn't unusual for Sarah to respond with "I love you" if we said it first, though that was still a rare and notable occurrence. But this time, *she* initiated the verbal love exchange.

During that same visit, Mom-Mom, Carl, the girls, and I went for a walk to the park. Carl brought a Frisbee. At the park, Carl asked me if I wanted to play Frisbee. I said yes, and Amy wanted to play, too. Then Mom-Mom came over because she wanted to play. And then Sarah came over! And she attempted to throw and catch! This was so huge. To join a game already in progress was a step that had at one point seemed laughably far away. To participate in a new physical activity was doubly huge. This was a serious first!

Sarah was participating so much more. Our small crowd was on its feet in celebration.

14

A Cat and a Stripe

Halloween when Sarah was six and Amy was two

IT HAD BEEN A year since Sonia joined our Sarah-Rise team, and we were delighted that she decided to stay working with us for another year, with the benchmark of Halloween helping us note the difference in Sarah from the previous year. This year for Halloween, both girls were into *It's the Great Pumpkin, Charlie Brown,* and were reading some other Halloween books too—and I got answers from both girls when I asked what they wanted to be for Halloween!

Amy wanted to be a cat.

Easy enough.

Sarah wanted to be a stripe.

How will we do that?

Carl and I came up with some ideas, and we made a plan, assuming we would have to make Sarah's costume ourselves in some way. Amy and I would go out looking for cat costumes while Carl did Sarah-Rise time with Sarah, and we would figure out how to make her into a stripe later. But when it was time for Amy and me to leave, Sarah really wanted to go on the adventure. We decided to make it a family outing. This felt like playing with fire, given that the previous year's family Halloween-costume-shopping outing was fraught with tension and unhappiness. As we drove down our street, Carl and I discussed the parameters and rules for this outing—for the girls and for ourselves. The rules were to stick together and not wander off and to be relaxed about the situation if we didn't find what we were looking for. We went to a used-clothing store first, where there was a striped outfit that Sarah loved, and it fit her, despite the tag claiming to be size 3T. It had some stitches missing here and there, but Sarah was so excited about it that I decided I could make it work. For Amy's costume, she and I went to the Halloween store, while Sarah and Carl waited in the car. We found a cat costume that Amy liked, and we returned home with our bounty. Sarah wore her costume for the rest of the day!

In a mostly traditional way, Halloween that year was a success. The morning of the Halloween preschool and day care celebrations, when everyone else was still sleeping, I felt like a quintessential mom as I sewed a ramshackle seam into Sarah's costume so it wouldn't fall apart. Both girls woke up excited to wear their costumes to school. I had made treats that the girls were allowed to have, and when they got home from their celebrations, I swapped out their bags of candy for the approved homemade goodies. After Carl came home, he and I took the girls trick-or-treating while Sonia, who didn't get any trick-or-treaters at her apartment, stayed on our porch to hand out treats.

"Going treating" is what Sarah called it. That phrase is probably more apt than saying "trick or treating." She also practiced saying "I am a stripe" and "Happy Halloween!" though she didn't say much to anyone when she was "going treating."

After trick-or-treating that night, I swapped neighborhood candies for homemade chocolate shapes and miniature pumpkin pies that were vegan and gluten-free. Both kids went along with it easily.

After the girls were tucked into bed and Sonia had gone home, Carl and I sat on the couch reminiscing about how well the day had gone. Even though in past years I worked to accept the idea that Sarah might never be into Halloween, this still felt good. It felt like we had finally achieved the quintessential Halloween experience with no major hiccups or upsets. I felt at peace, as if some invisible box had finally been checked.

When Sarah was twelve months old, a friend gave her an outfit decorated with snails. The shirt had one big snail, and the pants were covered in small snails of different colors. She wore the outfit, but at such a young age she didn't get attached to any particular article of clothing. When Amy was big enough to wear the snail outfit and we dressed her in it, suddenly Sarah was in love with the snail pants and wanted to wear them herself, even though they fit her like capris. The snail pants became Sarah's all-time favorite item of clothing, as necessary to her happiness as Linus's blanket is to him. She wore the snail pants 24-7 unless she was forced to undergo the torture of laundry. If the snail pants had to be washed, then Sarah would scream and cry, sometimes for an hour or more. Whether the pants fit petite size-six Sarah or not was not the question.

By now, Sarah had been wearing the snail capris for the better part of two years, and they looked like they had survived a shipwreck, falling apart despite my multiple attempts at sewing the holes and reinforcing the seams. They had also become snail *shorts*. I wondered how on earth I would take them away, and then suddenly the solution seemed obvious. The ragged garment would be worn only at bedtime and for naps! As we weaned her off the snails, I enjoyed seeing her in other clothes.

It didn't take long before Sarah set her sights on another clothing item: Amy's bug-print pajamas. In fact, Sarah got a lot of interaction and conversation practice asking Amy if she could wear those pajamas at night. I'd found them at a used-clothing store, so there was no way I could get Sarah her own pair—her only option was to ask Amy. Even though Sarah asked nicely and looked at Amy directly, Amy usually said no, and Sarah was always upset. This was still a huge win—they were having a tiny conversation!

I diligently reminded myself to celebrate Amy's "no" as much as I would her "yes." It was wonderful that Amy knew her own mind and could express it clearly, and it was wonderful that Sarah was learning to ask for things she wanted by phrasing questions rather than making statements.

Every once in a while, Amy said yes to Sarah wearing the bug pajamas, which made it all the harder for Sarah when the answer was no. She would yell and cry for several minutes before choosing to wear her ragged snail pants or being forced to wear some other pair of pajamas if the snails were in the wash. Sarah always had many pajamas to choose from, but nothing could compare to the bugs and snails.

"Nice work, Miss Magoo. Wow. Holy moly."

These were the words Sarah said while looking up at me after finishing her homemade carrot-celery-apple-kale-cucumber-parsley juice one afternoon, voicing the words she expected me to say. Miss Magoo was a nickname I'd given her when she was very young, but this was the first time she'd called herself Miss Magoo. The words were finally coming out of *her* mouth.

Sometimes, I felt especially grateful to Sarah for teaching me to cook. I mean, *really* cook. I could whip up a few things before we did GAPS, but from-scratch cooking and inventive baking were not a part of my regular skill set. Only in wanting to help Sarah and in wanting her to enjoy foods that no longer fit within her GAPS restrictions did I expand my repertoire and teach myself to get creative. Sure, she couldn't have regular pizza, but I could make a pizza that she could have. She couldn't have store-bought vanilla pudding, but I could make cashew butter vanilla pudding at the drop of a hat. She couldn't have store-bought cookies, but I could throw together cashew butter, eggs, and a little bit of honey to bake cookies she could enjoy. It helped that she was extremely flexible about the substitutions. I often marveled at how she could simultaneously be the most rigid person I knew and the most flexible. She could rigidly only want pizza but be flexible enough to accept my ground-pea crust with tomato sauce and shredded-carrot "cheese" as her pizza. I don't expect that most people would accept that substitution as readily as she did.

Although I was getting more adept in the kitchen, Sarah's diet continued to be a source of recurring frustration. As we slowly moved away from GAPS, Sarah ate a handful of new foods, until we ran into a snag with skin irritation. Backward we went, completely off most of the new foods until we reached equilibrium. It proved trickier than before to get in all the supplements suggested by a naturopath since Sarah now eschewed some of her old favorite foods, simply because they were not vanilla pudding.

I kept telling myself that I was happy and relaxed, that we'd get through this snag without subsisting on vanilla pudding, but the tension in my neck and shoulders begged to differ. I was tightening as I resisted feelings of sadness or frustration. It is great to feel good, but it is also okay not to feel good and to allow space for all the feelings. I had to learn and relearn this lesson.

One day, I found myself in the kitchen about to give in to Sarah's strong demand for vanilla pudding. I could make it just once more, even though she desperately needed to eat a variety of foods that day. Sonia was done for the day, and no volunteers were coming. Sarah whined for her snack, and Amy was hungry, too, both of them sitting at the table waiting impatiently to be served. I was dragging heavily, while telling myself I was upbeat, saying to the girls that I would get their snack and then we could play. What I desperately wanted was to sit on the kitchen floor and cry. This is one of my favorite places to give up for a few minutes and let the sadness and frustration flow out of me rather than fighting my feelings. But this time, I kept making vanilla pudding.

I stirred the ingredients, but I could not stop thinking about how frustrated I was and how much I wanted to throw in the towel and give up.

I knew it was good to have new information and a chance to clarify what Sarah's body couldn't process, but I wanted to be able to give her foods that she liked that were healthy. I hated needing to take these foods away again. It was the end of sprouted raw pumpkin seeds with sea salt, bananas, almond flour, and one bite of cheese. I knew I was supposed to go slowly with adding new foods, but it was harder for me than I'd anticipated. I wanted more options! I wanted to let Sarah have bananas! I was so sad! So pissed! *So fucking tired of this shit!*

The despair and frustration of the back-and-forth dietary mystery dance reminded me of the earliest years with Sarah, the failure-to-thrive years, the "I want to give up but dare not let up" years. All of this was my fault because if I had just gone more slowly with introducing new foods then we would have more clearly seen the cause behind the little blisters on Sarah's fingers. I felt trapped because I couldn't offer the many delicious options we'd worked so hard to create *and* Sarah was no longer interested in what she could have. Except, of course, this bleeping vanilla pudding!

Instead of resorting to the kitchen floor, I plunked Sarah's vanilla pudding on the table in front of her, gave Amy some dried apples that Sarah used to like but was currently refusing, and called my mom, who has always helped me deal with feelings of overwhelm, worry, or failure.

"Mom?" I blurted out as soon as she picked up. "This is all just too hard, and I can't do it. Sarah has had too many servings of vanilla pudding today, but she's hungry and doesn't want anything else that she is allowed to have!"

I poured out all my feelings and frustrations, tears, and grumps while she listened attentively. When I paused for air, my mom shared her wise thoughts: "Perhaps just as Sarah has had too many servings of vanilla pudding, you, my dear, have had too many servings of trying to figure things out for the day. I think it is time to stop."

I cracked up, and my energy shifted. I could process my thoughts again. I let the girls watch an episode of *Daniel Tiger's Neighborhood* after they ate their snacks, and I made a batch of pea crackers. I hadn't made any in a couple of weeks, but I hoped this old favorite would appeal to Sarah. I ground the freeze-dried peas to make flour; added an egg, a few roasted beet slices, and some coconut flour; and then pressed the mixture into small rounds that I baked until they were a bit firm but still chewy. The kids ate them readily. My mom's suggestion to limit my servings of worry and self-attack was a good one.

If I just did things the way Bears and Samahria did things, then I would also have a miraculous outcome. Two years into Sarah-Rise, this sentence was running through my head. Despite my best attempts to limit my self-attack servings, I spent a good bit of my time and energy down in an emotional valley, trying to crawl back up a mountain. I kept thinking I should be doing things better than I was. I was mentally and emotionally exhausted from my own criticism. Sometimes in the past when I would get to my lowest low point, I would ask myself, *If an angel suddenly appeared before me and told me that I was good, would I believe them?* If the answer was no, as it usually was, then I realized my only recourse was to change my thoughts myself because clearly nothing *anyone* else could say would have enough of an impact. So I reconsidered how much I was berating myself for not doing enough for Sarah.

What if . . . *just what if* . . . I needed to do things the way *I* did them to get whatever miraculous outcome was waiting for us? Each kid is different, and so each approach is going to be a bit different. What if the most helpful thing for Sarah was exactly the program I was running? What if I was exactly the right person to help her by muddling through in my way?

Whether any of this was true or not, thinking this way about myself and my program helped me breathe more freely and think more clearly. The idea behind The Son-Rise Program is that we choose our beliefs, whether consciously or not. While sometimes making a conscious shift feels like the most elusive and impossible task, sometimes I can do it with relative ease and clarity. When I get myself so deeply mired in emotional mud that I'm on the verge of getting physically sick, that is a significant wake-up call to move into more positive thoughts about myself, even if at first they may feel forced. It also helped me feel better about myself to look back on our past and see how far we had come rather than looking at what remained. At one time, just about everything that Sarah could now do had seemed unattainable.

It used to seem impossible that Sarah would have the dexterity to perform many fine motor skills. But now she was opening, reaching, unfastening, and fastening all sorts of things, some of which were new, some of which were old, all of which pointed to her growing independence and sneakiness. She could now unbuckle the top part of her car seat, and she was attempting to open the car door while the car was in motion. (Don't worry! Child safety locks were engaged.) She could unlock both the front and back doors to the house from the inside. She could open the upper cabinet doors in our large built-in cabinet that we use as a place to keep things away from children. She could reach the toothpaste that we thought was out of reach, put there because it was tasty. Maybe these were all small miracles.

It used to seem impossible for Sarah to have the dexterity to type purposefully on a computer. But during one of Carl's Sarah-Rise sessions, Sarah was climbing the plastic brick-and-plank stairs in the room when she said, "Going to work." So he asked what she was going to do at work, and she said, "Work on a computer." He then created a laptop out of two small whiteboards we had in the room. One was a keyboard and the other a screen. As Sarah pressed letters on the keyboard, Carl wrote them on the screen.

Carl coached, "'M,'" and Sarah pressed "m."

Carl prompted, "'O,'" and Sarah typed "o."

Carl suggested, "'M,'" and Sarah again found the "m."

"Great!" said Carl. "Do you know what you just spelled?"

"'Mom.'"

This seemed like another small miracle . . . the typing, the knowing what she'd spelled, the imagination play she initiated of going to work!

Sarah was now in that lovely, spongy pre-reading stage and liked paying attention and learning, the same way she'd soaked up and enjoyed learning to speak. This was so exciting and helped me feel more positive about everything.

Soon, Carl had another milestone experience in the Sarah-Rise room: He and Sarah were playing the cookie-matching game, where the pieces look like Oreos and you can separate them to reveal different shapes—a heart, a circle, a star, and so on. The top and bottom must match to make a cookie. This was something that I had explained and modeled and helped Sarah with many times in the past but without much traction. But on this day, when Carl spread out all the pieces and explained to her what to do, she independently matched every cookie correctly.

When Carl told me this, I nearly fell over.

Meanwhile, we continued seeing improvements in Sarah's social connection. Twice within one week Sarah apologized, without being prompted. The first time was to Sonia and the second was to me. She was in her toy car and accidentally backed up into me. In her defense, I had come in quietly to clean up, so I don't think she knew I was there. She immediately said, "I sorry," followed by, "Scuse me." It knocked my socks off!

A grandparent visit always provided a good vantage point on changes in Sarah's social connections. Her grandparents didn't see her every day, so they noticed things that changed so gradually that we didn't fully appreciate the progress.

When Mom-Mom arrived for a visit, Sarah ran up to her and said, "Hello. I love you, Sarah." She was saying what Mom-Mom often said to her, and the intention conveyed love toward Mom-Mom even if the name supplied was different. Meanwhile, Amy was so excited that she hopped on her red bouncy horse and galloped several laps around our first floor.

Next, Sarah went to the piano, followed by Amy, both of them plunking away enthusiastically. When Amy got up, Mom-Mom sat down at the piano with Sarah, and Sarah pointed to the music and said, "Music notes." Both seemed so excited to see Mom-Mom and show her what they could do. If you saw a pair of socks flying past you, they were mine.

Another time, when Grammy and Granddad came to visit, at dinner Sarah spontaneously stood up and took her painting off the wall where I had taped it.

"Paint at school," she said as she held it up.

We didn't get many of these moments, where she initiated showing something to someone, and this was the first occurrence of showing her artwork. It was the most blatant show-and-tell I had ever witnessed from her. *Wow. Holy Moly. Nice work, Miss Magoo!* I had no socks left!

The crowning moment of Sarah's dexterity, social awareness, and sneakiness was the day she locked me in the family room. The girls and I had been reading in the family room when Sarah got up and closed the door on her way out. I heard her helping herself to a Popsicle in the kitchen, which she could now do. When I got up to check on her to make sure she had returned the Popsicle tray to the freezer, I discovered that she had locked me in. Since that room has a door leading to the kitchen and a door at the other end of the room that leads to the house's front entryway, I wasn't *actually* locked in—our downstairs has a circular pathway of connections. Still! I already knew that she could lock the door, but it was her intention of sneakiness that impressed me the most—which was confirmed by the look she gave me when I came into the kitchen. She wore her normal, calm expression but with a hint of pride and achievement, a look saying that she had been caught and she was keeping her face extra relaxed. She knew I knew, and she was playing it cool.

While Sarah's skills and determination to control her world were progressing in fine form, sometimes even determination and imagination weren't enough to change reality. Carl rolled over on a lazy Sunday morning and was face-to-face with Sarah, who had come in to snuggle.

"The world is covered in snow," she declared with a glint in her eye.

"Well, it snowed yesterday," Carl said. "You'll have to check if it is still there."

Sarah bounced out of our bed and ran over to lift the closest window shade. Her face fell in disappointment.

"Did the snow melt?" Carl asked.

"Snow not melted!" Sarah said. "Close the shade! Try a different window!"

She did exactly that, but unfortunately her innovative plan for restoring the world to its proper state ultimately proved unsuccessful.

December, Day 7,582.
It felt like my time solo-parenting would never end. Carl was away in Australia for work, and Sonia was visiting friends in Seattle. By the week's end, I thought it had been a month or more. Initially, I rallied

and amazed myself with my own energy and resilience on these days where there was more on my shoulders than usual, but then I burned out.

The first few nights, I went to bed super early, and the girls slept well. I even had an epiphany: the door to the Sarah-Rise room was really the door to the house, rather than the specific room. More deeply, it was the door to my heart. I was extra flexible, creative, loving, and effective. And then . . . .

The nights with the girls were increasingly eventful and sleep happened less and less—for everyone. By the middle of the week, our nights were filled with fraught conversations and Sarah yelling in a way that made no sense to me. In the middle of the night, I didn't deal well with things that didn't make sense (not that I dealt well in broad daylight, either). Sarah wanted a different shirt or pants and then insisted upon what she had already been wearing. Or she wanted the snail shorts with the holes to the front . . . no, the back . . . no, the front . . . no, the back! That was where they had been to begin with! A couple of nights I was sandwiched between the girls with all of us in my bed. While this was deliciously snuggly, I did not sleep soundly.

Even though I still had volunteers coming and preschool and day care, the decrease in sleep, the continued days with Carl and Sonia away, and maybe other components I hadn't faced meant that my super-amazing, flexible, creative, loving self had gone AWOL. I was disappointed in myself, but I tried to balance that out with being gentle with myself, given the circumstances.

But what if there didn't have to be a "given the circumstances" to warrant gentleness? What if we didn't have to be disappointed in the first place? Maybe all of this was just *what it was*. I was ever seeking more peace and softness toward myself overall, noting my tendency to always need a reason to be okay with how things were but striving to not need a reason.

Regardless, I was very glad that my mom and stepfather came for the weekend. With Mom-Mom and Pop-Pop playing with the girls, I had time to cook, write, read, and sleep, and I had more time for me. It did take a village.

Even when we had challenging times, the girls and I were still quite snuggly. When the girls were babies, they never used pacifiers or sucked their thumbs. What gave them solace was touching my face in some way. My face still brought them comfort during our hard times. Sarah liked to feel my nose, or Carl's, with the back of her hand. He and I used to joke that when she felt our noses in the middle of the night, that was how she knew which one of us had come to her aid—"Identification by nose." Amy liked to cup her palm on my cheek. It seemed to be a physical reassurance of my presence beyond just sitting on my lap, and it brought me peace, too, to feel Amy's little hand on my cheek.

When Sonia returned, we talked about my experience while she was away and reminded ourselves about the Son-Rise Program perspective, and I had another epiphany: The best way to help Sarah respond easily and calmly when she didn't get what she wanted was for me to respond easily and calmly myself. Yes, this meant being happy or calm when I didn't get what I wanted. *Darn it all!* I loved and loathed this realization. In truth, I loved the challenge of it. I would have to be okay with not meeting all of my goals in one day, *and* I would have to be okay with the girls not doing everything I told them to do in one day.

Working toward my new goal—to be more relaxed and practice happy flexibility even if I didn't get what I wanted—did make some moments easier. If I wanted all of us to clean the family room before playing a game but the girls were determined to head outside, I could (sometimes) go with that flow and trust that the cleaning could happen later. If I wanted to sing a song and Sarah didn't want me to, I could let it go. I didn't have to take it personally that she didn't want me to sing. If Sarah really wanted to wear a certain thing and it was unavailable, I could remain calm in the face of her screaming and crying, trusting that my calm would help more than my upset even if I didn't want to be hearing her scream.

As much as I bristled in response to her daily screams, I did appreciate how Sarah kept me on my own toes, ever striving for more space within myself to allow us all to be our full selves—our screams, grumps, slumps, whines, and all. Sometimes magazines edit the photos of people to get rid of the extra curves and bumps, even though they are really part of the picture, part of the people. Maybe all the screams, grumps, slumps, and whines are part of the picture of a beautiful life and don't need to be edited out or removed.

15

Watching My Words

MUCH OF THE GIFT that we were giving to Sarah was time. Time to process our requests, time to respond, time to initiate, and time to be herself. Yet sometimes, giving her time felt like I wasn't doing anything. Yes, that was precisely what I was (not) doing. I was getting out of the way. I was inhibiting any urgent prompting. Time meant we didn't have to try to do everything at once. Time allowed us to work on the current goals for a while, and then, whether or not there was progress, we reevaluated and changed the goals so that we stayed fresh.

During one of my Sarah-Rise sessions in mid-December, when Sarah and I were singing songs together, I was struck by how much Sarah had progressed, specifically with singing the alphabet. I used to prompt her by asking her to sing or by starting the song myself, and then I would pause, giving her time to start saying each letter before I would chime in a fraction of a second behind. But now we were singing together, and it felt *real*. Twice the girls sang a few lyrics of "Jingle Bells" in unison, and I was stunned because it hadn't happened before. Sarah singing was one of the best sounds I'd ever heard. I'd catch her in moments when she was playing by herself, singing to herself, just as Amy often sang to herself. Sarah singing so independently was a milestone that I hadn't even acknowledged was on an invisible list of developmental milestones in my mind.

Almost everything we set as a goal eventually happened, and that was exciting to witness. Sometimes Sarah reached goals within days, sometimes within years, but our goals were almost always met. We had developed a framework that helped us focus and move forward without it feeling overwhelming. If a goal felt overwhelming, then that usually meant I was trying to climb a mountain in one big step instead of finding the path and taking the first out of many small steps.

There is such power to focused simplicity.

For as much as we'd been successfully singing the ABCs, writing them was not the same story. Sarah had learned to write the letter "A" perfectly! She also had a pretty solid "H" and "T" already. But there was one snag: Sarah kept writing her "A" upside down.

One evening when the girls were playing in the basement and Sarah was at the chalkboard, I went over to her and practiced writing an "A," my hand over her hand, many, many times. As soon as I let her have a go independently, she'd do it perfectly and upside down—again and again. I decided that instead of putting my hand over her hand, I'd coach her.

"Go up!" I said enthusiastically as soon as her chalk touched the board.

After saying "Go up!" many, many times, it seemed like we had rewired her habit. She could now write her "A" correctly, right side up, without my even needing to continue with the verbal coaching! If she could write her "A" so clearly and correctly, I expected she could learn to write all the other letters, too. It seemed to help to focus intently on a small detail, such as the upstroke on the "A," until she got it. Next, we tried working on "S," which felt much harder to coach her through. Despite the challenge, it was beautiful to see how ready Sarah was to practice and learn to write her letters.

Sarah's fine motor abilities and attentiveness continued to expand. Carl found Sarah wearing my pajama shirt, fastening and unfastening the buttons repeatedly and all by herself.

Holy moly, Miss Magoo!

We also noticed that Sarah was making puzzle progress. A year earlier, puzzles seemed impossible, and coaching Sarah to manipulate a piece correctly seemed impossible. Now, she easily completed her wooden puzzles, the kind where you put a piece in a hole of the same shape, so I added a small challenge: Instead of a wooden puzzle with holes and shapes to fill the holes, I gave her one of the three-piece jigsaw puzzles we had. The puzzles had one picture with a three-letter word, one letter per puzzle piece. I arranged the three pieces spelling "cat" so that they almost fit together, which made her role very clear. She put them together. Next, I moved the three pieces farther apart. She fit them. Then I rotated one piece. Again, success! Then I turned one piece over. Yes! Finally, I turned all of them over and rotated them differently, and that was the only setup where she needed help, which she asked for after trying by herself for a while. I gave one verbal suggestion, and she got it!

Sarah's enjoyment of manipulating the pieces of the puzzle made me think it was a good time to get out Mat Man. Mat Man is the name of a kit from Learning Without Tears. The kit has wooden pieces that can be used to make a flat person or flat letters. I had been modeling it and letting her have free play with the pieces for a while, but this time I handed her the pieces *and* explained to her what they were for. She placed them all by herself. This was her creation:

January kicked off with me trying to make a new breakfast dish. It was supposed to be baked eggs in avocado halves, with the raw egg neatly held in the space vacated by the avocado pit before the assembly went in the oven. This did not go as smoothly as planned.

"Oh, poop!" I said when the raw egg spilled out of the avocado.

"Oh, poop!" Sarah said.

"Hara haid, 'Oh poop!'" Amy said.

At least my word choice was tame!

A few days later, the girls had their first inside joke:

"Oh, coffee!" said Sarah.

"Oh, coffee!" said Amy.

They had been saying this back and forth and giggling for minutes on end.

I had no idea how it started with "coffee," but it became a family joke—and a useful alternative to cursing. Anytime I got mad at something inanimate, Sarah would come up next to me and say, "Oh, coffee!"

"Oh, coffee, indeed," I'd reply.

The girls continued coming up with jokes together that were a mystery to me. When they both tried to go in a small space at the same time, Sarah said, "No, no key!" and Amy cracked up. Then they both repeated the phrase several times while laughing. "No, no key! No, no key!"

I had no idea what was so funny.

The two would sing, "Baba doink doink," which was a spin-off of Carl's version of the Sandra Boynton song "Perfect Piggies."

Sarah and Amy were feeding off each other. I delighted in this bonding and creativity.

Sarah had recently turned seven, and I spent a few days in February trying to wrap my mind around an idea that might help me stay more present with myself and with the Sarah-Rise program. I have struggled my whole life with having high expectations of myself and being disappointed when I don't meet my own goals for any given day or task. My new idea was very simple and also profound—at least I thought so. When the day was done and I noticed how much I did or did not do, maybe I could see that as information only. Unmet goals and undone tasks didn't have to be judged harshly. If I could accept Sarah's speed of learning and doing, perhaps I could accept my own. This would certainly feel better than being the jockey with a crop on my own rump.

In support of being at peace with what I had done rather than always thinking I should have done more, I received these affirming words from my stepmom:

What if you knew that The Extraordinary Miracle has already happened? That MANY of them have been happening? And more are continuing to happen? That what Sarah has already achieved in her short life is a miracle? Would you feel a huge high? A sense of "I am good at this"? Could you sit back, relax, and calmly soak in the radiance of success? I ask this because . . . Sarah's progress does seem to me like a miracle. We have no "benchmark" that is appropriate for Sarah, thus one could say she is "behind" the "typical" child . . . or another perspective is that she is growing her skills by (extraordinary-Sarah) leaps and (extraordinary-Sarah) bounds at fantastic Sarah speed.

The "fantastic Sarah speed" meant that we were playing games in a way I'd never dreamed possible. Sonia, Sarah, Amy, and I played three rounds of the Hat Game. Three rounds of using up all the cards! Taking turns and acting out the activities! The Hat Game was a game Sonia and I created involving a hat filled with little pieces of paper that described some moment from the girls' favorite books. Then there was a question or a direction to follow based on the description. For example, "Toad makes delicious cookies. Can you pretend to make cookies?" I was able to expand it as we played, writing out new cards based on our latest batch of favorite books. We could keep adapting the basic idea as much as we wanted, for the game involved taking turns but there was no winning or losing. The Hat Game was simply fun, and it created structure for our time together and a chance to witness that fantastic Sarah speed.

Sarah could do the zipper and buttons boards we'd set up in the Sarah-Rise room all by herself. She'd mastered snaps a while ago, but the latest achievement was that she could zip her sweatshirt with only the tiniest bit of help. Yes, that was my entire sock drawer flying past your window. A few years ago, such accomplishments seemed completely impossible.

Not only did her zipper prowess showcase that Sarah speed, but it was also a great reminder to trust The Son-Rise process and to respect the ism. Isms, the repetitive, exclusive behaviors, which were performed for Sarah's own enjoyment or self-soothing, were often Sarah's way of practicing skills. During all that isming, she had been taking the time she needed to teach herself how to snap, button, and zip. Our biggest gifts to Sarah were to allow her time and space and to get out of the way but to be there to help when she asked for assistance.

Our collective team used to get five to eight hours a day in the Sarah-Rise room, but two years in, that number dropped for various scheduling reasons. I was going in the room much less myself, but I realized that even if I wasn't in the Sarah-Rise room, it was still important to set aside official time to be with Sarah where I wouldn't be distracted by other things. I found setting aside time and distractions was possible, but the room made it so much easier.

I decided to recommit to doing Sarah-Rise time at least five days a week. There was a magic that could happen there in the quiet space that I didn't get elsewhere. I could focus in a different way, just as Sarah could. I also continued to learn things from observing my volunteers when they worked with Sarah.

"Make a crib," Sarah said to Abby one day.

Abby was our newest volunteer. For those of us who had been in the room a lot, we assumed that Sarah wanted to build a crib out of materials in the room. So that's what we always did—we'd build cribs from blocks and blankets. Abby didn't know this. She thought maybe Sarah wanted to draw a crib, since they'd been busy drawing. Surprisingly (to me!), Sarah went with it.

This is central flexibility! I thought.

Central flexibility showed that Sarah was okay with changing an aspect of the main activity. Sarah already had what is called "peripheral flexibility," which is being okay with changing an aspect that is tangential to the main activity, such as not minding if we wore a hat or sang along with an activity. For instance, if we were building a crib, I could wear a hat and sing a lullaby, neither of which would change the main activity. Hats and song lyrics were tangential to the activity itself;

however, changing the central activity, such as *drawing* a crib instead of *building* a crib, might not fall within Sarah's comfort range.

Yet, here she did it with a new volunteer who didn't make the same assumptions the rest of us might have made. This was a good reminder for me to not always do what I *thought* Sarah wanted me to do, even if it was the umpteenth time she requested a certain thing. Maybe I, too, could find a new way to play an old game and shake things up for both of us.

I could also relearn my own wisdom from my children. Sarah's current favorite conversation to have with me involved climbing onto my lap and saying, "Mom sad sometimes. Get tissue. Tears go in ears. Snuggle with me, help to feel better."

While the pronouns sometimes got confused, she was mainly clear. She was referencing what happened once when I felt sad. The next time I felt glum, I decided that instead of rallying through my sadness, I would slump into it. I told the girls that I was feeling sad, and I had a good cry on the kitchen floor while both girls snuggled into me for the duration of my tears. Soon I did feel better, and we all had a harmonious dinner together.

Recognizing that the girls knew that if someone is sad you can just be with them until they feel better was the best testament that I could ask for that I had been doing an okay job parenting.

With school for both girls in full swing in the spring, we had to make our morning routine a bit speedier, so we were not racing to get out the door on time. I made a list for each girl, akin to Toad's list in Arnold Lobel's Frog and Toad story called "A List." I'm not sure it helped with speed, but the kids did enjoy crossing things off their lists. Amy was faster and more willing in general with her morning to-do items, so the primary target with the lists was Sarah.

What actually helped Sarah speed up was the word "wonderful."

"Wonderful!" I said one morning when she took off a sock.

She whipped off the other sock, and she and I cheered.

"Wonderful!" we said in unison.

Next her pants came off.

"Wonderful!" we whooped again.

Then, her shirt . . . "Wonderful!"

"Wonderful" was the secret ingredient to Sarah getting dressed and ready on time. "Wonderful" was repeated each time she removed an item of clothing, put on each new item of clothing, used the potty, brushed her teeth, or brushed her hair. With "wonderful," so much of the usual struggle was gone, having been replaced by exuberance.

Along with increasing my exuberance to increase Sarah's speed, I was working at giving myself more time to slow down and be still. Usually, when I decided to be still and center myself, I realized that first I had to sharpen all my pencils! Clean everything! Do anything else but nothing! Yet when I was still, I found a lovely calmness, and I thought that would ultimately help me connect more effectively with Sarah. When I was more centered and gave myself time to breathe, my interactions with Sarah throughout the day had more time to breathe. I exuded less impatience or pressure in her direction when we were trying to get ready for something.

I was skilled at doing a lot of noisy running around and thinking that we as a family must do more, more, more. But, maybe, less was more.

To help Sarah with language, this same principle applied. Less is more. When I cut down my own language use, I was able to make space for her language. At dinner one night, I described to Carl some of what Sarah did at preschool: "Sarah was the Weather Bear at school today, and she made a Shape-osaurus at the craft table."

"Sarah," Carl asked, "what shapes did you glue on the paper for the Shape-osaurus?"

Silence, for twenty very long seconds.

"Triangle," Sarah piped up clearly. "Circle."

While I had been uncertain that Sarah knew the answer, Carl was giving her time.

I sincerely loved such moments when I underestimated what Sarah could do and she surprised me. I also loved that Carl asked her the question, not underestimating her at all. Maybe to help her succeed more in other ways, I first needed to give her space. After all, when I felt someone pressuring me to do something, I was known to dig my heels in and not want to do whatever was asked of me. Perhaps Sarah felt pressure from me to be normal, typical, smarter, faster, less screamy, and more cooperative. Perhaps I put the same pressure on myself to be more capable, flexible, prescient, and efficient. Maybe we both needed more space. What would happen if I could just stop pressuring her? The pressure wasn't necessarily blatant, but I know that if I felt it inside me, on some level she felt it too.

I vowed to work, or rather un-work, toward more stillness and to allow her more space to do more things on her own.

Sarah continued loving doors, and she would regularly open the door to our backyard. Since our yard is enclosed, this was perfectly safe, but I still wanted her to ask first, and I didn't want her out there when she wasn't dressed for the temperature or potential mud. It's not that she even wanted to go outside all that often, she just wanted to play with the door. I didn't want her to play with the door at all. It was loud, and I didn't want the cat to get out.

One day Sarah was playing with the door.

Slam!

"Sarah!"

Slam!

"Please don't play with the door."

Slam!

"You can be in or out, but not in and out over and over again."

"Why?"

I sat on my mental butt.

Sarah had never asked me that. She usually asked if she could have things or wear things, and often that was in response to my prompting her to ask.

She just asked me why! I marveled.

"Because the door is loud, and I don't want the cat to get out," I replied. "I also don't want anyone's fingers pinched if you and Amy are both going in and out."

After that, Sarah opted to play outside for a while.

16

The Great Bed Transition

IN APRIL, WE DECIDED it was time to transition the girls to sleeping in their own beds all night long. For the Great Bed Transition, Carl and I purchased a new twin mattress for Amy to match the one we already had for Sarah. We had already transitioned them from going to sleep with us sitting in their room to going to sleep without us, and that went more easily than we'd expected. I assumed that getting them to stay in their own beds all night would be a much bigger feat. They were used to starting in their own beds but moving into our bed sometime within the night, staying with us until the morning. We talked to them about transitioning to their new beds in positive terms—going to bed on their own and sleeping in their very own beds all night long with no grown-ups allowed. Carl and I were fully committed to making the Great Bed Transition, knowing that if we wavered, then we wouldn't have a leg to stand on.

Upon seeing their new beds, decked out with Hello Kitty–themed sheets, comforters, and stuffed animals supplied by Grammy, the girls jumped up and down with glee. They were not so thrilled about what the new beds represented, and that first night involved many short journeys. Each child came into our bedroom multiple times, and Carl and I took turns putting them back in their own beds. The second night involved no relocations but did include many instances of the girls calling out for us. Each successive night got better, with few relocations and very little calling for us. It wasn't long before all of us were sleeping better, and I was once again amazed at how easily we'd met such a milestone.

In addition to sleeping independently, riding a bike is often seen as another monumental milestone as a child grows. Carl helped Sarah get started riding her new bike on the sidewalk in front of our house, and she loved it! At first, she had some trouble with the pedals, but that came along beautifully with practice. I was grateful for training wheels, which made it easy for her to go at her own pace and meant we didn't have to hold on to the bike to help her balance. She could be independent, aside from needing an occasional push when she got stuck on the uneven areas of the sidewalk. When I watched her, I felt teary, remembering the days when I despaired of her ever learning to crawl.

Now we were doing all kinds of things with Sarah—all kinds of activities outside of the Sarah-Rise room. Sonia and I took the girls on field trips together. This way we had a good ratio for giving good attention to each child and flexibility if the girls didn't want to do the same thing or go at the same pace. The four of us went to various playgrounds and libraries, the Children's Museum, the Kidsburgh play area of the Heinz History Center, and the Schenley Park Carousel. For one field trip we went to the Center for Creative Reuse and stocked up on a multitude of supplies, including two large wooden bears and a bag of buttons. When we got home, I got out the glue and the girls made button bears.

I had been leery of art projects and the potential mess, but the button bears went more smoothly than I could have dreamed. The girls loved them, and we began doing art projects each day. The kids sat patiently at the small table that I set up in the dining room, waiting for many minutes while I gathered whatever supplies they needed. In one week, they made button bears, painted bears, painted clothespin dolls, dot-painted papers, and crayon-colored pages. We also pressed Play-Doh onto laminated letter cards from the Handwriting Without Tears materials.

While I had been worried about getting glitter, glue, paint, and marker everywhere in the house and on the children, in actuality, it was not such a big deal. Yes, there were some things to clean, and glitter did get everywhere, but the kids were patient and listened well when I asked them to wait for my help. I also had Sonia to lend a hand with cleaning kids, tables, and floors. This contained level of mess seemed totally worth the effort, given that the girls were getting creative sister-bonding time while simultaneously working on their fine motor skills and individual artistic expression. Amy was clearly an artist at the core of her being and had been so from the moment she could grasp a crayon.

Over the years, there have been many mornings when Amy started an art project before breakfast. Art was also how she calmed her soul after anything stressful. Sarah didn't love art in quite the innate driven manner that Amy did, but she did enjoy it. Sarah especially liked the tactile experience of picking up buttons or sifting glitter through her fingers or rolling crayons under her fingers. My journey was to remind myself that both ways of interacting with the art supplies were valid and wonderful and helped my children express themselves.

Since the Handwriting Without Tears materials were a hit, I wanted to borrow the "Without Tears" perspective to create a hair-washing experience that went beyond using Johnson & Johnson shampoo. Sarah hated having her hair washed and would cry and yell in protest when it was time to do so. I knew I had to increase my own efforts around the whole experience if hair washing was going to be more amenable to Sarah.

For our next Sarah-Rise session together, I brought in a laundry basket, our bath bucket, a washcloth, and a couple of bath toys. I climbed into the laundry basket.

"Sarah, can you wash my hair?"

She reached out tentatively to rub my head.

"No! No! No!" I said playfully.

She laughed.

"Sarah, this is so nice to be in the tub!" I said. "I love having clean hair. Can you get my hair wet?"

She pretended to pour water on my head with an empty plastic cup.

"I love it! That feels great. Can you add some shampoo?"

She pretended to put shampoo on my head.

"I love feeling you washing my hair! Can you rinse out the shampoo now?"

She poured more pretend water over me.

"Your turn. I'll get out and you can get in."

We traded places so she was in the empty dry laundry basket of a tub. She had no tears or troubles, allowing me to pretend to wet, wash, and rinse her locks.

The next day, I got into our regular tub, with water, with both girls in attendance outside of the tub, and I asked them to wash my hair. Sarah didn't want to get my hair wet, but Amy wet a washcloth and put it on the back of my head. I asked Sarah to help by using a washcloth to get the top of my head wet. She did so, though tentatively.

"Yes! Yay! Sarah, can you open the shampoo bottle?" I asked.

"No!"

I opened it and put some in the palm of my hand and offered my palm to her so she could touch the shampoo. She did, very tentatively. I put the shampoo on my head, and Amy helped suds my hair. When it was time to rinse my hair, Sarah helped with the washcloth a tiny bit.

"Girls!" I said, getting out of the tub. "Thank you so much for your help! I know that was a new experience. Maybe the shampoo felt a little weird. That was brave and courageous to try such a new thing."

If Sarah was that tentative about the process when it wasn't even her own hair, no wonder having her hair washed was such an anathema. We clearly had a long way to go to make bath time more palatable.

Eventually, with time, patience, practice, and singing songs, we were able to wash Sarah's hair in a way that she usually tolerated. Singing "The Bear Went Over the Mountain" often helped. In truth, it took years before this became an easy part of her week. The more she took over the tasks of getting the washcloth wet and using that to wet her hair, the more she tolerated the process. When we eventually got a new showerhead and tub, that helped, too. Somehow the novelty or possibly the different sensory experience with the rainwater shower-head helped. She eventually shifted from baths to showers and even began washing her hair on her own, but that was many years after the initial time of practicing washing my hair.

I started noticing that Sarah had conversation isms. Isms can be very clear when they are exclusively repetitive physical behaviors, but when isms involve eye contact and conversation, they can be harder to detect. Initially, at least. The key is to look for repetitive loops of statements, in place of novel conversations, or statements that seem to come from nowhere.

What I started understanding was that Sarah reached for certain statements or topics of conversation when she wanted a safe zone, perhaps because we didn't give a physical ism enough space or because we challenged her instead of bonding.

Sarah often quoted *Olivia Acts Out* by Jodie Shepherd.

"Oh no! The play be ruined!" she said one day, midconversation.

We had been talking about the schedule for the rest of the day.

To bond with her statement, my best response was, "Oh no! The play will be ruined!" adding as much dramatic flair as I used when reading the book.

Her eyes lit up and we connected, repeating this line back and forth until I attempted to challenge her a bit. I asked her a question: "Could Pig Number Two jump over the moon to save the play?"

"Oh no! The play be ruined!"

It was as if I hadn't even said anything different, so I said the original phrase again. Joining.

"Oh no! The play will be ruined!"

"Oh no! The play be ruined!"

"Oh no!"

We shared delighted eye contact and exuberance about that line as I recognized that she wasn't ready to move beyond that phrase at that particular time.

When Sarah was isming, the best thing to do was to bond through joining. That helped her feel safe enough to have flexibility to follow a request or rise to a new challenge later. With an ism involving physical activity, the go-ahead signal that she was ready for a request or challenge was when she looked at me for a while or said something to me. But how could I tell when it was safe to add something different to a conversational ism if she was already looking at me? I had to test the waters. I could try inviting Pig Number Two to say or do something, but if there was no bite, then I returned to joining.

Sometimes we had sessions with more verbal variety where she was ready to rise to my challenges. One started with her commenting on a picture of someone carrying flowers. I said it was a bouquet. She attempted to say "bouquet." I offered her a bouquet of markers to smell. She said they smelled like tulips. I said my bouquet smelled like lilacs. Then my bouquet made me sneeze! Then hers made her sneeze. Then my bouquet consisted of roses, and I pricked my finger on a thorn. She giggled a lot while practicing saying "prick" and "thorn." She put a pretend Band-Aid on my finger. When I held my bouquet too tightly and pricked my hand on a thorn, I threw my bouquet in the air. Markers went everywhere. She threw hers in the air too.

This moment is a perfect illustration of play when Sarah was fully ready for my builds, challenges, and requests. She was fully engaged and flexible, enjoying each new idea I introduced—until I put the marker flowers in a vase, which led to a few moments of isming with putting the markers in and taking them out. I did the same thing with a different container, and then Sarah shifted to wanting to make a pretend milkshake, which was interactive again.

Everything was going along so well, and Sarah was progressing so well, but sometimes I just felt so tired. I wanted to pause and rest. I wanted to not think or plan or make food or question my food decisions or come up with new games or goals. I *loved* our program, and I *loved* spending so much time with my girls. I loved cooking good food for them and shopping for good ingredients and thinking about how to make their growing up wonderful.

I also wanted to scream and turn in my resignation. I wanted to walk away from it all. I was so tired of Sarah's screaming and so tired of Amy's whining. Sometimes, I wondered how it could possibly be time to make more food again, because didn't I just make food yesterday? Sometimes, I was so tired of the mess that our house so often was, and that was with Sonia's diligent help! There was just so much to do all the time, and sometimes I was just so very tired.

But would I want to step out of my role and give it to someone else? No way! Hands off!

I may have wanted a break, but I felt proprietary about who was running the show.

On Mother's Day, I shared with Carl how tired I was, and he suggested that I go to our bedroom to rest and write my weekly update. On my way upstairs, I stopped by our chocolate stash and picked out a Chocolove dark chocolate bar, intending to break off a small chunk to enjoy as I wrote. Then I thought, *Why not indulge?* it being Mother's Day and all, so I put the whole bar in my bathrobe pocket. Carl witnessed my less-than-sly moves, and I looked up at him after pocketing my generous snack, and we burst into gales of belly laughter.

I have always been my true self around Carl—my genuine, messy, tired, chocolate-loving self, ready to giggle even when things might feel tough—and Carl has always helped me find my laughter by supporting me in whatever feelings I have rather than needing me to change them.

I was thankful for a good laugh before going off to write and eat chocolate and nap for two hours. Those two hours were glorious and helped me feel kinder toward my family members and the whole world.

By the end of May, I had created a new intention that I kept for a whole week. My new intention was to feel like I was on vacation all the time, to live with that ease and joy and no time pressure. I had a truly, deeply, amazingly wonderful life, and I wanted to embrace that and revel in it. I was the one making the schedule and most of the rules, so why not be gentle instead of beating myself up to go faster or do more? Interestingly, that week I did eight hours of Sarah-Rise time in the room. Easily! With fun and joy! Sarah didn't resist it at all, as she sometimes did if she was busy playing elsewhere in the house.

I asked Carl to help me remember my intention, and he asked how he could do that, because if I needed a reminder then I might not be in a frame of mind to take a reminder kindly. I didn't have an answer, so after a few moments Carl created The Intention Dance, in which he cavorted around ridiculously.

How could anyone stay uptight in the face of The Intention Dance?

A couple of days later, after the girls had gone to bed, I was venting to Carl about things feeling hard again. He got a gleam in his eye and began The Intention Dance. I laughed and let go of my tension, suddenly able to be present again and have a nice evening together to sit on the couch and watch a bit of TV before we went to bed.

17

Climbing the Walls

By June, Sarah had grown so strong that she was literally climbing the walls. We wanted to support Sarah's physical play, so we got a small trampoline. It was sold as personal fitness equipment for an adult and had a protective covering over the metal springs. It also came with a bar, to hold on to while you jumped, unless of course you were a small child, in which case the bar could be used to do a flip. Amy figured out flipping around the trampoline bar first, and Sarah got it shortly thereafter, though it was harder for Sarah because her legs were longer. Watching the girls flip was something I never tired of doing.

Sarah's language dexterity continued to evolve with her physical dexterity. Early one evening, I found Sarah in my bedroom holding the home phone.

"Want to call Mom-Mom by yourself."

She meant she wanted to call by *herself*, and so I told her what buttons to push, and then when the voicemail started, I suggested what she could say. She happily left her message: "Hi, Mom-Mom. Hi, Pop-Pop. I love you. This is Sarah. Bye."

Every thirty days the voicemail system tells my parents that the message will expire and asks if they want to save it again. For the past many years they have been listening to her sweet words again and resaving it. They will save it forever, on their voicemail and in their hearts.

Sarah's newest thing was answering questions with "Um . . . ." We thought it was the cutest! But more importantly, it was functional because "um . . ." gave Sarah more time to answer while signaling that she had heard the question and was working on an answer, which Megan pointed out during our next Outreach.

Megan observed most of our team playing with Sarah in the Sarah-Rise room, but where I learned the most was watching Megan play with Sarah. I noticed that Megan continued with play scenarios for much longer than I did. She didn't stop when Sarah's only participation was watching what Megan was doing.

For part of my Megan-observed session with Sarah, I brought out several sheets of paper and had Sarah write down some of her favorite sounds. She wrote "la," "ma," "wa," "yip," and "gah" on different pieces of paper, and I added a couple more. The sounds were from a different game I'd created, so I knew she liked them. Then I spread the papers on the floor and hopped on them, saying the sounds as I hopped. I lost my balance and grabbed for Sarah to help me. I encouraged her to hop, and she did so with two feet. The papers stuck to her feet a bit, but she didn't mind. Then we switched to sitting and hitting the papers with our hands and saying the sounds. I rearranged the papers at one point so she couldn't just memorize what sounds went with certain locations. This game was a great reading exercise. When her attention began to wane, I packed up the pages and put them away.

What I now understood from Megan's play and feedback was that when Sarah began to lose interest, I could have continued the game with more nuanced variations. For instance, I could have held one page and run around the room making the noise. I could have tossed the paper in the air. We could have worn the pages as hats. I could have written a song with only those sounds. We could have made more pages with new sounds. We could have made smaller papers with sounds and played a memory game. We could have written a story about the game we'd just played, drawing pictures of ourselves hopping on paper and making noise.

The day after her first session with Megan, who always came for at least two days, I heard Sarah playing by herself, and she was quoting Megan's play about being stuck in a tree. I could tell that Sarah was drinking in all the new imaginative scenarios that Megan had introduced, from the tree to making the three little pigs out of Play-Doh and having the wolf try to blow down their plastic house. I, too, was expanding and developing. I could now build ideas within a game in all sorts of directions. I was also aware of how much more effective I was when I had an idea for a game or play scenario *before* I entered the Sarah-Rise room.

The day I created the dungeon game, I had one of my best play sessions with Sarah. It all began when Sarah said something about "Poor Sarah

Bucket Head in a dungeon," which was a reference to Snow White and Prince Bucket Head, as he is called in a comic book version of the fairytale that we had. I started building a dungeon around Sarah, using our milk-carton blocks. Milk-carton blocks are an invention by Grandma; she'd made them for Carl and Sonia when they were little. The sturdy blocks were wonderful for stacking but could also be stepped on by young kids, absorbing the child's weight without collapsing.

A milk-carton block is made with two paperboard cartons of equal size. Start by opening the tops of both cartons, and then wash and dry them. Then remove the top of one carton by cutting around the edge where the carton begins to slope upward toward the top. Take the second carton and fold the top inward at the same edge where it slopes upward. To make the block, stuff the carton with the top folded in inside the carton with the top cut off so that both ends are carton bottoms.

Sarah crawled through the space between two of the milk-carton dungeon blocks that were on the rug, and I said she had squeezed through the bars. She found this funny and did it again. I then took on the role of the prison guard, picking her up, rocking her a few times, and gently placing her back into the dungeon. She escaped again! I continued to expand my responses, always acting as the prison guard, throwing her over my shoulder, going down an imaginary spiral staircase, having rats scurry over her feet, slamming the milk-carton door closed, sliding an imaginary bolt, and locking several locks. Sarah kept escaping and coming to stand right in front of me, waiting for recapture. It was so cute! And so fun! And so tiring.

As soon as my energy waned, Sarah started isming, stepping in and out of the dungeon but without the interactive play. Maybe she was tired, too. Eventually, she used the potty and escaped to her room, but I had created the perfect scenario for bringing her back. I went in, captured her, threw her over my shoulder, and we resumed interactive play in the Sarah-Rise room.

We returned to the dungeon play many times that week, and we had many times of isming and joining, stepping in and out of the dungeon without further interaction beyond our amicable co-stepping.

When joining an ism, I often went on a thought journey. I reminded myself that it was perfect, that it was a way to say *I love you, Sarah,* that it was exactly the most helpful thing to do in that moment. What was interesting was that once I had my own thoughts clear, Sarah was usually ready to reconnect with me.

Milk-block cartons also made for good ice cream, with markers for spoons, and Sarah and I ate a lot of pretend ice cream together. I often offered her peanut butter ice cream to help her practice saying, "No, thanks, I'm allergic." Or we would add several toppings, including "shush," which is what my family calls ReddiWhip because of the sound it makes coming out of the can. Sarah made the *shushhh* sound, and then we added cherries. When we ate our ice cream, we were careful not to eat the cherry stems.

Another day, we made money to buy our ice cream. I held the paper, and Sarah cut along the folded line I had made. She had improved immensely with her use of scissors. She could do it with one hand! I dictated the denominations, and she wrote the numbers on the money. Then she came to my ice cream store and sorted through her purse to find the correct bill. She bought three different flavors from me! This took some coaching on my part, but she was willing.

"Hello! Welcome to the ice cream store," I said. "What flavor do you want?"

"Va-ni-la"

"Here you go. That will be two dollars."

Sarah paused. I pointed to two of her dollar bills. She handed them to me.

"Would you like anything else?"

"Choc-lat and mmmint!"

"Great. Here you go. Four dollars, please. . . . I see you have a five-dollar bill in your purse. If you give me five dollars, I will give you change."

Sarah handed me the five-dollar bill. I handed her one dollar in change.

"Bye. See you next time," I said.

We tried switching roles so Sarah was the ice cream vendor. That sort of worked, but I drove more of the interaction, and she had less input. I noted this for the future so that we could work on it.

It was a hot day in June when Carl really excelled as a parent, beyond even his usual excellence.

I caught Sarah drinking water from the water play table in the backyard.

"Ewww!" I yelled. *"Nooo!"*

I pulled her inside, and she started crying because I had yelled at her and stopped her activity. Carl delayed leaving for work to sit with her and wait for her to regain equilibrium. When she was calm enough to talk, he engaged her in many loops of conversation about the situation.

"Sarah, the water outside is dirty. It is for playing, but not for drinking. The water inside is clean and is for drinking. If you drink the water from this table, you might get sick, and we will also have to take the table away. Do you understand?"

"Yeah."

"So next time you get thirsty, and you are outside, will you drink from the table?"

"Yeah."

"Well, wait. Remember, this water is dirty. You might get sick. Don't drink this water. Drink the water inside the house."

"Yeah."

"So, if you are outside and thirsty, what will you drink?"

"Wah-ter."

"At the water table?"

"Yeah."

"No. Water table water is dirty. Not for drinking. Water in the house is for drinking. Where is the clean water?"

"In the house."

"What kind of water is in this table?"

"Di-rty."

"Next time you are thirsty, will you go in the house?"

"Yeah."

"Next time you are thirsty and outside, will you drink the water from the water table?"

"No. In the house."

I was so impressed listening to Carl's patience and his method of mixing explanation with questions and the fact that he kept going until Sarah appeared to have learned the lesson. This time, if you saw my socks flying past your window, it was because of Carl. Ultimately, he got her a drink of fresh water (from inside the house), gave her a hug and kiss, and went off to work. By that time, I had regained my equilibrium too, and Sonia had arrived. Our day could officially begin.

Many situations with Sarah required persistence and patience, some involving her behavior, à la the water table, and some involving her physical health. One persistent struggle we had over the years pertained to Sarah's fingers.

Sarah would get these tiny blisters, or a rash of some sort, and I couldn't help but wonder if this irritation had something to do with her diet—because in my mind, everything was feedback about Sarah's diet. But try as I might, I could never figure out the source of the blisters. Carl, the girls, and I went for a walk one day, and halfway through our perambulation I realized Sarah's blisters were back—and she had a new rash on one arm. Although different from the finger blisters, the arm rash might have been in response to the heat of the summer day, and I didn't know if Sarah's finger rash was the same thing as it had been the last time her fingers had flared up—something that had not ultimately healed—or whether it was a new reaction to food or something in her environment that I had yet to identify. Every time the rash flared, I despaired and assumed it was somehow my fault. I felt like I was two inches tall as I trudged along on our walk.

Carl gently suggested that maybe, going forward, I could see myself as a scientist instead of a terrible mother.

A scientist?

Now that was a radical notion I could consider.

I spent the rest of our walk adjusting to this new perception of myself as a full-height scientist mom rather than a two-inch-tall failure mom. Certainly, I could think more clearly about the situation when I wasn't berating myself. I could take stock of what I knew and didn't know regarding foods that worked or lotions that seemed to make things worse. I could consult a dermatologist. I could make a chart to track ingredients in soaps and lotions. I could make sure I was slow to add new foods. The overwhelm was still present, but at least I had a direction in which I could capably channel my efforts.

18

Not "If" but "When"

I HAD BEGUN APPRECIATING the perspective of "when." It was not "if"; it was "when." For anything. It was not *if* Sarah would be able to play with other kids; it was *when* she would be able to play with peers. It was not *if* she would learn to independently wash her hair; it was *when that would happen easily*. It was not *if* Sarah would attend kindergarten; it was *when* she would move beyond preschool.

Not "if" but "when." How could we do our best to continue to help her?

Carl had a new experience with responding to Sarah when she was upset. Sarah loved a car across the street deeply. It was an ordinary silver sedan owned by our neighbor. If it was not parked outside, then from her perspective all was not right with the world. One night, Sarah checked on the car's status after bedtime and was chagrined.

"Oh no! The car! Car, come back!" Sarah cried.

Carl went in to comfort her, and he did so from a shared belief that all was not right with the world because of the missing car.

"Oh no! Sarah, the silver car isn't there!" he said. "Where do you think it could be?"

Pause, pause, pause.

"Target," Sarah replied at last.

"Oh, that's a great idea," said Carl. "Maybe they went to Target to get something."

Pause.

"Pizza," Sarah suggested.

"Yes! That would be delicious. Maybe they went to Target to get a frozen pizza."

He was really with her. This creative brainstorming about where the car could be was new. This was not "*if* she could think flexibly while being upset," this was the moment of *when*. She was thinking while moving through her feelings instead of being frozen in her sadness. She was exhibiting a more connected upset.

One new development I wasn't thrilled about was that now when Sarah played with Sonia, she tried hitting Sonia, or she talked about hitting Sonia. No one had any idea why this started, and it wasn't how we wanted things to be. Sonia certainly wasn't pleased about it and found it a bit more challenging to want to do Sarah-Rise time. To her credit, Sonia continued showing up for her Sarah-Rise time with love and patience. While Sarah spent time with other volunteers, Sonia and I had many conversations in an effort to sort through what might be going on for Sarah, why she was hitting or wanting to hit, and how to address it. And why was it only Sonia? Sarah didn't attempt to hit or talk about hitting anyone else.

We wondered if Sarah was mad at Sonia for enforcing rules around the house, which she did with more firm assurance than I did. I was often in awe of Sonia's ability to wait Sarah out on finishing a cleaning task or eating a certain food before others were given. Sarah was probably less in awe. Sonia could enforce things without getting her own tailfeathers ruffled, whereas I often had grumpy, rumpled feathers because I doubted myself much of the time when I attempted to enforce things, and I got frustrated when the kids resisted me.

Sonia and I decided that we would do joint Sarah-Rise sessions to help Sarah with her "hit Sonia" comments and actions. In the first session, Sarah was very upset after an attempted hit. Her upset seemed to be twofold. She was upset at us for making her stay in the room and upset about hurting Sonia. It was as if she did and didn't want to hurt her. She was mad, thus wanting to hit, but didn't want to cause harm. She wanted to leave the room but couldn't, because I was sitting in front of the door, blocking her exit. She sat on my lap and cried for twenty minutes. When her attention cleared, she got up and ate a snack, talking to both of us easily about her snack.

For the next joint Sarah-Rise session, when I told Sarah we were going in the Sarah-Rise room with Sonia, she gave a sudden angry look at both of us, as if she was mad at Sonia in general and mad at me for suggesting such a situation. But once in the room, there was only a little hitting talk, no attempts at actual hitting, and less upset overall. The third joint session involved no mention of hitting and no attempt at hitting. We played for twenty-five minutes with the same toy, enjoying a three-person connection, with evolving ideas that came from Sarah's suggestions. Sarah, Sonia, and I played with foam shapes, creating food, pretending we had variously shaped whistles, and throwing them as Frisbees.

The plan of us doing joint sessions worked! We were able to help

Sarah move through whatever was going on regarding the hitting, and it gave Sonia a reset on what it was like to be in the Sarah-Rise room without anticipating hitting or adversarial energy from Sarah.

Around the time that I was getting the girls ready to go back to school, I had an epiphany about self-care. Was I to let my lettuce wilt or let myself wilt? Was it more important to make yogurt so we didn't run out or to make sure I didn't run out of my own oomph? My answers had always been to save the lettuce and make the yogurt! After all, both were also a form of self-care, to have all food prepared and feel less overwhelmed the following day. That was care for my future self. But the to-do list never ended, so I had to put a stop to it. I had to let the veggies wilt.

For most of my life, I'd wanted to get all my work done before I relaxed so I could fully enjoy the relaxing. It was time to reverse that pattern. Relaxing and having an excess of time for me had to come first. In fact, the first ingredient to having the Sarah-Rise program of my dreams was to fully take care of me. I would have to pay attention to the nuances of when I started to get overloaded in small ways *before* I got overwhelmed in a big way. I would have to take breaks as soon as I felt myself slipping under 90 percent of my targeted good energy and good feeling.

What was extra noteworthy about this self-care epiphany was that after a few days of what felt like indulgent, excessive self-care (naps, reading my own fun books, going for walks by myself), Sarah started spontaneously giving me kisses or coming up next to me with a smile as she nuzzled in for a cuddle. This may have been a coincidence, but I'd place a solid bet that it wasn't. The same day that Sarah started giving me tons of kisses, Amy changed her usual "Hey, Mom, I love you" to "Mom, I am loving you." The cockles of my heart melted all over the floor.

After Labor Day, Sarah started preschool as a seven-year-old, and Amy started preschool for three-year-olds. We were two and a half years into Sarah-Rise. Carl and I opted to have the kids attend different preschools so they could each have their own school experience. They spent enough time together at home. Sarah would attend the same preschool she'd been enrolled in the year before. This year, she would go three mornings a week from nine to twelve. Sonia would be there, but instead of shadowing Sarah as she did before, this year Sonia would sit in a chair in the hall outside the closed classroom doors. She was not in Sarah's sight but was instantly available for things like snack time, bathroom trips, and the occasional meltdown. I was excited about this new arrangement. I hoped Sonia would be able to focus on other things, such as planning curriculum for our home activities. I also thought Sarah could own her independence a bit more without Sonia present in the classroom.

Even though I was excited about our arrangement, there were some days when I felt sad that we were doing yet another year of preschool. I knew that other kids with special needs who were also developmentally learning at preschool levels, like Sarah, were moving through higher grades, yet I wondered about the reality of their situations. How much of what they were actually learning warranted the higher grade label? I wondered what the grade labels meant, other than the kids were "a certain age" and had completed "a certain number of years of school." Each year that Sarah was in preschool was different for her, and I firmly believed that preschool was where she was developmentally. It felt like a huge success that she was there now and that she continued to grow and learn. *What do grade labels matter?* I asked myself. When I was in my Sarah bubble, I saw our progress and was amazed. That felt hopeful. When I was reminded that other kids her age were in second grade and doing second-grader things, I felt like I was standing on a road having been left far behind.

No one was leaving me in the dust except the person painting the picture in my mind. I was aware that everyone has challenges in their lives and that the challenges come in different forms at different times. I was happy for my friends who had second graders. That was truly wonderful. I wanted them to share what their kids were doing. From that road I was on, I could turn, start walking, and arrive at the door to my beautiful house with my wonderful family and continue building from where we all were right then.

I could leave the labels behind in the dust.

Sarah did beautifully for her first week of preschool. I was there the first day, sitting in the hall behind closed doors. I only helped when Sarah needed to stay in a line, with snack time, and with outside play-time. During the prayer before her snack, she kept sneaking peeks back at me, which felt very kid-sneaky-wonderful. From behind the doors, I couldn't observe her for much of the time, but what I did see felt full of a clear, present, calm, healthy poise. On the playground she watched the other kids, but with a mostly calm demeanor, whereas a couple of years earlier, she would have had her head tilted down while she watched the feet passing her, and her jaw and hands would have been moving a mile a minute. Now she stood, head and body upright, jaw mostly still, hands mostly calm, watching.

A month into her time in preschool, I realized that Sarah had acquired a skill that at one point had seemed laughably far away. She was contributing at least two spontaneous ideas within a game or play activity. She had probably been doing it before I even analyzed our playtime with an eye for that particular ability, but the day I noticed was when, after playing the Snail's Pace Race game, Sarah folded the board and said she was reading a snail story. I asked her to tell me what it was. She said, "Once upon a time . . . ," and I got a pen and paper so we could write her story together. I did the writing and the filler words, but I asked her questions, and she provided the details. Our story was about a red snail named Pink who wore pants with a heart pattern and a shirt with dots. For dinner, Pink liked to eat a green cracker and a graham cracker.

Other goals were for Sarah to join a game already in progress and to play more games as they were intended to be played. Amy and I were playing Colorama one afternoon. This game involves rolling dice to determine which color and shape you pick and then placing your piece in the corresponding space on the board. Sarah came into the room, sat down, and joined our play! She could play it correctly with very little help. This was huge, but it was also slowly becoming less noteworthy because it was more of a given that she had this capability. In fact, a skill becoming something that we could take for granted was an even bigger achievement! The only challenge left for Sarah now seemed to be staying interested for the duration of the game, and that fell under the goal of increasing her interactive attention span.

With school underway, the year had been flying by, so fast that I realized it had been five months since Sonia and I filled out the developmental model provided by ATCA. We had planned to do this monthly, so every five months seemed rather lax until I realized that waiting five months was the perfect way for me to do it! The developmental model is a form that takes a parent through questions about different areas of social development. You assess where your child is for each area—whether they can do that skill easily, whether they can do it with some help, whether it's a struggle, or whether you aren't even at the point of considering that they could do such a thing. In a month, we didn't chart much change, but in five months there was room for big changes. I'm sure the path to "two spontaneous ideas" and "joining a game already in play" involved a steady, slow increase over time, but from one month to the next we might not have observed much progress. This would be an increase like noticing the difference between five and six miles per hour—not much to notice. However, if you go from five to ten miles per hour, it's easier to perceive the change in speed and motion.

Another metric for assessing Sarah's progress was some annual preschool homework. Sarah's class at school was putting together a display about each family, as they did each year. Each child was asked to bring in a family picture and a small paper that detailed some of their favorite things. This year, I asked Sarah to provide the answers.

I placed myself right in front of her while she was in the Cozy Coupe toy car to make eye contact easy, and I proceeded as I did with our snail story, asking her questions and being her scribe. She looked at me while I asked, considering each question, and then answered clearly and appropriately.

Favorite food: chocolate bar.

Favorite color: pink.

Favorite animal: Hello Kitty.

Favorite toy: Connect Four.

Once again, this was huge! Or maybe it was something that was becoming a given. *Of course* she could answer such questions.

I signed the girls up for a gymnastics class again. This year would be the first time they were in the same class as each other and without a parent accompanying them as they moved around the room. Yet another step forward. Another *when*. Though I wasn't accompanying Sarah, I stayed in the room as requested by the staff. I only had to intervene a few times when Sarah tried getting to new equipment before it was time. But Sarah sat on the line at the beginning, and she said her name when it was her turn to introduce herself, and she followed one-third of the warm-up movements before getting more interested in other things. This was another huge improvement. Her behavior was so different from when she first took a gymnastics class a few years earlier.

I was struck by how proud I was of Sarah's participation that day and almost immediately aware of how much I took for granted that Amy participated so easily. More so, the fact that Amy's easy behavior garnered less awe and less appreciation yet was no less amazing. It came relatively easily for Amy, whereas I knew it had taken a lot of work for Sarah to get to this moment. Still, I wanted to notice the miracle of Amy at the same time as I noticed the miracle of Sarah.

There was so much that Amy did that I marveled at with loving wonder because, in part, it seemed to be evidence of brilliance or creativity. What if I had the same loving wonder toward Sarah's yelling or any of her isms? I trusted Amy to thrive and be in charge of when she wanted to learn new things. What if I trusted Sarah the same way? I mostly did trust Sarah now, especially in the Sarah-Rise room, but there were certainly places where I didn't trust Sarah's interests to lead where I wanted her to go.

In *The Runaway Bunny* by Margaret Wise Brown, there is a page where the mother bunny tells her little bunny that if he becomes a boat to sail away from her, then she will become the wind and blow him where she wants him to go. When I was little, my mom rewrote my copy to have the mother bunny say she will blow him where *he* wants to go. What a difference a word can make.

Ultimately, my goal for Sarah was for her to be as capable as she could be in her own unique, creative, playful, sparkly way. I wasn't going to force her to have "good behavior." I wanted her desire for connection to foster her cooperation, participation, kindness, and flexibility. I wanted to trust her isms. I was blowing her where she wanted to go, because that was the way I wanted to reach this ultimate goal.

The Son-Rise Program helped me figure out how to be the right kind of wind.

19

Pretending

THE GIRLS LOVE PRETENDING. One day, they walked around the block riding small broomsticks, pretending to be witches. Another day, Amy started making monkey sounds, saying she was a monkey. Sarah heard this and started pretending to be a monkey, too. Other times, Amy said she was a cat, and Sarah said she was a frog.

In college, I had a role in a play where I performed the opening monologue, and then during intermission, I did improv interactions with the audience. I was nervous on opening night, but to get into character, I had to pretend that I wasn't nervous—because my character was not nervous. Pretending that I wasn't nervous actually helped me let go of my nervousness!

Now, in my mothering role, I was trying to sort out how I could honor my experience of feeling overwhelmed while at the same time giving myself wiggle room to pretend that I was not overwhelmed. What if I could pretend that I wasn't overwhelmed by kids yelling a lot or by the idea of homeschooling? Could such pretense actually change the situation? Maybe. Could I pretend the screaming didn't feel like worms burrowing under my skin? What if Sarah's screaming didn't make me want to lie down and give up . . . or scream back with all of my being?

Sarah's prowess in screaming had been a constant throughout her life, which was not exactly in line with the cozy vision of motherhood that I had before becoming a mother. My own angry response was also a surprise because it wasn't part of my parenting model. I thought of myself as being kind and loving. I *am* kind and loving. I also get mad and sometimes screamy in response to loud screaming, whining, and complaining.

Sarah screamed on a daily basis, but it varied in frequency and duration. She screamed in protest if she didn't like what she was told to do. She screamed if she was impatient for something to happen. When she was very little, she would scream a high-pitched screech to protest diaper changes. One of my friends gave her the nickname "Sarahdactyl" because the screaming was so intense that she might as well be a pterodactyl flying overhead screeching at you.

When I told Sarah that a volunteer couldn't come or would be late, she often launched into her screaming of protest and upset, yelling the name of the volunteer and demanding that they "get here *now!*" Fortunately, our volunteers were usually on time and usually came for their regular time slot each week. But there were times when they were sick and couldn't come, or they were stuck in traffic and thus late. Sometimes, I could listen to Sarah's screams and have space. Other times, I couldn't.

Another common situation was needing to get dressed to go

somewhere when we weren't in our normal school-morning routine, such as on a weekend or during vacation. If the thing she wanted to wear was in the wash or had a stain, she screamed loud and long about wearing something different. Sometimes she just yelled the word "No." Other times it was a sustained, high-pitched wail. If I really needed her to function and get dressed, then the screaming felt like an insurmountable mountain. Or it felt as if I were treading water and had no idea how to make it through a given moment other than to grit my teeth and try to breathe.

I really didn't enjoy the screaming. Sometimes, I really didn't enjoy being a mom or an adult with responsibilities for other humans. Other times I could pull up my mental and emotional bootstraps to pretend this was all okay. And then, at the other end of things, sometimes I had full capacity and capability to hear the screams, remain easily calm, and creatively encourage forward movement.

In our non-screaming, peaceful times, it was pure heaven to have both girls climbing on me, Sarah giving me chin presses and Amy cupping my face gently with her palm. It was heartwarming when Sarah would give me kisses and Amy would say, "Mom, I love you." And if I happened to make a meal that both of them equally liked and snarfed happily (a minor miracle), then watching them chow down filled me with contentment.

Thank goodness for the balance. Even on the hard days, I tried to remember how healthy we all were, how much loving one-on-one time Sarah received thanks to our team of volunteers, and how much our life was richly full even when I might not meet my ideal standards of a life at every moment. We had a supported, bountiful life, and I tried not to take it for granted.

We now had a new climbing apparatus for the girls in our family room because they outgrew the small trampoline bar. This became evident the day they both ran to swing on the trampoline bar at the same time and the whole trampoline levitated toward the wall, girls and all. The trampoline was promptly retired to the basement. Our new climbing structure had rings, a trapeze bar, a rope, a gymnastics bar, and a tall ladder that went all the way to the ceiling. Carl painted a blue sky and white puffy clouds on the wooden boards that protected the ceiling from the pressure of the gym apparatus, which was held in place by nothing more than pressure against the floor and ceiling. The girls loved it, as did we. We were always aiming to get whatever could help Sarah with her physical strength and coordination. We knew that physical and mental aptitude were often linked and that supporting her nervous system in any one realm could help in all areas of development.

When Carl took Sarah to an outdoor equipment store, she saw the climbing wall, wanted to do it, and Carl said okay. She just barely squeaked by with the minimum weight requirement, and she only climbed up a very short way, but I loved that she saw the activity and wanted to do it—and that Carl arranged it so she could. He loved going on expeditions with Sarah. He had her help pay for purchases and parking and hold the parking garage ticket. I didn't do such outings often, and when I did, I didn't have the internal space or thought to let Sarah participate as much as Carl did. I was glad he had that level of comfort to let her be more independent.

Another way that we supported Sarah's development was through Anat Baniel Method lessons. Since Sarah was a baby, she received these gentle bodywork sessions a few times a year. The sessions help strengthen neural connections and create new neural pathways by doing small, slow movements to help a person notice and process subtle kinesthetic differences. My mom heard about the method and found a practitioner for us. I knew that these lessons had helped people with various challenges, sometimes making a tremendous difference. The lessons for Sarah never garnered a hugely obvious change, but I saw subtle shifts of muscle control after her lessons, and I believed the lessons could be doing big things inwardly even if I couldn't see big changes outwardly.

I used to sit in the room while Sarah had her ABM sessions, but one particular time three years into Sarah-Rise, Sarah told me that she didn't want me in the room during her lesson. What growing independence on her part! As soon as I left, Sarah eagerly climbed onto the table, ready to watch buses while the lesson progressed. The office where we went for her lessons was on a prime bus route, and Sarah loved watching city buses pass by. To this day, I am never quite sure what she loves more, the ABM lessons or the buses, but she knows that one comes with the other, so she is always eager for her lessons.

For Halloween that year, both girls were Dora the Explorer. Carl was The Map from the Dora show. I was going to be the Grumpy Old Troll, also from the Dora show, but I didn't get that costume made in time. I certainly felt like I had that troll's personality down pat sometimes though! Instead, I wore a dirndl my mom had purchased when she was in college while traveling through Europe, and I pretended to be a dairy maid who had lost her cow and needed Dora's help.

This year Sarah had mostly moved beyond her love of pencils or wanting to give away her candy. She still had some desire to go into people's homes, but she was also interested in getting candy, which meant that she came home with quite a haul! To trade for the Doras' bounty, I made a bounty of treats. Melting cacao powder, coconut oil, and maple syrup together and pouring that mixture into molds, I made chocolates in all sorts of shapes that I wrapped in red and orange foil. I bought maple sugar candy, and I made mini vegan pumpkin pies with homemade whipped coconut cream. I traded these goods for the trick-or-treated candy because I wanted to make sure the ingredients were simple and healthier than the usual store-bought fare—especially for Sarah.

Halloween was a success—costumes, candy, and all!

Upon my entering the room one Wednesday, Sarah started saying, "A bicycle!" in her usual super-excited way.

"Bi [garbled sound] cle!"

Sarah lost her clarity of speech when she said some words because she got so excited. "Bicycle" was one of them. I often requested that she slow down a tiny bit so we could understand her better, and she almost always did so.

"Yes!" I said. "Bicycle! I totally know what you are going for! When you are excited, then sometimes you lose some of your clarity, and I want to make sure anyone can understand your beautiful words. Let's practice slowly. Bi-cy-cle."

"Bi [garble] *cle!*"

"That was wonderful! Let's try again even slower. Bi . . . cy . . . cle."

"*Bi*-cy . . . *cle!*"

"Yes! Again! Give me a 'bi'!"

"*Bi!*"

"Give me a 'cy'!"

"*Cy!*"

"Give me a 'cle'!"

"Cle!"

"Yes! Bi-cy-cle!"

"Bi-cy-cle!"

"*Yes!* That was so clear! And I love how you looked at me as you said it!"

Gregory figured out that Sarah maintained more clarity with words similar to "bicycle" rather than "bicycle" itself, since that was her favorite word at the time. The two of them did a lot of practicing with "motorcycle," "unicycle," and "tricycle." That, plus asking Sarah to slow down and practice a word broken into components, helped her speak ever more clearly.

"Make bi-cy-cle!" she said.

"Yes! Let's make a bike. Here's some paper. Can you draw two circles to be the wheels?"

She did.

"Great! I'll draw the seat." I drew the seat, paused, and then asked, "Can you connect the seat to the wheels?"

She did, although the connections weren't completely direct or solid.

"Wonderful! Here's you." I drew a sick figure. "Can you add hair and a helmet?"

She added scribbly crazy hair and a rudimentary but oh-so-earnest helmet.

"I love it! Here is a line for you to write your name so you can sign your artwork. Can you add your name?"

She did!

The next day, when Sarah asked to "make a bicycle" with Carl, he opted for a 3D creation. They made a bike out of large plastic bricks and planks. Sarah had to get the bike the right height for the seat. She said it needed handlebars, so Carl added those. Then he put blue magnetic boards from Handwriting Without Tears against the bike and asked Sarah to add wheels, which she did using magnets shaped like arcs. Then she said it needed a light stick, and so Carl drew a rectangle on paper. Sarah colored it, cut it out, and taped it to the back of the bike—entirely by herself! They practiced directions as she pretended to bike around, turning left, turning right, and staying straight. Such imagination on both of their parts had me mentally barefoot as my socks once again went flying!

When Sarah was focused, she could now do many things correctly and easily. When she was not focused, she struggled to do the very same things correctly, and if you didn't know she could do the required skill then you would think she couldn't do it.

We had a game called Quack Quack with eight little flat wooden animals, each made up of a unique color combination. There were three dice, and when you rolled, you'd look for the animal that matched the color combination of the dice. Sarah and I played a little less competitively than the rules dictated—we just took turns rolling and finding animals. One time when we played, she found her first three animals quickly and correctly. Several turns later, she was, in theory, focused on the game with her body and head orientation, but her mental focus was not there anymore. She couldn't get the last animal at all.

If Sarah hadn't played her first three turns so cleanly, then I would have deemed the game too challenging for her. Maybe she'd used up her focusing oomph, or maybe she'd lost interest. I wasn't sure, but I knew she had the skills. It was a matter of harnessing the right moment and environment for her abilities to shine. We realized we could help strengthen her abilities if we made our own games that capitalized on her interests.

Sonia and I made a new board game called Around the Wheel. You rolled a die and then moved your person (borrowed from another toy) around a poster-board wheel with different colored sections. When you landed on a section, you picked a card from the deck with the corresponding color. Sarah and I played a few rounds of this, and she picked the correct card perfectly for each turn. She liked almost all the prompts from the cards, until we got to the instruction to have another player (me) draw a shape and for Sarah to color it in. The shape I drew was too big. I soon realized that to help her move toward the goal of coloring in a shape fully, I needed to start small so that she could achieve it easily. Maybe I could start so small, so teeny-tiny, as to be ridiculous, and we could laugh about it together. It wasn't just about the right moment or environment; we also needed to help her feel capable and successful.

One evening, Sarah was isming in the family room with the Minnie cards from a Minnie Mouse matching game. I didn't often join her when she ismed outside of the Sarah-Rise room. Honestly, I figured she was occupied, so I could do some cleaning or cooking. But this time I joined her. Sarah was taking the cards out of the box, spreading a few of them on the floor, pressing on the pictures, and putting them back in the box. I sat down a couple feet away from her, took some of the cards (there were a ton), spread them out in front of me, and pressed on the pictures. I used the half of the box that she wasn't using to put my cards away and then took them out again to repeat the process. She immediately looked at me and started smiling.

"Play Minnie Mouse matching game."

I was smiling too.

"I would love to play with you!"

We played for at least thirty minutes, maybe even forty-five. Amy joined us as we spread out all of the cards face down. After a short time, Amy brought a toy elephant into the game to take turns, too. I told Sarah she could have a toy elephant take a turn, and I had an elephant myself. It was really like six people playing. I found it very hard to make any matches because there were so many cards, and small individuals sometimes moved cards to new locations. (You know how those toy elephants misbehave!) I was the one to end the game before it came to its actual end. I was getting too frustrated and tight about enforcing turns and instructing small people and elephants to leave the cards in place, but I think the girls would have kept going had I stayed with it. The elephants definitely would have.

Although Sarah mostly turned over the same two cards each turn, unless I prompted her to turn over a new card, she stayed with the game the whole time. *This* was real progress, and I decided to set a goal for myself. My goal was to be more relaxed about enjoying the process of the time together rather than worrying about playing the game correctly, quickly, or efficiently.

The following morning, I got out supplies for the girls to do an art project with pastels and watercolors. Amy, who loves to color, immediately got down to business. Sarah did a few cursory scribbles but mainly wanted to hold a handful of pastels and then slide new pastels into the bundle in her hand. While I usually allowed this, I also usually felt disappointed that she wasn't doing the activity I'd envisioned.

This time, with my new goal in mind, I was able to genuinely let go of judgment, and I felt a peaceful acceptance with what Sarah wanted to do. Amy drew with the pastels and Sarah gathered them by the handful, and eventually both girls added watercolor to their work. Two hours later, Sarah independently returned to the art table and asked me for new paper. She proceeded to color with intention and focus.

We were working with Sarah to say "yes" instead of "yeah," because sometimes her "yeah" sounded like "no."

When she said "yes" clearly, we celebrated.

"Yes! That was such a clear 'yes'! Thank you!" we'd say, or "I love it when I can understand your words so clearly!" Or we gave her a thumbs-up and a big smile while nodding our heads vigorously.

Amy, who was just starting to be able to pronounce "s," but only if you didn't draw any attention to this fact, started saying, "Hara, you did a really good job haying 'es.'" Amy, now a few months shy of being four, would pronounce the "s" sound in maybe half of her words.

I was so curious about what would happen to how she said Sarah's name when she did get her "s" sound. I adored how Amy called her sister "Hara." As we encouraged Sarah's yeses and as Amy's "s" words increased, it seemed that we were reaching the end of an era. A few weeks after Amy started with more "s" sounds, she switched to saying "Sarah" and "Sonia" instead of "Hara" and "Honia." This was exciting, but I also felt a little sad. I had so wished for progress, and it had been so painful when progress was slow, stilted, or seemingly nonexistent when Sarah was much younger, but still . . . time was passing, and my little ones were growing up. As exciting as that was, I was sad that certain sweet moments were coming to an end.

Sarah was going to turn eight at the end of January, and Carl commented that in just over two years, we would have a ten-year-old. I don't know how to spell the sound of air being sucked out of me and feeling internally thrown backward, but that was my experience. I'm not sure why this age information was such a stunning revelation, but it was. It was moments like these where I felt like I was standing on the top of a mountain ridge, buffeted by wind from all directions, forcing me to work a bit to keep my balance. I could look one way and see a chasm between Sarah and her age peers. I saw how far behind she was, and I felt all my fears of messing up on this path we were on, as if we would fall later because of my choices now. If I turned the other way, I saw how far we had come. I knew that if my choices now meant homeschooling for Sarah's whole school career, then I would do it wholeheartedly. Which way to look was my choice. I could compare Sarah with some norm of what *should* go with a certain age, or I could be present and move forward peacefully from where we were. It was such a strange sensation to see the stark differences between my choices of thoughts. It was not always so clear. When I saw my choices clearly, then I more easily moved toward a clearer yes: *Yes, this is the path I want to be on. Yes, here we are, and yes, things are changing, and yes, let's keep going.*

20

Goals

Recently, I've hit a very nice groove with Sarah, in the Sarah-Rise room, with our Sarah-Rise goals, approaches, and guidance. Our interactions have been quite authentic . . . playful, dramatic, and fun . . . and Sarah has remained connected nearly fully. Indeed, today she hit me with a mildly sarcastic and completely verbal reaction. Hiding under 'the tent' she demanded, 'Read another book.' I countered with a dramatic, 'But I can't even see your face!' She immediately countered, 'Yeah, you can,' with an almost teenage-girl tone. It was fast, it was brilliantly timed, it was funny. I turned to laugh, and when I turned back she had popped out, smiling at me and at herself, I think, hair a mess from the static . . . quite proud of her accomplishment.

—Gregory

WE AIMED TO HAVE a group meeting once a month, but sometimes it was once every two months depending on when we could coordinate schedules. We started our meetings by having everyone share any recent good or funny moments with Sarah, in addition to asking any questions or sharing recent difficult moments. The room was always filled with tales that invited loving and laughter and sometimes tears of poignancy.

At one meeting, I told everyone about a moment when I'd felt upset about something unrelated to the kids and Sarah called me a grumpsicle. That was so unexpected, clever, and funny that my grumps dissolved almost instantly. I talked about how Sarah was very good at making connections and word substitutions to further her play, as many volunteers had already noticed. Carl and I play and substitute words ourselves. If she was cold, we might call her a Sarah-cicle, or if Amy was grumpy, I might call her a grumpalupagus. Sarah joyfully played with her own words with a glint in her eye to tell us she knew full well what she was doing, such as when she launched into a rendition of "Old MacDonald Had a Farm" while she was sitting at the dinner table. Instead of naming the animals on the farm, she sang, "Old MacDonald had a fork . . . ."

After everyone shared their good moments and all their questions, we would talk about our goals going forward. We had a lot of goals for Sarah because we wanted to help her develop in all areas, but it helped to narrow our focus and not go after all our goals at once. Three goals seemed about right.

Every meeting, I was in awe of my volunteers, in awe of their creativity, their thoughtfulness, and their dedication to our program. I had the best volunteers! We would brainstorm to come up with our three goals, make plans for upcoming Sarah-Rise sessions, and decide on any changes to make to the room itself.

In our December meeting that year, we decided that we wanted a slightly bigger table and two chairs, so we could work on having Sarah do an activity at the table. We'd bring back some old games and introduce some new games for which she might be ready. And I would paint a portion of one wall with special paint to make it into a dry-erase board. We established three goals:

Goal number one: help Sarah express herself verbally to let us know that she didn't want to keep doing an activity. She was clear about this with body language, but we wanted her to use verbal expression, in which case we would honor it immediately. Or when she suddenly switched from what we were doing to discussing bicycles or sock marks, we would encourage her to say, "I don't want to do this anymore," or "This is too hard," or "Help."

Goal number two: help Sarah attend to an activity while sitting at the table, because sitting at the table, rather than on the floor, would be good preparation for school. She had a small table at which she sat for some snacks, but we wanted a table with more room for games and for an adult to sit in a chair rather than on the floor. We also agreed that sitting at a table to practice writing was far more ergonomic and in line with how she would practice writing at school.

Goal number three: encourage a longer interactive attention span with games, such as what I was already experiencing sometimes while playing Colorama or the Minnie Mouse matching game. We would pick games we thought she would like or games we knew from the past that she liked. We would remain as focused and interesting and encouraging as we could and would invite her to stick with the game and play to the end even when it seemed like her interest was beginning to wane.

Goal number three was an interesting goal to have alongside goal number one, but, zooming out, the two were more in alignment with each other than not. We could celebrate her pushing a tiny bit past her limit of interest and cheer her on to stick with a game to the end. However, the moment she verbally said, "No," we'd honor that. We did not intend to force Sarah to do something she didn't want to do, and so we'd always encourage her to be clear with verbal communication.

One of Sarah's newest Sarah-Rise volunteers was Jason. Since he was new, I observed all of his time with Sarah and then gave feedback as we gradually increased how long he was in the room.

"The curtains are closed," Sarah said during one of their sessions one day.

Jason didn't understand her pronunciation of the word "curtains," so after a few attempts Sarah said, "The shutters are closed."

Shutters!

I didn't even know she knew that word! We always encouraged volunteers to smart-up their time with her, rather than dumbing it down. The more varied our vocabulary, the better. I loved that Sarah had the calm, thoughtful flexibility and the determination to be understood, which is what allowed her to think to say "shutters."

Even seasoned volunteers—like Laura, who had been with us for the entire program—could be surprised by Sarah, just as I continued to be. During one session with Laura, Sarah was talking about a red bicycle, so Laura brought down paper and markers. Laura asked what came first, expecting Sarah to tell her what to draw. Instead, Sarah said, "'R' . . . 'e' . . . 'd.'" Sarah's response may have been predicated on her time with Sonia earlier that day. Sonia had been asking Sarah how various words were spelled, and Sarah nailed many of them. She was quite attentive to Sonia's help for the ones she didn't know. Sarah was like a sponge, soaking up new ideas and skills in one session and squeezing them out into another.

Sarah's favorite item in the Sarah-Rise room that winter was a set of number flash cards from Handwriting Without Tears. Sarah counted the items on the flash cards and traced the numbers. She also did some addition with one of our volunteers. Sonia created a game around Sarah's love of having the cards spread all over the floor. She gave Sarah a task to do with a certain number, such as finding the ten and touching it with her left pinky finger. Sarah was fully responsive and enthusiastic about this game. I continued it some during my Sarah-Rise time, but when I prompted Sarah to give me a task, the game fell apart. But then she let me use the Cuisenaire rods in conjunction with the flash cards. Cuisenaire rods are small rectangular wooden or plastic blocks of different colors, and they are excellent for learning math and colors. In one way or another, we were all playing and learning with Sarah's love of the number cards.

I didn't always know where ideas originated in the Sarah-Rise room, whether from Sarah or a volunteer in a previous session. One example was the geography elevator, a game Sarah now initiated with multiple volunteers. She used the number flash cards to select the floor for the elevator, and then the elevator took Sarah and the volunteer to a state on the map of the United States that we had taped to one wall. One time with Gregory, the elevator game involved making a blue elevator out of a blanket and taking that elevator to the tenth floor. At that point, they had a snack at a pretend rest stop.

When I came into the Sarah-Rise room, we continued with the elevator theme. Sarah asked for the number flash cards, and while she started taking them out of the box, I got down the art supplies. I drew a line down a piece of paper, and Sarah cut along the line. Together, we taped the paper over a small piece of cardboard, and I suggested that she draw circles to be the buttons for our elevator panel. She did. Then I asked her to write numbers in the buttons. She did a few, and I did a few. I asked her to color the buttons. She did so, even following prompts to color some buttons in more fully.

I put the art supplies away, and we were ready to go with our button panel. We used the number flash cards to determine our floor and to label the floor (putting the card on the windowsill). She pressed the buttons on the button panel, and I said, "*Ding!*" Sometimes the buttons were broken, and the sounds went haywire, or I stuck my tongue out. When she wanted to go to a floor that was higher than our buttons on the panel, we did math to get there. I told her what to press, and she did it. To get to floor one hundred she pressed the "ten" ten times. At each floor, she got off the elevator and completed a task that I gave her—for example, she found a picture of a bicycle or a label that read "table." She only got caught in the doors—comprised of my arms—a few times and much to her giggling delight.

Next, I spread the small word flash cards around on the floor, and when she got off the elevator, I told her to look for a certain word. When she found it, I flipped it over, so it became a new word (each card had words on both sides). She found the word almost every time. When it was very clear that she was done with the word searches, I threw the number cards all over and we had to put them in order from one to ten to make the elevator work.

By then, we were both tired, so we had some quiet time where we each did our own thing and weren't interacting with each other. When I started putting the larger number cards in order, Sarah came over and started tracing them with her finger. She was more careful and deliberate with this task than ever. It was a rejuvenating moment of quiet companionship for us both.

During another session with Sarah, I used the number cards to work on counting squares. She often struggled to count with a one-to-one correlation of pointing and verbal counting. Sometimes when she counted, she didn't touch each object being counted or she counted some of them twice. On this day, I made a huge hammed-up deal about the importance of not missing a single square. She ate up my dramatics, gave me many chin presses, and spent a lot of time correctly counting each square on the number-ten card while pointing to the squares. Internally, I felt like I had shifted from needing her to do the task correctly to wanting her to enjoy doing it, which of course made it more likely that she would do it correctly.

That night after the kids were in bed, I made new flash cards with the number written on one side and squares on the other. I made cards for eleven through fifteen and then skipped to twenty, and then I made cards for each multiple of ten from thirty on up through one hundred. Let me tell you, that was a lot of small squares to draw and color!

In addition to helping with counting, these number flash cards were a testament to the fact that anything can be anything in a person's imagination. We could expand Sarah's interactive attention span with games created from the number cards, thus working on goal number three from our group meeting. We pretended to taste the numbers and say what flavor they were. We made number cakes (both sheet and layer), and we frosted our number cakes with number frosting. We pedaled number bicycles. We wrapped number presents and then put them in a box that served as a truck, a plane, a boat, or a sleigh, and we delivered them. We canoed in number canoes with our number paddles. I learned that Sarah loved it when I gave her a choice between two numbers. She said which one she wanted and pretended to taste it.

Once the girls were on their winter break from school, our holiday was filled with Christmas celebrations and visits that brought us into the New Year. During our travels, Mom-Mom had some beautiful moments with the girls. When one of the girls was busy getting ready for bed or getting dressed for the day, Mom-Mom invited the other up to her room for "a conversation." Both girls loved it—they adored the one-on-one time, and I'm guessing the idea of "a conversation" felt very grown-up. Conversation topics ranged from bicycles to fish to hanging plants. They even pretended to bring new hanging plants into the room for watering.

When we were saying our goodbyes at our last family holiday stop, Amy didn't want to go. She was heartbroken about leaving. I hadn't seen her act that way about a goodbye before. Then, later at home that evening, Amy started having a meltdown about getting into pajamas, but when I sat down and held her, she switched to saying how she was sad about leaving Grammy and Granddad's house. Sarah didn't seem to mind so much that our trip was over. In general, her upsets about people were about being impatient for someone to arrive or for us to get somewhere. Amy had an easier time with the anticipation but a harder time with the parting.

In our family, we are well versed in feelings and do our best to make space for them rather than shutting them down. I tended to have an easier time with Amy's feelings because they were usually sad and full of tears. Sarah's feelings, while sometimes sad, were more often full of anger and dynamic screams. I had a much harder time listening and making room for her expressions of deep emotion.

I had a very humbling moment one evening; the girls were supposed to be in bed, but we heard footsteps coming down the stairs. I felt myself getting grumpy and stern. I braced myself for the yelling. When it turned out to be Amy, I was immediately soft and easy and okay with things. *Egad! Say it ain't so!* In my defense, Amy didn't usually yell about being told it was time to go back to bed; Sarah often did. However, this was a startling moment that shed light on my assumptions and the inequality in my responses to my children.

Sometimes the kids and I needed metaphors to help us talk about our temper clashes. In the past, we'd talk about being "borkupines" (porcupines). "Borkupines" is a reference from *When Mommy Was Mad* by Lynne Jonell. Now, with the same sentiment, I would say, "We are on the wrong bicycle," because Sarah brightened at the very mention of bicycles.

One day, I said we were on the wrong *tandem* bicycle, because we were clearly together in our upset. After we had "put our prickles away," as Amy pointed out, we were able to ride on the right tandem bicycle all the way to the bathroom to finish getting ready for the day. Riding the right tandem bicycle involved me holding Sarah under her armpits or around her waist and walking with her while she pedaled and I said, "Pedal, pedal, pedal." Sometimes I had her put on her pretend helmet first.

While I did not love our angry clashes, I loved our way of pedaling out of them and reconnecting with shared play. This clash-and-recovery aspect of our lives is still something we navigate to this day—and perhaps will be navigating our whole lives. The important part is that we do deeply love each other and are always able to come back to that in relatively short order.

When I described the different energies of Sarah (taut) and Amy (soft) to a friend, this friend, whom I had known for at least twenty years, shared that she saw both of those energies in me—and had always valued the combination. She also observed that I often had more trouble accepting my taut side. That comment of hers was so insightful. It was a truth so largely in front of my face that I couldn't see it until someone else described it. So I took the first baby step toward accepting my taut energy, and I think that helped me accept Sarah more. I had more compassion for Sarah and the times when she felt so emotionally tight that she just had to yell.

I certainly still had my grumpy moments—with both children—but I felt like I was getting better at seeing past Sarah's yelling to the child that she was. When I was mad at her for being mad or upset, it was because I was expecting her to know better and for her behavior to represent her numerical age instead of seeing her at her own developmental age. And more recently, it felt good to hold her instead of stalking off. Instead of angrily thinking she was being upset just to get at me, I saw that maybe her nervous system was taxed to the max and she just needed to be snuggled and listened to. I had so often expressed this softness in response to Amy's upsets, and it felt good to have this softer response with Sarah now too.

One night, I was in a relaxed mode about getting the girls ready for bed. Instead of sternly reminding them for the tenth time to put on their undies, I started singing and dancing.

"Underpants, dah, dah, dah, dah, dah, dah, dah, underpants!" I sang.

I didn't know what to expect, but I kept singing.

"Underpants . . . dah, dah, dah, dah, dah, dah, dah . . . underpants!"

What I didn't expect was that both girls would not only comply but also start singing and want to keep singing. When Carl came home, we greeted him by lining up at the banister and singing the underpants song, with three voices gleefully chiming, "Underpants . . . dah, dah, dah, dah, dah, dah, dah, underpants!"

I eased up on mornings, too. For what seemed like forever, Sarah had been asking—every single morning—to go downstairs in her pajamas. Normally, we reserved this special attire for Sunday mornings. I believed we needed the pull of breakfast to make the girls get dressed during the week, so we always had them get dressed before going downstairs. But Carl and I decided to experiment. We switched things up, at Sarah's request. We let them eat breakfast first—on a weekday.

Astonishingly and humblingly, this change made our mornings much more enjoyable and efficient. There was much less yelling, and everyone was ready for the day earlier than ever.

I stood happily corrected.

When my computer shows the spinning rainbow pinwheel, I know that I must wait. Sure, I might feel annoyed, but I know there is nothing I can do except . . . wait. Perhaps, I could visualize Sarah as showing me that spinning rainbow ball when she seemed distracted, and I could wait, trusting and knowing that there was nothing else for me to do except possibly close some activity windows.

If she was focused on my getting dressed, then I needed to finish my activity and then make whatever request I had of Sarah, such as for her to get dressed. After all, if Benedict Cumberbatch were suddenly in the room with me, I would have some trouble continuing with my work. I would be rather distracted and in awe. Similarly, when Carl fastened his belt or I put on my bunny-print pajamas, Sarah had trouble continuing with what we asked her to do. After finding a metaphor to which I could relate, I understood her distractions in a new way, and it was easier to have more patience. Perhaps, this new understanding could help me yell less, too, remembering that sometimes her system just got overloaded.

From bicycles to spinning balls, figuring out my metaphors was helping me to see my actual life more clearly.

21

Reading

I WAS AS EXCITED about the How to Teach Your Baby to Read protocol as I was when we started the Sarah-Rise program. I'd learned about this different approach to teaching reading from some friends who had a child with developmental challenges. The Institutes for the Achievement of Human Potential designed this approach to reading, which is different from phonics. We had tried using phonics to teach Sarah to read, as had some of her preschool teachers, but it always felt difficult and useless. How to Teach Your Baby to Read involves making large word cards and showing a small group of them briefly each day with joy and enthusiasm. The cards quickly rotate, so new words are introduced every day. The method is geared toward babies, but can be used with anyone.

I bought the book and kit, and I also made a lot of cards myself, buying more poster board than I ever had before or ever will again! We started in January, a week shy of her eighth birthday, and the next day Sarah read the words "swimming" and "Grover." Amy read the word "spaghetti." This was after *one* day! I wanted to run from room to room whooping in delight. This was so easy and fun.

The words that we covered in our first week, most of which Sarah knew by the end of the week, included:

mail	the
night	blowing
Dora	oranges
boots	hippopotamus
troll	Benny
map	seat
delivery	in
red	helps
her	roller skates
spokes	scooter
brakes	with
bicycle	rides
gears	bathtub
cherries	bubbles
strawberries	spaghetti
ice	carrots
reading	no
swimming	oh
sleeping	backpack
play	

Oh my goodness!

I eagerly made many more word cards, keeping them in a big box in the basement. I loved that I could put any word I wanted onto a card and that I didn't have to make the words easy or similar. In fact, the more different and interesting the words were, the better. Every night I retired a word from each of the five packs around the house and replaced it with one from my basement stash. The retired words went into a different box that I eventually moved to the Sarah-Rise room closet.

Usually, Sarah was eager and interested in looking at the packs of word cards several times a day, as the method suggested. Every once in a while, though, she wasn't so interested. My strategy for these moments was to tell her that I had items to go in her dump truck. One of Sarah's favorite songs was about a dump truck, with the lyrics, "It's so cozy to ride in my dump truck." I gave her the card while I said the word, and then she placed it on the floor to her side—in her imaginary dump truck.

By the end of our first week with the word cards, we had an eight-year-old who was learning to read!

Birthdays are such good opportunities for growth and for me to see my stuck spots. I was trying to celebrate Sarah as she was, but I couldn't stop judging how she did certain things. I judged when she didn't open presents because she was having so much fun with the package itself. I judged how loud or weird her excited sounds and movements were. I judged how she wasn't at all near her age peers developmentally. Perhaps, all my judgments were more about myself as a parent. If only I had done more or done things differently, then Sarah would be different, farther along, or more neurotypical. I was being hard on both of us instead of fully celebrating our efforts.

That year, I made a special book for Sarah for her birthday with only one or two large words per page and a few pages with only pictures. I had made sure that we'd covered all the words in the book with the word cards—I had a vision of her reading the book all the way through, easily and delightedly, with focus, intent, and purpose. I used a blue plastic folder with fasteners to hold plain white three-hole-punched paper. I wrote with black Sharpie, and each page had only a simple sentence or part of a sentence on it, reminiscent of the word cards.

Sarah opened the present and immediately tossed the book aside, asking for another present, which she then didn't open for many minutes. The two times we encouraged her to read the book, she got a few of the words, needed help with some, and stopped before reading the word "spaghetti." She never found out that Dora rode her bike through spaghetti!

In theory, I knew that this didn't mean the reading program was a failure or that I was a failure, but those were my internal knee-jerk responses. I was doing a better job than before at noticing that these feelings were not truth and that what I had been given was *only information*, such as, Sarah wasn't quite ready for such a book. This didn't mean that she wasn't loving the word cards or that she wasn't learning the words on the cards.

For goodness' sake, we had only been doing the reading program for one week! She just wasn't yet ready to transfer her new knowledge to a smaller font in a bigger book, especially when there were other exciting things to look at or do. Remember the spinning ball of distraction? It was her birthday, after all.

Why was it that when I observed that Amy wasn't remembering all the words, I didn't worry about it? I knew that she was smart and would learn to read at some point. Perhaps, I could hold that belief regarding Sarah as well. It's just that when those word cards had started working so successfully, so quickly, I'd started imagining Sarah reading chapter books within a month. Although my envisioned time frame needed work, this didn't mean that Sarah wouldn't eventually read chapter books. We just weren't there yet. Still, I hid the tears behind my eyes. One more reminder that ours was not the typical path. Why was I not just okay with this?

Whenever I was sad and crying, and not hiding it as I did on her birthday, Sarah would come to my side, put her hand on my forehead, and look into my eyes. Sometimes, she even did this when I was trying to hide it. She knew when I was sad. Could I ask for more of a sweetheart? No, I could not.

For Valentine's Day, Carl gave the girls valentines with a few words on each. Sarah read hers all by herself except for the word "from." *Wow!*

"To Sarah [from] Dad," she read aloud. "I love you."

Despite my momentary book frustration, the word packs continued going well. Whenever I gave Sarah the option to read them, she almost always chose to do so. She often knew all the cards except for the newest word, but sometimes she even knew the newest word after only seeing it once. Occasionally, there was confusion when two words were slightly similar, such as "piggie" and "piano" or "snake" and "sneeze." One day, I dumped out several retired words onto the floor of the Sarah-Rise room and pretended they were snow and that we had to shovel the snow. I asked her to shovel specific words to me, and she did at least ten before wanting to switch to snow made of number cards.

Other times we played a game of squishing words. During one of my sessions, Sarah and I went through the entire box of retired words, taking turns squishing them, pressing down on the flat surface of the poster-board material of the word card. When it was her turn, I held the cards out so she could read them before I gave them to her to squish. As with other opportunities for her to show what she knew, she got most of them right and a few wrong. When she got a word wrong, she would always say a word that started with the same letter as the word on the card I was holding, and Carl pointed out that this was huge progress for her to look at the initial letter to help her know the word.

One day, I took Sarah to the library with me to pick up a book that was waiting for me. We headed to the shelves of books being held for patrons, and I offhandedly mentioned that we were looking for my name. She pointed to the book with my name before I had found it! I nearly fell over right then and there. I didn't know she knew my name in print.

I was thinking a lot about Sarah's birthday and my feelings about the book, which had me thinking about my life in general and how I assessed my world. It occurred to me that just because I might be unhappy in a given moment or feel like I was struggling with something in our life or our program, it didn't mean that I was failing. This may have been obvious from the outside, but when something was challenging, on a deep level I was sure this signaled that I was failing. I held tight to a belief that absolute, unadulterated success would mean a completely joyful Jenny at the helm at all times. And yet, the reason Sarah-Rise was so wonderful for our whole family was that we all learned, grew, and changed alongside Sarah. That meant that the whole process, grit and all, was what this successful journey looked like.

To give us more opportunities to work on reading and writing, I painted a whiteboard on part of one wall in the Sarah-Rise room and now kept a pile of washable dry-erase markers on the floor under the board. Sarah's favorite book at the time was *You Are (Not) Small* by Anna Kang, so during some of my Sarah-Rise time, I wrote "big" and "small" on the board in various sentences, such as, "Sarah is small." "Sarah is big." "Amy is small." "Amy is big." "Mom is big." Sarah read them all and wrote her own "Big" in the clearest writing of "B" and "g" that I had yet seen from her. Not long after that, there was water on the kitchen counter, and Sarah dipped her finger in the puddle and started writing numbers with the water on her finger. She wrote her clearest "5" ever.

One night, Carl was reading from a book of *Peanuts* comics for Amy's bedtime story. The story involved Linus having trouble with math.

"For Linus!" Sarah said suddenly. She had been trying to go to sleep but was now holding out her hand.

"What are you giving him?" Carl asked.

"Math cards," Sarah said.

Such thoughtful and flexible imagination. Not only could number flash cards be anything, but a handful of air could be pretend math cards! Along with doing the reading cards, we had been attempting the How to Teach Your Baby Math program. We started the math-program cards shortly after we started her with the word cards. These cards were not the same as her beloved number flash cards from Handwriting Without Tears or the similar flash cards that I'd made. The How to Teach Your Baby Math cards had varying numbers of dots spread randomly on cards. The idea was to help kids associate images and amounts with numbers. Sarah was willing to look at them, but the cards didn't work as magically for her as the reading cards had. In fact, we are still seeking the most effective way to help her with math. We do know that it is worth experimenting with different learning approaches because we never know which one will work.

22

Flexibility

Sarah asked to play with the project. (Project, what project? I've never heard Sarah use that word. How does she know it? Does she know what it means? How am I ever going to figure out how to come up with a project?)

Sarah guided me, unerringly, to the shelf in the closet. No, not the pink sheet, not the blanket, the box. (One mystery solved, the box is called '101 Electrical Projects,' or something like that. But, yikes, it's a serious science project, not a toy. What's it doing here? How can Sarah be interested in it? Should I be letting her play with it? Maybe it's just about the box.)

Sarah saw that I had the box and had a look of happy anticipation. Once I gave it to her, the box got only a cursory glance. "New box." Then it was open, and we were ready to play (Sarah was; I was madly looking for directions to see if this was dangerous. I was concerned that the pieces seemed so delicate or intricate somehow).

Sarah started building a circuit, she took out the pieces, snapped them in place (making a good effort of it), she showed me the motor, and then the fan, told me what they were. Then she asked for help, very clearly expecting that together we could make the motor work so the fan would go round. (I can't do this! I have no idea how to do this! How can I get this box back in the cupboard?) *Then Sarah asked for help again, and I noticed one of the pieces had a switch* (okay, maybe I can do this. Let's give it a try).

Once it was built, Sarah knew exactly how to start it with the switch. When she toggled it over, the little motor started, the fan quickly went round, then it launched. The preciousness of those few seconds! Sheer delight, from both of us, solid, joyful eye contact, squeals of joy from both of us, the absence of doubting voices in my head.

Sarah never doubted there was a project, she never doubted that I would help her build it, she never doubted she could build it, she never doubted me and my support. I'd brought all of that doubt into the Sarah-Rise room with me.

Doubt. Now that I've noticed that habit in my thinking, maybe I can more readily recognize it when it creeps into my thoughts and choose to replace it with a more Sarah-like trust.

Thank you, Sarah.

—Laura

WILLIAM HOGAN, ONE OF the people who taught me to run a Son-Rise Program and with whom I had multiple helpful consultations about potty training and control, was undergoing treatment for cancer. I was sad, disbelieving, and hopeful all at the same time. I loved and appreciated him so much. Within the Son-Rise Program Facebook community, comprised of families from all over the world, there were hundreds of prayers circulating for him. I read a post where someone suggested doing everything we did as an act of love and prayer. When I tried it, it led to the most Sarah-Risey day I had experienced in ages. I felt more loving, creative, and patient than I had in a long time.

I found myself doing things as an act of love and prayer often. I realized I could do this as a prayer in honor of Sarah, too, imagining her thriving and learning with ease, reading voraciously, writing up a storm, responding to "no" with calm grace, and connecting with others with increased clarity and creativity. Creativity abounded within the Sarah-Rise sessions, and I felt extra appreciation, as if the creativity could pour love toward William.

With Sarah C., Sarah initiated taping a small circular container of hand lotion to the wall—she said it was a smoke detector. With another volunteer, Sarah played a little bit of Twister and then made the Twister mat a boat. Noah and Sarah often created all sorts of "edible" concoctions from Play-Doh, using whatever container was at hand to serve as a blender or oven.

I loved the conversations I had with my volunteers after their sessions, where they said things like, "After we went to the store . . ." or "When we were at the coffee shop . . ." It was as if those things had been real. Because they were. Pretend real. Real pretend. Full, real wonderfulness. Real, wonderful pretendfulness. Like the play with Mom-Mom, which involved pretend tea parties and thunder parties, regardless of what the weather was doing.

On their most recent visit, I noticed how Sarah was connecting with Mom-Mom and Pop-Pop at every opportunity. She was playing games with them *and* joining in on games that they were playing with Amy. To join a game already in progress was still notable and to be celebrated.

Sarah's participation in simple games increased and improved by the day. One afternoon, Sarah, Amy, and I played Busytown, a cooperative game based on Richard Scarry's books, and all three of us got through half the game together—and it can be a long game.

Sarah's ability to play more games was echoed by her increasing flexibility with language.

"Go ahead, tell me I have new jeans!" Gregory said enthusiastically as he walked in the door one day.

He had just arrived for one of his sessions, and he was wearing new jeans. Sarah loved jeans and always noticed when people had new pants.

"You are wearing new jeans!" Sarah said excitedly.

This was correct grammar and pronoun use! Such a development was as exciting as her first words, because every bit of clarity with her language helped her be understood more fully. In the past, Sarah might have said, "I am wearing new jeans," when she meant that Gregory was wearing new jeans. It is hard to coach someone with pronouns because pronouns change based on who is speaking. We usually exaggerated correct pronoun use or used Sarah's own hand to point to whomever she was referring, speaking as if we were her to model what she could say. Sarah was always open to being corrected with her sentence structure, just as she had always been open to us correcting her pronunciation.

Within this more sophisticated stage of language development, Sarah started asking simple questions. When Sarah was with Laura, the two of them created a game where Sarah greeted and asked after each number card and book in the room; for example, she would say, "Hello, ten, how are you?" and "Hello, *Pigs Make Me Sneeze!*, how are you?"

Our next step was to help Sarah expect, and wait for, answers to her questions, at least those posed to people.

One day, Sarah knocked on the laundry room door and *waited* until she heard Sonia say, "Come in." Next, she easily answered Sonia's "How are you?" with "Good."

This was definite progress and was not to be sneezed at.

For the first time since we'd started the reading and math programs, I went to bed one night without refreshing my piles of cards in preparation for the next day. And I lived.

"I'm worried if I don't do the word cards tonight then my whole system of nightly word rotations will fall apart," I told Carl as we got ready for bed. "I don't like not being prepared! I feel like it is a slippery slope and the whole organization of our house will fall apart forever."

Carl looked at me with a warm twinkle in his eye.

"Well, I know that is how it feels, and it is a very Jenny-ish way to feel, and that is why you are so prepared so much of the time, but I will say there was one night when you were away, and I didn't prepare the word and math packs. So far, eternity is going pretty well anyway."

It was just what I needed him to say, showing his appreciation of me while also helping me gently laugh at myself.

As my flexibility around being prepared increased, Sarah's flexibility around music decreased. That was rather disappointing, since our overall goal was to increase her flexibility. I once had played all sorts of music, and Sarah had enjoyed it all. Now, all she wanted was an album of *Disney Children's Favorite Songs* that she called "dog music" because of the picture of Pluto on the cover. Any other music was met with screams and protests. Amy preferred that no music be played. Of course.

I wanted to sigh loudly in frustration about their impasse, and sometimes I did, but that still didn't resolve the situation. My only solution was suggesting a compromise. We'd listen to dog music for a bit and then have no music for a bit. Conveniently, if Amy forgot about turning it off then so did I, because when I did turn off the music, Sarah yelled, or asked politely, anxiously, and repeatedly, for it to be played again. If I played Sarah's music again, then Amy got upset. I saw they were both playing me to a certain degree, but sometimes all I wanted was peace and quiet. Or peace and dog music. *Just please, no yelling!*

With the return of Sarah's passion for dog music came an intensified desire to wear, all the time, a pair of snail pants that I'd made for her. We had thought that it was important for us to work on her flexibility by presenting the reality that clothes do need to be washed—that Sarah couldn't wear one pair of pants all the time—but this led to intense amounts of yelling and screaming at each laundering moment, unless the pants were taken away completely. If she knew she never got to wear them, then she would be upset for a while but would then adjust and pick a new item of clothing about which to be passionately attached. Sarah didn't do half measures well, so wearing snail pants only some of the time didn't work well for her.

One premise of The Son-Rise Program is to give control as often as possible, especially where it is clearly, desperately sought. This can help a person relax enough to foster future flexibility. In the spirit of supporting Sarah enough that she could feel calm and relaxed and then move forward from that point, I changed my thinking about snail pants and the reality of laundry. What if I could change that reality so she never felt the sorrow of laundry hour? I wanted to surround her with an abundance of snail pants so that when one pair was being washed, she could be wearing another pair. I decided to make Sarah enough pairs of snail pants that she could wear them every day. Laura offered to help me make some of the pants. Snail pants or bust!

The fabric was called "Summer Snails," and once we had a plethora of Summer Snails pants, shorts, and capris, Sarah started choosing to wear her other clothing! Not always, but sometimes. This not only proved that the approach of abundance rather than scarcity did help with flexibility, but it also showed that making an abundance of snail pants was joining the ism rather than fighting it. I just hadn't seen it that clearly in the past.

I have my moments.

I have moments of inspired, patient, loving brilliance, and I have moments of losing my shit!

I had a couple good, hard cries one week in April, which helped clear a few emotional cobwebs. Carl is a wonderful listener, always sitting with me during these moments. He didn't try fixing me or the feelings I was having. He didn't run away either. He accompanied me as I had my feelings, offering tissues and a shoulder to lean on. Carl did with me what I aspired to do more frequently with the girls. I did such relaxed, present listening often but not always. What never ceased to amaze me was that after a good cry, I could then easily do all the tasks that had previously felt overwhelmingly impossible. Perhaps, if I didn't resist my own tears so often, if I allowed a light rain on occasion, then I wouldn't require a thunderstorm to empty my clouds.

Of all our moments, I preferred those of laughter and delight, though I realized those sometimes flowed more easily after a good cry and getting our sad or mad out.

One of my favorite moments was when Sarah and I were in the Sarah-Rise room and she wanted to pretend we were in a sleeping booth on a train, so I asked a pretend conductor for a pillow and blankets, and we tucked ourselves in under the covers. I was concerned that we would fall asleep for real, so I put my hand on her middle and moved her gently while saying, "Chugga, chugga . . . ," and then I yelled, "Screeeech!" I moved my hand with more force so her whole body moved toward her feet. I looked around with an expression of exaggerated concern and bewilderment.

"Sarah! Someone must have pulled the emergency brake!"

Sarah was laughing so hard that she could barely speak, but she wanted to repeat what I had said because she liked it so much.

"Sssccc [laugh] rrrr [laugh] ss [laugh] ssscreeech!"

We continued replaying that scenario with variations for the rest of our time together—me pulling the emergency brake, Sarah pulling the brake, Sarah *chugga-chugga-ing* my stomach and moving me when the train *screeeched*. Mainly, Sarah liked saying "screech" and liked it when I physically jostled her, appreciating my faces of mock alarm and consternation. What made the moment even better was that while we were playing, we were working on interactive attention span, eye contact, copying facial movements, imaginative play, asking questions, and speech clarity.

My less-than-favorite moments were those of judging Sarah, often without even realizing it. This is something I realized when I was observing Gregory. When Sarah was with me in the Sarah-Rise room and pulled her pants down a bit to look at the depressions on her skin from the elastic, I would get annoyed that she had her pants too far down and that I had to keep telling her not to do that in the Sarah-Rise room. Gregory, too, reinforced with Sarah that she needed to keep her pants all the way up, but then he kindly pointed out to her that she had been so interested in her pants marks that she hadn't realized how far her pants had moved down.

Oh. At that moment, I saw how Sarah wasn't being bad or intentionally embarrassing.

Oh. At that moment, I wasn't proud of being judgy, but I was grateful to notice it and know that I could change my perspective.

It was around this same time that I also considered the suggestion that we "be the change we want to see in the world." If I wanted Sarah to be more peaceful, then I needed to be more peaceful. Perhaps this was obvious, but it felt profound. And I was certainly not achieving it in all my moments. However, having this refreshed intention did help me because it clarified my purpose in peacefulness. In a very selfish way, I wanted to be peaceful so that Sarah would hurry up and be more peaceful, but I was also more of the parent and person I'd always wanted to be when I maintained my own inner calm.

Most school mornings were met with resistance about getting dressed, so one morning, when Sarah was refusing to get dressed,

I told her I wasn't going to force her to get dressed and that I just wanted to talk. She calmed down immediately.

"Sarah, when you are focused, you get dressed so quickly," I said. "I know you can get dressed in just one minute and brush your teeth in one minute. I can do your hair in one minute. That means in three minutes, you could be back to playing."

Remarkably, she responded to my explanation by getting dressed and ready in three minutes. I was stunned. This breakthrough did not, however, carry forth to other mornings. Still, for something to happen twice, it must happen once, so one morning of success was important and to be celebrated.

That same day, Sarah went to school without a personal attendant in the wings. This was not the plan, but Sonia was sick, and I had a client, so I asked her teachers if they were okay with Sarah attending on her own or if I should put her in the day care that was in the same building. They said she could be at school. Apparently, it went well. Sarah did a beautiful job participating as the calendar helper, and Sonia and I imagined dumping tubs of Gatorade on each other in celebration.

23

Tiny Huge Progress

When our volunteer Maiti came to play with Sarah one day, Sarah talked about her new favorite play scenario involving Baby Bear. Maiti drew a huge zoo on the whiteboard.

SARAH WAS TAKING FLIGHT with new things in the Sarah-Rise room. There were days where she traced dotted letters that I wrote and other days when she inscribed letters with my hand over her hand, me guiding her. She initiated writing freely on her own more often. One day, before she did a project with Carl, I asked her to write the word "tool." And she did so clearly!

Sarah's flexibility around how certain games were played also increased. Toward the end of the school year, she and I played a creatively adapted game of Zingo, changing many aspects of how and where we typically played the game. Zingo is a kind of bingo. Manipulating the game pieces, or chips, was good for finger dexterity, while the pictures and words were good for reading and matching practice. Playing any game at all was good for Sarah's interactive attention span and connection. Usually, when we played Zingo, it was the chip holder that consumed all of Sarah's attention, but the chip holder wasn't with us on this particular day. The chips and the boards were, and I assumed Sarah would want the holder.

"Do you want to go to the Sarah-Rise room to play?" I asked her. "That is probably where we left the chip holder."

"Stay here," she replied.

"Okay. Sure. Let me just wedge my rear into this tiny seat."

Sarah was sitting in a small wooden armchair at the small wooden table that was used for art projects in our dining room. She began playing with the Zingo chips in a cup that was on the table, so I wedged my butt into the other small armchair and selected a few chips myself. The chips are yellow plastic and are printed with pictures and words in black letters. I started putting them down while saying the words out loud. She did the same. Next, I started putting each chip on my forehead, where it stuck, thanks to the humidity. She looked at me with delight and said the words on my forehead. Then we put all the chips in the cup and took turns picking up a chip and seeing if it matched a square on our boards. This was flexibility on both of our parts (and I mean, really, don't underestimate what it was like to squish into a child-size seat!) regarding how we played the game, and I could also tell that Sarah's reading skills were getting stronger.

Sarah's reading progress was rapid. Now, her word cards had two or three words per card. She was reading phrases, and sometimes, she made verbal connections between words all on her own. One morning, Carl showed her a new word card with "black cat" written on it, and then he showed the already familiar "red rose" card, and Sarah spontaneously said, "The black cat is holding a red rose." My jaw dropped as far as it could toward the floor.

Another thing that floored my jaw was Sarah's increasing ability to express empathy.

Sarah C. had had a hard day. When she was joining Sarah by pressing on book pages, each with their own book a few feet away from each other, she felt sad and got a bit teary. Sarah immediately stopped what she was doing and came over to comfort her, which included calling on a pretend phone to say, "Hello, Sarah C. is sad." She then pretended to drop off a bag of stuff to help her feel better, as we sometimes do for friends who live nearby when they are dealing with hardship.

While this showed Sarah's increased empathetic social connection, and while gymnastics class provided a clear reminder of how far Sarah had come in her physical abilities, we were all most excited that she finally seemed ready to graduate preschool. It was the end of May, and eight-year-old Sarah was about to go to her last day of preschool ever. She had been in preschool for five years—two and half years in a public-school class just for kids with special needs, followed by a stint of no school (other than the Sarah-Rise room), before she started at the church preschool where she had been for the last two and a half years with neurotypical three-, four-, and five-year-olds.

At every decision point for a new school year, we had many thoughts and feelings to consider, always wanting to support Sarah optimally, but knowing our choices would have repercussions. No matter whether school is public or private, the age limit is twenty-one, so after you finish the academic year in which you turn twenty-one, you are no longer able to be in the K-12 school system. During the Sarah-Rise years, we felt strongly that the best thing for Sarah was to keep her with her developmental peers rather than age peers, though this is not the model that any schooling typically follows. We cared about her social connection more than academics, understanding that she wouldn't be ready for academics if she couldn't pay attention well to another person.

After so many years of preschool and so much progress thanks to Sarah-Rise, we felt that she was developmentally ready to move to kindergarten. It helped that her church school was creating a kindergarten class that would be small and half-day, taught by Ms. Michelle, who had been one of her preschool teachers. Ms. Michelle agreed with us that Sarah could start the year without a personal assistant, and that we could see how that went. It seemed like the perfect transition out of preschool.

We were all excited! Amy would attend her preschool three mornings a week and day care the other two mornings. Sonia was eager to have more time to be at the house making food, doing laundry, cleaning, and planning Sarah-Rise activities or field trips, and I would happily fill my morning schedule with massage therapy clients.

The night before Sarah's last day of preschool, I was overwhelmed with emotion, like I had made it to the finish line of a long race. I certainly still had my visions and hopes for the future, but this was a huge moment worth celebrating. I had not followed a traditional path, but I had gotten us to this moment that I'd envisioned long ago—the moment of Sarah being in a class with her developmental-age peers and only moving to a new level of class when she was truly ready.

Another achievement that I'd recently discovered was that we had already surpassed the Pennsylvania state requirement for nine hundred hours of homeschooling. This didn't change our daily routines or goals, but it lifted a bit of weight from my shoulders. Next year, I planned on officially homeschooling Sarah, in addition to her attending kindergarten, because the kindergarten was half a day and the state required her to be in full-day schooling based on her age. Even if I didn't need to officially homeschool, I would have stayed with this plan because we saw that a blend of regular school and Sarah-Rise time (our version of homeschool) worked so well for Sarah. She was thriving and learning and edging closer to transitioning fully away from the Sarah-Rise room and fully into school.

Alongside Sarah's progress, I had a few seemingly small yet huge breakthroughs myself. When it came to the word and math packs, I often forgot to connect with Sarah first. My breakthrough was remembering to join her if she was isming and to wait for her to be ready for my input. I was good at that in the Sarah-Rise room but not always outside of the room—and all our word and math packs were outside of the Sarah-Rise room. When I waited for us to connect through play and then worked the words into the play scenario, our academic practice time became more effective and fun. It was far better than me asking her for her attention outright and getting grumpy if she was unwilling or unavailable to give it to me. Connecting was the key to everything.

As is my wont after any epiphany, I was instantly and hugely ambitious. I wanted to parent with perfect connection, at all times, no matter what. The problem with that goal was that it was born from seeing my usual mode as lacking, and it set the bar impossibly and unspecifically high. To rein things in, I set a specific goal: to connect first when it was time to request something of Sarah, whether it was word or math cards or something else. That was all. That was doable. No more perfection at all times.

Getting Sarah to get dressed in the morning often involved many requests on my part. So on one morning after I'd set my new goal, to connect with Sarah first, I sat next to her on the sofa and waited for her to look up from her book. When she looked up at me, I proceeded.

"Sarah, time to get dressed," I said.

Minutes passed. Nothing.

I tried again: "My sweet Sarah, let's go to your room so you can get dressed. Are you gonna take off your shirt, or am I?"

Sarah giggled while walking to her room and didn't answer. I prompted, "Sarah?"

Sarah took off her shirt.

"Wonderful! You will do it! You can tell me, 'I'll do it!'"

I put a shirt for her to wear on my head.

"Mama!" she said with a giggle, and then took the shirt off my head and put it on.

"Great! Now, what about those pajama pants? Are you gonna take them off, or am I?"

"I do it."

"All right! That's what I like to hear!"

She took off her pants and then decided to look at a book that was on the floor. I went to brush my teeth. I came back a few minutes later and handed her a pair of underpants. She took care of that clothing swap and then wanted to go back to her book, so I put a pair of her pants on my head as if they were hair.

She smiled, swiped the pants from me, and put them on. I sang a made-up song: "Put on your pants a leg at a time. Put on your pants and things will be fine!"

Then I continued, "Great! Now the only thing left is socks. Do you want help?"

"No. I do myself."

I left the room again, and when I checked back a few minutes later, I found her looking at the book, feet still bare. I put a sock on my hand. At that point she took both socks and put them on her feet, with minimal help to get them rotated appropriately.

Sarah is dressed!

Success! And the process had been fun and connected.

Sometimes, I was desperate for everyone to be happy and connected, forcing and faking it but not really feeling it. This never actually got people feeling happy, relaxed, connected, or motivated despite how many times I tried. It was always better when I acknowledged the real feelings everyone was having without needing to change them. I had to remind myself that it was okay if the kids were upset. I didn't have to cave to their clamoring, nor did I have to censor it. I could have limits and boundaries and be at ease when those were met with resistance. I forgot and relearned this lesson many times.

Limits around technology were often where the kids and I clashed with conflicting desires. Sometimes I handled it calmly, and other times I didn't. I would turn off the TV, and they would complain, and I would inwardly cringe as I anticipated screaming. But now I had logged a few times of being inwardly calm when I turned off the tube, letting them voice their consternation while either easily listening or calmly leaving to tidy the kitchen. Just as when I celebrated Sarah for doing something once because then it could happen a second time, I celebrated my calm moments as stepping stones toward more calm moments.

Another situation that I was able to handle with more calm than before was a sibling rivalry that involved our toy car. Amy was driving the Cozy Coupe, and Sarah got upset as usual. Instead of bracing myself for her screaming, or getting annoyed at the situation, I went over to her, feeling easily comfortable with her upset and looking in her eyes.

"I know it can feel hard to wait. Amy, can you move to another room, so Sarah doesn't feel so jealous?"

Sarah loved the word "jealous" and began talking about feeling jealous, shifting into sparkly-eyed contentment.

In many of the situations when I was overwhelmed and couldn't find my flexible, calm self, I realized I was usually hungry.

My stepmother used to say to my dad, "There is no quitting your PhD program after 10:00 p.m.," and I have since translated it: "There is no quitting on an empty stomach."

I was not allowed to give up or feel like a failure if I was hungry, since hunger and feeling like I was failing often went hand in hand. First, I needed to eat or drink water or pee or nap or turn on the AC or put on a sweater, whatever it took to meet the need of the moment. Then, and only then, could I evaluate the situation.

Once my basic needs were met, if I reminded myself that if the kids were upset, then they were allowed to be upset, and it wasn't my responsibility to keep them from feeling their feelings, then I could feel okay. I had to remind myself ahead of time that feelings would pass and that everyone would feel better once the mad and sad were out. I had to remind myself of how much I valued the time, space, and lack of judgment that Carl gave me when I was upset. To maintain the equilibrium I sought, I needed these reminders.

As I learned in part with the Alexander Technique, it's not like there is a magical end point to be reached where everything is figured out forever, much as I desperately wanted such an end point of wisdom. It is about rewiring one's habits and anticipating the patterns that may happen before they happen. For instance, if I knew that Sarah was attached to a certain shirt for some period of time, when it got dirty, I would remind myself ahead of time that she would probably get upset when it needed to be washed. I could better welcome the screams and tears, knowing she would be clearer and freer emotionally afterward. I could sit with her if I had time and emotional space to do so. And if I didn't have either, then I could do other things without getting myself all worked up into tension and anger about her feelings.

When I was growing up, my mom and dad often made space for me to have my feelings, always explaining and modeling that tears were okay and that I would feel better after they were out. Why making space for all the feelings was harder to do in my own parenting, I don't know. This is still a journey. I am learning that I handle tears better than screams, but whenever I can make space for all of us to genuinely feel how we feel in the moment, everything seems better.

24

Summer

ONCE SCHOOL WAS OUT, Sonia and I filled the summer with many field trips, which was definitely easier with two grown-ups. We had fewer hours in the Sarah-Rise room, but it felt like the right step at the right time. We were doing Sarah-Rise the lifestyle way, being as flexible and supportive as we could be while introducing new and outside activities. Field trips afforded many opportunities to practice having the kids stay close to us without always holding our hands and to practice safely crossing streets and parking lots.

With our eight-year-old Sarah and four-year-old Amy, we went to the Trolley Museum, the Children's Museum, the Heinz History Center, and the Carnegie Science Center. We had picnics and went to various playgrounds. One of the many times we went to the Schenley Park Carousel, there was a gigantic beach ball with which all were invited to play.

When we were at home, Sonia and I spent more hours playing with both kids at the same time, which often looked like navigating between two activities in one room if the kids wanted to do different things. It was the right next step to help Sarah connect with kids and stay connected in social situations involving multiple people. I often played with both kids in the Sarah-Rise room with the door closed even when we were the only people in the house. It helped me focus and kept me from being pulled to cook or clean.

With Amy in the room, I took more of a back seat and let Amy drive the play because you couldn't get more kid-like than Amy. Amy had vast amounts of energy, so she joined some of Sarah's play scenarios more physically and wholeheartedly than I usually did. One day, the three of us played Hello Kitty Bingo. Whenever it was time to roll the dice, I started singing made-up lyrics to the tune of "Rawhide" (original lyrics by Ned Washington, music by Dimitri Tiomkin, 1958):

> *Rollin', rollin', rollin',*
> *Keep those dice rollin'.*
> *Hello Kitty!*
> *Daniel, Fifi, Squirrel,*
> *Gum ball and watering can,*
> *Hello Kitty!*

Eventually we all sang together, Amy adding dramatic flair as she sang "Hello Kitty!" at top volume. Later in the day, Sarah requested that we play the game again, specifically with Amy. We did so, playing and singing our way to someone saying "Bingo!" many times. This was huge for Sarah to not only request a game and play it all the way through but to want Amy to be a part of it and attend to a game with two other people.

That summer, the girls decided they wanted to take ballet together. It was a small class with only six students. During the first class, Sarah was focused for nearly the entire time. I only had to block one of the doors for the last fifteen minutes so she wouldn't leave. Sarah then ran farther into the room when it was actually time to leave, and then she tried leaving through the main door without me, but the whole experience was a good metric regarding our participation goals for such a situation. I wanted her to easily attend to the class without trying to play with doors, to not leave early, and to leave easily when it was time.

Above and beyond my goals, Sarah did an amazing job with the actual ballet in the class (at least on day one)! Both girls did. Sarah easily participated, listened to the teacher with minimal prompting, engaged in pretend play, answered questions, and repeated ballet terms flawlessly when asked to do so. *Wow! Holy moly, Miss Magoo!*

Ballet class wasn't always as smooth sailing as it was on day one. After a few classes, I spoke with the teacher about Sarah staying longer at the end, if she wanted to, to help her transition more easily. The teacher was supportive of this idea. But in the next class, though there was no screaming or running away, Sarah was distracted throughout and didn't want to do some of the activities. Toward the end, I went in and told her that she could "leap over the pond" with the other kids or she could sit outside of the room with me. She opted to sit with me and enjoyed watching traffic, so she didn't even finish class that day, let alone stay longer at the end.

Ballet class, a bit like gymnastics, helped me access a range of feelings—from pride and happiness to frustration, anger, and hopelessness. It was refreshing to notice that I used to feel all those negative emotions often, but now I hardly ever felt that whole packet of feelings. Ballet class was an opportunity to practice being happy and calm regardless of Sarah's participation. Sometimes that was easier said than done. It helped that the girls' teacher appeared happy to have us there, and *that* was not to be taken for granted.

Carl and I had a rule that we couldn't have two weekends in a row with either hosting company or being out of town. But sometimes, there were important events that meant going against this rule, and that is precisely when I was reminded of why we had the rule in the first place. Two in a row was too much.

In July, I had two weekends in a row of travel. The first weekend was just me, going away for a memorial service, which also served as a family reunion. Carl stayed home with the girls. The next weekend, the four of us traveled to Minnesota for Carl's high school reunion. We got to see lots of family members, which was nice, and the weekend went as well as possible in terms of food, thanks to my mother-in-law, known to the girls as Grandma. Since we flew, I couldn't bring supplies like I normally would, so I was very grateful that she prepared everything for us when we arrived. She baked Sarah's chocolate zucchini cupcakes and filled a cooler for me with other things that Sarah could eat. Grandma and Grandpa also provided excellent babysitting and assistance overall. Still, I found it stressful.

It seemed that on any family trip, I ended up feeling much tighter about Sarah and her behavior. I felt like I said "No!" all the time. But I did something different for Carl's high school reunion trip. I accepted my stressed and grumpy state a little more than usual, and instead of wondering how I'd suddenly become a failure of a mother, I was able to say, *Oh, this is what usually happens with trips. It is going to be okay.* This new mentality then allowed me a sliver more of calm while away and to appreciate how nice it was to get back to some normal routines once we were home.

Reentry to normal life was not without its challenges. The Thursday after we came back from Minnesota, I had the girls for the entire day—just me—and it went surprisingly well. But toward the end of the day, I felt done. Just done. I was burned-out and feeling bad that I felt burned-out, because I was a parent who had so much help overall. I had to remind myself that the first step toward feeling better was to stop fighting the burnout. And perhaps to have some water and eat some food.

Hot on the heels of Burned-Out-Thursday, on Saturday we went to Point State Park, where there was a festival that included a big Ferris wheel. We stood in line for a long time to ride the Ferris wheel. In Carl's words, "The girls and I had a great time, and Jenny was there, too." True. I was stressed and wanting to be done for most of the time we were there. It was hot and crowded. There were cars on display for part of the festival, and Sarah wanted to be in the cars and didn't take kindly to leaving the car display. However, the Ferris wheel was both better and worse than I'd expected. The height bothered me less than I thought it would, but Sarah wanting to stand up had me very anxious for the last, painstakingly slow revolution. I had no capacity to be nurturing or supportive when I was scared. In fact, I even kind of shut down verbally, covering my eyes with my hand in some moments and in others just looking imploringly at Carl to fix the situation.

"No! Sarah! Please sit! Sarah, can you just . . . ," I implored. Tension permeated my voice. I took a big, deep breath of frustration and fear. "Can you sit? It's important to . . . *sit*. Can you—"

"Hey, Sarah, can you sit down?" Carl asked, relaxedly. "It's important to stay safe on the Ferris wheel and stay sitting. You can still see everything if you are sitting."

Sarah sat.

"Thanks, Sarah!" Carl said, cheerfully. "Nice job!"

All I could muster was an audible sigh of relief.

I was a hypocrite. I had my team of dedicated volunteers who came to my house to be loving and focused with Sarah, but I myself was having a hard time being loving with her. In hindsight I can see that there had been too many trips and outings with my stress level through the roof. So, of course, I wasn't feeling loving and, of course, she was feeling frustrated at how often I said no. We had nice moments, sure, but my overall impression of our relationship was that of frustration, sternness, and yelling at each other. I knew that Sarah and I had gone through phases like this, and that this, too, would shift, but I was impatient for it to change and frustrated with myself for not being able to change things on my end sooner.

Why couldn't I just allow her more room to be herself? Why couldn't I be more okay with her upsets, and why did I feel the need to control her activities and timing? Why couldn't I feel love instead of judgment? I would frequently resolve to be more loving in general, especially after we had a good make-up snuggle, but then the next time she protested about what I served for dinner, I would go from zero to sixty on my tense-grumpy meter. I'd slam the fridge door as I put back what she didn't want, stomping off to get something new while saying she would just have to eat what was there. I knew in theory I could enforce rules around eating without getting grumpy, but in practice I seemed always to be grumpy.

I was not just mad at Sarah's whining and yelling. I think I was also mad at her for her condition. For her delay. For her challenges. For her neurodiversity. Instead of having compassion for her when she had a hard time with transitions, I was angry with her. And this anger was immediately followed by considering myself to be the most horrible, rotten person imaginable for having those feelings.

I wanted a break, a time when I was not on call in any way in my own home. I wanted to be at home unneeded so I could deal with piles of stuff or just read my book all day. I wanted a day where half of what I said wasn't met with whining by Sarah or Amy or both together. Once upon a time, there was some version of me that was totally fine with whining, crying, screaming, and general upset. I don't know where that version of me went that summer, but I was trying to find her.

Perhaps, yet again, the first step was to be okay with my own disgruntlement.

My mom wisely recommended taking some small but concrete steps to change things in my life. One of the changes was to make

Post-its, which involved writing messages to myself on Post-it Notes and sticking them around the house so I could be reminded of my intentions. Some of my notes read:

"I am doing enough."

"Connect first, then request."

"It's all okay."

"Breathe."

Another change was to call my mom daily, except when I was traveling. Calling my mom meant talking to someone who I knew, beyond the shadow of a doubt, always loved me, always cheered for me, and was always interested in my deepest, maybe-not-so-pretty emotions as well as any not-so-deep thoughts. I got to talk about any and all of it during our now-daily phone conversations. My mom helped me keep my attention out in the world—so I didn't get bogged down by life feeling too hard.

The Post-its helped, and although I had many supportive people that I saw daily, the addition of the phone call with my mom was what I needed. My mom could tell when I was about to set my expectations too high. She knew when I was creating impossible standards for myself, and she'd nip them in the bud before I even got going. She knew that sometimes I needed to aim for being a "mediocre mom," so that I wasn't frozen and tense trying to be a great mom.

Even though I may have been struggling, many things with Sarah were going well. On the way home from Minnesota, Sarah lost her first tooth! Sarah didn't get her first tooth until she was one, so while many kids already have lost teeth at age six or seven, Sarah was eight. While not quite a developmental milestone in the same way one might think of walking or talking, a first lost tooth was a big deal, as was the new development of having word cards with four words per card! There were many instances where our toothless Sarah could read new cards perfectly without having seen them before. Sarah was also willing to try new things that seemed physically daring. We went to a playground, and Sarah went down the firefighter pole several times, with Sonia helping just a little.

Sarah's language skills continued blossoming, and we noticed that she was able to ask "where" questions with more fluidity and ease.

"Where's Dad?" she asked me one morning.

"He's downstairs."

"Bye," she said, before heading down the stairs.

That may seem like a very typical kid moment, but it was one of those huge moments for us, because nothing like that had happened before.

On a balmy day in July, Sonia and I decided to take the girls on a Just Ducky Tour of the city, the one where the tour bus is also a boat so it can drive down the street and into the river. When the boat was in the water, all the kids were allowed to take turns sitting at the wheel. Amy wasn't interested at all, but Sarah took to it like a duck to water. Most of the kids kept their hands immobile on the wheel, but when it was Sarah's turn, she steered for real. I think she surprised the driver a bit because he chuckled as he straightened our course a few times. Sarah didn't want her turn to end, but she handled that transition well considering the level of protest she sometimes had in situations like this.

A few weeks later, we had a fabulous time at Bald Eagle State Park in central Pennsylvania. We were there with Carl's cousin and her family, all of us enjoying swimming in the lake and playing in the sand and on a playground. The weather was perfect, and the scenery was beautiful. But, as usual when on a trip, there were many, many, many times when all Sarah wanted to do was what we didn't want her to do. Regardless of our saying no, she tried again and again. When we were at a visitor center, she wanted to go in and out, in and out, in and out of the doors. She wanted to stay in the bathroom using the loud air hand dryers seemingly forever (note that Amy particularly hates the sound of air hand dryers). She wanted to play on ramps, going back and forth, back and forth, and back and forth.

What if that *is part of her diagnosis?* I thought. *What if all of the repetitions and all the fixations are par for the course given her genetics and autism?*

You may be thinking, *Of course that is true.* But the epiphany was for me to realize that those behaviors didn't mean something was terribly wrong with my parenting or with Sarah. They meant that she wanted to do certain things over and over and over, especially on trips, which were filled with her favorite things. Ramps, doors, and air hand dryers were present in new forms, and we seemed to encounter them at every turn.

With my epiphany came the relief to acknowledge that it all was okay. After all, didn't I already know that her relentless repetition often served her? This was so clear in the Sarah-Rise room when practicing with snaps or isming to regain equilibrium after a challenge, but somehow, when we were out in the world at large, I missed the connection of how she needed to ism for her own practice and peace of mind. She also found doors, ramps, and air dryers fascinating, so why not spend time with the most interesting thing around?

This all clicked into place for me while watching her running up and down a ramp at the Bald Eagle State Park visitor center. Perhaps, because at that moment I didn't have to tell her no. She was safe and not in anyone's way. I could even play on the ramp, too. Whether with fine motor skills (for instance, zipping and unzipping zippers) or gross motor skills (for instance, running up and down ramps), I knew that repetition served Sarah's learning ability. She needed many repetitions with a skill before she attained it, and my goal was to make space for all the repetitions she needed—in all the spaces she encountered.

At home, it was easier to routinely make time and space for such needed repetition. Sarah loved playing on our backyard playground, especially going across the monkey bars many, many times with Carl's help. Inspired by watching *American Ninja Warrior*, she tried and tried and tried climbing up the side pole of our indoor climbing structure. The more she repeated all these activities, the stronger, more capable, and more independent she became. She was also becoming more independent with her bathroom use. She wanted to do her potty trips *by herself*—with the door shut!

Meanwhile, I was learning that the more often I introduced (and reintroduced) new foods, the more the girls were willing to try. It had been my own assumption that they wouldn't want certain foods, and Sonia reminded me to go ahead and offer them with enthusiasm and the assumption that of course they would like them, and then offer them again and again and again.

We were now seeing that all the practice and repetition in the Sarah-Rise room was making a very big difference in how Sarah moved through the world.

"Open it, please," Sarah said one evening.

Carl was getting Amy ready for bed when he saw Sarah standing in the doorway with a toothbrush in one hand and a tube of toothpaste in the other.

The significance of this was threefold. The fact that Sarah initiated brushing her teeth before being told to was notable. The fact that she went to find Carl to ask for help instead of whining and yelling in the bathroom was what we dreamed of. The fact that she looked at him while saying a clear and full request was amazing!

"Sure, Sarah! Wow!" Carl replied. "I love that you came to find me to ask for help and that you are brushing your teeth without my even saying anything!"

Sarah smiled and commenced brushing her teeth.

Wow! Nice work, Miss Magoo!

25

Kindergarten

SARAH STARTED KINDERGARTEN!

By herself!

With no extra helper in the wings!

She was eight and half. She loved it. Ms. Michelle, the assistant preschool teacher from the year before, was Sarah's kindergarten teacher this year. Her class had four students, and it was half-day kindergarten, a rare find in Pittsburgh. Two of the students were girls who had been in Sarah's class the year before, and the third was a boy that was new to the school. I saw the other families when we did drop-off and pickup, and I knew Sarah was in the right place. Everyone was so friendly and welcoming. I really couldn't have designed a more perfect situation for her.

She never wanted to leave when I picked her up in the afternoon, and every morning she looked forward to reading the paper arrows taped along the hallway that had the words "kindergarten" and "Sarah" and the names of the other students written on them. When Sarah walked down the hall, she liked to touch the arrows and read the words.

Her kindergarten situation was so good that I found my heart overflowing, in the same way that my heart overflowed with appreciation for my volunteers. In the past years when I'd visited other kindergartens to consider for Sarah, I'd never felt quite certain they would be the right fit. Her preschool experience at this church school had been so positive that I was thrilled to extend it into kindergarten. I only wished they had grades beyond that!

Sarah's independence continued to grow in realms beyond school, too. As a family, we watched *American Ninja Warrior*, and the girls often pretended to do courses around the house, scaling window ledges and hopping off couches. We went to an outdoor festival that had a bouncy house and a bouncy obstacle course. The girls were clamoring to go through the obstacle course together.

"I want to do it!" Sarah exclaimed.

"Me too! Me too!" Amy added excitedly.

"Yes!" I affirmed.

And then I read the rules.

"Oh . . . Amy, sweetie, I'm so sorry. It says you must be at least six years old," I explained. "But, Sarah, you can do it. Dad and I are too big to get in there to help you. Do you think you will be okay on your own?"

She looked at us and uttered her customary "yes-no" blended word of mystery.

Carl clarified, "Was that a yes?" He knew it probably was, but we wanted to encourage enunciation especially regarding "yes" versus "no."

"Yes!" she declared.

Carl went with Sarah to help her get in line and get ready, taking her shoes off in preparation. I snuggled Amy and smoothed the tears off her cheeks. Eventually, she recouped and happily took some turns in the bouncy house. Once Sarah completed the obstacle course—all by herself!—she joined Amy in the bouncy house.

Later that day, Little Miss Capable walked into the kitchen, picked up her water bottle from the drying rack, and filled it at the water-spout on the fridge. It seemed that Sarah's independent abilities were galloping apace, and I needed to get out of the way so she could gallop past me. I would stay nearby to assist when needed, but I wanted to let go of assuming she would need my help.

Sarah was getting more fluid and fluent with her speech too.

"Sarah C.! Your eyes look like tunnels. Want to go through!" she said one day.

This was rather poetic and profound.

Meanwhile, Amy's language also progressed—especially her "s" sounds. Sarah C. asked Amy who her best friend was. Amy said, "Sarah. Because she's my sister." Amy also told me I couldn't eat Sarah because Sarah was her sister, when I was pretending to be so hungry I might gobble them up. This sisterly devotion Amy had was probably part of what supported Sarah's ability to connect with her so often. There was such love.

Gregory, who had now been with Sarah for five years, was seeing changes, too. He wrote:

During our conversation, Sarah's thoughts were almost poetic in reminiscence. At one point we found the photo with Amy sleeping on Carl. Sarah started, "Has glasses on." I didn't get it.

"I don't see glasses, Sarah."

"Great-Grandpa." I still wasn't there. Then, "Amy as baby Daddy."

"Oh. You're thinking about the photo with baby Daddy with sleeping Great-Grandpa wearing glasses."

Her smile encompassed her entire head.

Gregory then wrote about a time when Sarah said, "It getted to zero":

I've never heard her make that kind of a developmental error. That is, using the regular past-tense form with an irregular. Typically, Sarah either knows a word and uses it, or she doesn't use it. I rarely hear these wonderful little errors.

Making a little error that might be associated with any kid learning to speak felt like an accomplishment or another step toward some sort of "normal," whatever I thought that meant.

As well as demonstrating more language flexibility, Sarah was becoming less rigid in some of her daily moments. One September evening, Sarah spilled a small bit of applesauce on her snail capris at dinner. There was a collective pause, waiting to see how Sarah would respond.

"Oh no!" she exclaimed.

"That's okay. You can keep wearing them, or you can take them off, and we can wash them later," Carl assured Sarah.

"Pantless!" Sarah happily sang in reply.

She used her napkin to wipe off the excess applesauce but remained sitting and proceeded with her meal. In the past, this spill might have resulted in screaming and upset on her part, especially if we asked to have her clothing to wash it. Even if we assured her she could keep wearing her clothes, she often would get upset and feel the need to change them anyway. *This* was definitely progress.

Sarah was suddenly reading beginner-level books, and I figured the word cards might soon be obsolete. One week she read a line from *Pinkalicious and the Pinkatastic Zoo Day* by Victoria Kann. The next week she read entire Pinkalicious books and entire Elephant and Piggie books by Mo Willems, with me pointing to the words to help her stay on track.

Sarah had been making such reading progress that we made books for her during our next team meeting. I provided a pile of blank paper, different kinds of tape, yarn, scissors, markers, and a multitude of photographs of the kids, various family members, and volunteers. It was exciting to see how we each approached the task and the completely different books we produced. Sarah wasn't immediately interested in reading them, but we adults all had fun making them and delighted in reading them ourselves, enjoying the creative venture and the pictures. I made very simple books. One was about Sarah's anaphylactic reaction to pecans and her visit to the hospital. The other was called *Sarah and Amy Love Books!*

We didn't discuss what books we were going to create before we made them—we each dove in to do our own thing. What is remarkable is that with no explicit coordination, we wrote in varying levels of difficulty. Whereas my books were quite simple, Carl's book had more words than mine did, and Gregory's book was filled with words and flaps for Sarah to lift. Sarah was able to read them all when she decided to give them the time of day. Sometimes to pique her interest, it was most effective for me to read a book out loud to Amy in Sarah's vicinity. Later I would see Sarah perusing the book on her own. That is what happened with these books. It seemed that they needed to marinate or steep first in proximity with Sarah, and then she became interested and read them often.

Even though Sarah's reading ability was steadily growing, and we had our newly made books for her to enjoy, we still reviewed the word cards. We were up to six cards per word pack, changing two cards per pack per day, and using all the cards that we'd used in the past. Sarah often got the renewed cards right away without any help, and when she didn't know a word, she could make a good guess based on one or more letters in the word.

Sarah was also getting more fluid with her ability to ask questions. One morning, when Grammy and Granddad were visiting, she picked up a bag of coffee beans.

"Mom, Granddad, what is this?" she asked.

Indeed, the only place the word "coffee" appeared on the bag was in tiny print within other tiny words. I was so pleased with Sarah's ability to address both adults in the room and then ask a question. Just as if it were the most natural thing in the world to do.

Kindergarten had barely begun, and already Carl, Sonia, and I were discussing what to do about the following year for first grade. Sarah's kindergarten situation was so dreamy and perfect, but alas, that church school didn't go beyond kindergarten. I started visiting schools again, thinking about what would make sense. There was a disparity between what I wanted to believe Sarah was ready for and what she was actually ready for. I worried about all my past and present choices while simultaneously wanting to roar like a mama bear defending myself.

She was thriving because of my choices, and I wanted to trust my intuition for moving forward. Then there was deciding what was best for Amy and what made sense as a balance for both girls. As usual, it felt a bit early to tell how Sarah would be developmentally in a year, but that didn't stop me from trying to know the answer *right now*. I like to know things yester-minute.

I knew that I did not want to homeschool Sarah for the next school year. I had loved running a Sarah-Rise program and doing what bits of academics made sense as part of a school-homeschool joint effort, but I knew that I did not want to fully homeschool—not even a little bit. It felt good to come clean about this and to realize that there were many options for schooling for Sarah. She could attend a public school in a life-skills classroom, or she could attend one of the public schools devoted entirely to kids with disabilities. There were also some options outside of the public-school realm.

School quandaries aside, there was no question that we had the best Halloween yet. By "best" I suppose I mean the most typical-feeling Halloween we'd ever had. The weather was good, and we were costumed and ready at the start of trick-or-treating. I wore a skeleton dress, Amy was a ballerina, Sarah was Dora, and Carl was Mr. Fusion from *Back to the Future*. Carl took the girls out, and I stayed home to hand out treats. Carl was able to stay back on the sidewalk while the girls went up to each house, interacted with our neighbors, and then came back to him. Sarah tried eating some of her bounty immediately, but she accepted the repeated reminders to wait until she could make her trades with me for homemade treats. We missed Sonia, but she had just moved and wanted to hand out treats at her own house.

The girls and Carl came home happy, and then we had dinner, a chocolate treat, and pumpkin pie. In addition to swapping out Sarah's haul for homemade chocolates, I gave her store-bought applesauce pouches and maple sugar candies and some freeze-dried strawberries for future days. Amy traded with me for a few things, but I didn't force any trading since I felt okay about her eating what she got from our neighbors. Our house was also left with an abundance of fruit leathers and stickers—the treats I had chosen to hand out.

Amy and I often talked about how there were certain treats that she had to eat when Sarah wasn't next to her, such as any peanut items, even though Sarah's flexibility around foods she couldn't have was notably impressive.

She was usually completely okay with other people eating things around her that she couldn't have, and she accepted substitutes with grace and ease. The times she got upset about food were when she couldn't have one of her usual things, which was most often due to the fact that she'd already had enough of that food during the day.

When Carl, the girls, and I went to a Halloween party that year, Amy had some very sad moments. I wasn't sure why except that maybe it was a bit overwhelming to be in a house she hadn't been in before with many kids she didn't really know running all around. I suggested that she might like sitting next to Sarah in a large toy car that had two seats—a deluxe version of their Cozy Coup.

Amy readily went over, saying, "Sometimes when I'm feeling sad, I like to do the same thing as my sister because that helps me feel better."

It was clear to me how much it helped Sarah to have Amy to play with and learn from. Seeing how Sarah helped Amy, especially in some social situations where Sarah was less overwhelmed and more confident than Amy, warmed my heart.

In November, William Hogan died, and I felt deeply sad. He was one of my most beloved teachers at ATCA. I loved and was inspired by him. I read the news of William's death in the morning as I helped the girls get ready for the day. I started crying hard as soon as I saw the subject line of the email. The girls were sweet and attentive. They sat with me, listened, and gave me hugs and kisses.

That day, I had much more time with Sarah than I normally would have had, and that felt like just the right thing for my soul. I also had time to sit in the sun and think and be. I was deeply grateful that William had existed, and that I had the honor of learning from him, and I was sad and having trouble comprehending how such an inspiring and wonderful person wasn't living in his same form anymore.

I like to think that the whole world is a better place with William Hogan's spirit now spread throughout. During my time of sitting quietly in the sun and watching the individual blades of grass gently swaying in the breeze, I felt as though I was placing him in the sunlight, in the grass, and in the air. Even now, when I have a moment of similar quiet reflection outside, it is as though I am visiting William and remembering the poignant peace of that afternoon.

"Because Sarah can read . . ." Ms. Michelle was saying, but I missed the rest of her sentence because I was thinking, *Did I hear Ms. Michelle right? Sarah "can" read?*

I was in a parent-teacher conference with Sarah's kindergarten teacher. Month after month and year after year, Sarah's skills across many areas continued growing stronger. While being able to read is expected of neurotypical children, this was something we never took for granted with Sarah. Up until this moment, I had it in my head that Sarah was *learning* to read, but I hadn't let myself fully cross the threshold into "Sarah *can* read."

By November, four years into Sarah-Rise, Sarah had been "reading" books all by herself at home. *Miss Bindergarten Has a Wild Day in Kindergarten* by Joseph Slate was a book that was easy to memorize, but now it was clear to me that Sarah was reading it and not reciting it. We were rapidly reviewing all the old word cards, too. I was changing three words per pack per day, and Sarah was recognizing parts of her memorized words in new words by looking to the first letter of a word to help her know how to start.

By the end of the month, Carl and I decided to change how we did the word packs for Sarah's reading practice. First, we retired all the word cards made on poster board and made the new packs on index cards. We also returned to single words. Originally, I didn't do many words that were similar ("hat," "cat," "sat," for example), because the program we were following advised against this, but by this point Sarah was so adept with getting things from their context that now we wanted to have words that were similar. This would encourage her to focus on the letters she was seeing. We wanted to help her a bit more with the phonics aspect of reading so she could figure out new words. Did you know there are a ton of words that sound like "I"? Take all of these, for instance:

aye	high
by	lie
buy	lye
bye	my
cry	nigh
die	pie
dye	rye
dry	sigh
eye	tie
fie	vie
guy	why
hi	

I also made a few packs of fruit and vegetable cards, including words like "banana," "pepper," "strawberry," "broccoli," "raspberry," "carrot," "avocado," "kale," "chard," "apple," "pear," and "cucumber."

As words on the page became easier, Sarah's spoken language continued becoming more fluid, and her eye contact with others easier, yet some moments still caught me by surprise and warmed the cockles of my heart. One such moment was while I ate breakfast on a Monday morning. I was talking to Carl, and Sarah came over, nudged my arm out of her way so she could get closer to me, looked me right in the eye, and said with bright enthusiasm, "I have kindergarten today." Her speech was clear as a bell, and to have that coupled with such deliberate eye contact and drive to communicate was a most notable and exciting moment.

"Yes! Yes, you do!" I said. "Thank you for telling me!"

"That's great, Sarah!" Carl said. "I'm so happy for you!"

Later that day, when Carl was outside with the girls drawing with sidewalk chalk, Sarah saw that one of our neighbors was also outside. Sarah walked right up to her and said, "Say hi to George." With no hesitation, the neighbor invited all of them to come into her house to find her son so Sarah could say hello. Sarah was becoming quite the social butterfly. We greatly appreciated our neighbors and neighborhood for fostering such a welcoming and safe space for Sarah to grow.

After returning home, Sarah said she wanted to climb onto the hood of Carl's car. He said no and then turned his attention to Amy. A minute later, Sarah was on top of the hood. As soon as she climbed down, Amy tried climbing up. But Amy couldn't do it and called out for help. Immediately, Sarah assisted Amy by giving her butt a boost. Then, Sarah climbed back on the hood. The two sat there with expressions of triumphant glee, reclining as if on a beach. Although this was hilarious, Carl informed the two of them that this was the first and last time this activity would happen. He then suggested everyone go inside and play Candyland together.

That night was the first time the three of them played Candyland all the way through. For real, the *entire* game! Sarah only needed a bit of prompting to go when it was her turn and some advice on what direction to move. This game-playing progress was both expected and astonishing: expected because Sarah was sticking to her general trajectory of progress, and astonishing because every step forward with Sarah was notable and exciting. Every step knocked off our collective socks.

It was also becoming more common and expected for Sarah's progressive play to involve Amy. Sarah C. began her Sarah-Rise sessions with Amy in the room for the first half hour, though sometimes Sarah didn't want Amy there. Other times, she didn't mind but she didn't engage in play, so Sarah C. had to navigate interacting with each child independently rather than facilitating a group game. But increasingly, Sarah, Amy, and Sarah C. played games together, like Candyland, Candy dominoes, Hello Kitty Bingo, or Hello Kitty Uno. When Sarah got upset, the Sarah-Rise room was the perfect setting to help her work through the upset with support and love.

One night when I was singing the songs from *Blue Moo* by Sandra Boynton, Amy started singing with me, and then Sarah did too! Singing *with* us—singing what we were singing—was not something Sarah did easily or often. Sarah also sang "Happy Birthday" with us multiple times, and it was the most fluid, clear, confident singing I had ever heard from her.

Not long after the evening of song, I was out seeing a client, and Sonia was watching the girls. When I came home, she told me that the girls were dancing to songs with movements together while they cleaned the family room—for over an hour! In the past, if Amy or I were dancing, then Sarah would usually stop her own dancing to watch us. So, for Sarah to dance along with Amy and participate in cleaning for such a long time was a huge achievement.

Eggs! We tried eggs!

We started working with a naturopath because I wanted someone to help us look at Sarah holistically. The naturopath did some blood work and met with us in person, suggesting various supplements and a specific way of reintroducing foods. We would give Sarah the new food two or three times on day one, take forty-eight hours off the new food, and then pay attention to any changes in Sarah.

On Friday afternoon, I gave her scrambled eggs, and later we would have cupcakes made with eggs instead of my usual egg substitute made of ground flax seed and water. Once she'd eaten the scrambled eggs, I explained to her that she should tell me if she felt sick.

A half hour later, Sarah said, "Mom, I am feeling sick."

She'd been watching a show with Amy, reclining on the sofa with no obvious signs of distress.

"Are you going to throw up?" I asked.

She said yes, but nothing happened, and she continued watching the show. After a bit of time, I reminded her that if she was truly sick, then we wouldn't be trying the *cupcakes* made with eggs but that she could have something different. A few minutes later, she was up and about as her usual self.

She may have felt sick, or that may have been a fabrication. When she told me she felt sick, her phrasing was a little too perfect, a little too precisely copying my own wording. We had cupcakes with eggs that night, and I decided that the next time we tried a new food, I wouldn't ask her to tell me anything. She could volunteer information, but I wasn't going to offer her wording for feedback along with the new food. That week, she had a renewed itchy area on both sides of her right wrist. I didn't know if this was from the egg or not, given our previous experience and her general skin sensitivity. So I gave eggs a rating of "maybe."

We then retried bananas and fruit leather for what felt like the billionth time, which both received a tentative "yes." For our Thanksgiving feast, I found coconut milk ice cream that Sarah could have (Coconut milk ice cream from a store! Coconut milk ice cream that I didn't make!). So while this wasn't exactly a *new* food, it still had the potential for Sarah to have issues with it since it wasn't homemade. There was no reaction. I did make whole wheat bread from scratch because that allowed for the most control—wheat needed to be the only new ingredient. Sarah had one piece and didn't seem to have any bad reaction. Not that we needed to go crazy with an abundance of wheat and gluten, but wheat gave us more freedom in Sarah's food options in our life, especially when traveling.

I was also on a quest to find soaps and lotions that would keep her hands from getting tiny blisters. I continued learning how much I didn't know or understand about the ingredients in various soaps and lotions, so I decided to make a huge spreadsheet to catalog all of the ingredients in the soaps and lotions we had tried. I had no idea what most of the ingredients were! I realized that an overlap of ingredients in products that seemed to cause irritation didn't necessarily mean those were the offending ingredients. In fact, almost every product had some ingredients that didn't overlap, and maybe some of those were the problem. Then again, I noticed a significant overlap of ingredients between the 365 fragrance-free foaming soap and the Kiss My Face olive oil soap, both of which were suspect. While at times this method of discovery was overwhelming and frustrating, it was a potential game changer if I could figure it out. If this meant that all the times I thought foods were causing the blisters it was actually soap that was causing the blisters, then we could retry so many foods! I was determined to find the soap culprits or solutions.

I wrote about our struggles in my blog and email update to friends. I had a flood of possible solutions and ideas from my readers. My friend Monika called me to share her similar situation with her hands, and that made all the difference. Vanicream bar soap was what worked for her, and lo and behold, Vanicream bar soap was the right soap for Sarah, too! Her hands were noticeably healthier when she used this soap. We could move forward with adding more foods to Sarah's diet without the perpetual hand-blister surveillance.

This Vanicream experience, among others, is why I share so many details about our experience with Sarah and with Sarah-Rise. If I don't say I need help, then how can people help me? And if I don't share about our journey, then how can I be of help to others? Many people keep their issues private, which I can understand and respect, but I have learned that the best thing for me has been to share openly and honestly about basically everything. Every story, every detail. Every win, every loss. Every step forward and every step back. Not only do I gain support and ideas, but I also hear from other people that what I share is inspiring, helpful, and relatable.

My weekly writing is a way for me to preserve and remember the many details about my kids' lives and my journey through parenthood with Carl. There are so many precious memories that would otherwise be lost, and when I write about struggles, they often ebb. Frustratingly, sometimes the opposite can be true. When I write about everything going well, such as when I think I've determined the answer to life forever after, that usually is a sign that things are about to fall apart. I write about it all and have a supportive audience of readers to cheer us on and to hold me up. I am forever grateful for that support network.

That year we learned what Sarah was grateful for: her sister! Near Thanksgiving, Sarah made a paper turkey at school where each feather represented something she was grateful for. One of her feathers had the word "Amy." When Amy and I saw this, we were very excited.

"That means Sarah likes me!" Amy said, several times. That feather really meant a lot.

"Mom," "Dad," "food," and "iPods" were the other four feathers.

While Sarah may have been grateful for Carl, that didn't stop her from getting frustrated with him. Around this same time, Carl and Sarah were looking at family photos on the computer and listening to her favorite music. Carl also had his work laptop open, and Sarah wanted it closed. Repeatedly she tried to shut his laptop, and repeatedly Carl told her she couldn't.

Sarah reached to close Carl's laptop.

"No, Sarah," Carl said. "You need to leave my laptop alone."

Sarah made the sound of a mad whimper.

Carl didn't say anything.

"When Sarah gets older, be Dad," Sarah said. "When Sarah grow up, be Dad."

"Oh really," said Carl with joyful surprise. "You want to be like me when you grow up?"

"Yeah," said Sarah.

"Oh . . . that's great," Carl said. "What would you like to do when you grow up?"

"Shut the lid."

26

A School Dream Dashed

Each kindergarten student was asked to write a card to someone of their choosing. The big deal was that their card would get mailed from school. When Sarah's card arrived in the mail that week, it was the best part of the week. I believe she wrote it all herself with maybe the tiniest bit of help, and it read, "My Dear Sii [sister] Amy Merry Christmas Love, Sarah."
Sarah chose Amy.

JUST AS SARAH CHOSE Amy as the recipient of her letter, I made some big choices myself. I chose a school for Sarah for the next year. I had a dream school and a dream vision of Sarah at this dream school. It was a small private school, and the feel of it reminded me of my small private elementary school. It was what I wanted for both of my kids. It had narrow halls with art on the walls, the math teacher was playing a game with a bouncing ball to make math fun, and the kindergarten room had a slide. This was where Amy attended preschool, so I sat in the hall often while I waited for her. I attended an open house, and I loved the teachers, their creativity, and the whole vibe of the place.

I had really, really, *really* hoped that Sarah could go to this dream school next year. Maybe she'd be able to repeat kindergarten and then continue to first grade—all without an assistant. The classes were small enough that I thought it could work if the teachers were on board. I met with the kindergarten teacher, the first-grade teacher, and some of the administrators of the school in December, and they seemed open and willing to consider the possibility of Sarah as a student. We scheduled a three-day visit, increasing the number of hours she would be there each day, because I knew her first day might not be her finest. It turned out not to matter though.

The email came just hours after her first visit. The school said that it didn't feel that it was the right place to meet her needs. I felt like my crush had broken up with me over email after our first date. I tried to balance not feeling too bitter with allowing myself to have the emotions that were coming up.

First, it was, *Drat! Now, I don't even want Amy to go there!* This was big because this school had long ago been my dream school for Amy, too. But now it was tarnished, cruddy even in memory. So . . . .

Now what? I asked myself in complete exasperation.

Then: *Why? I work so hard to have our life feel normal, to see Sarah as normal. Of course, I know she is older than her classmates at school—and at gymnastics—but she is able to be both places now with either no help or minimal help, which makes me feel normal, and normal feels good. I explain all the time that she has special needs and that I run a program to help her, and yet I hate having it reflected back to me by any other mirrors that she is not neurotypical, that she is not catching up, and that she may never catch up.*

The more I thought about it, the more I stewed. I was furious. When I was honest with myself, I reflected that I knew even from the visits without Sarah, when I met with teachers and described her, that the answer from the powers that be would be no. While some teachers were open to meeting her and then deciding, it was clear that others became veritable deer in the headlights at the mere idea of having someone like Sarah in their classroom. They felt they couldn't meet her needs without even meeting her and knowing what those needs might be! In hindsight, I can see they were perhaps right. But the main reason they were correct that it wasn't the right place for Sarah was because they were already closing their hearts to her. I wanted a place where the teachers would love and delight in Sarah for exactly who she was and believe in all that she could be.

I was furious that we were dismissed without following through with the original plan for her visits and without more clear communication. I sent a response to their rejection email asking for more details.

Days passed with no response. I fumed, ranted, and raved. I felt disrespected and ignored. After one week, I finally received a reply, and I thought, *Was it really so hard to respond? Were you really that busy?* Maybe. The response was respectful and kind but was still disappointing. The admissions director explained in more detail that their understanding was that I didn't want Sarah to need a helper, which was why they didn't bring Sonia in to be with Sarah during her visit. *Argh!* They wanted to see how Sarah would be without a helper and after those few hours decided that she would need a full-time helper, which was not something the school could provide. *I could have provided that!* Still, I was not going to fight their decision. I didn't want Sarah anywhere where I had to fight for her acceptance. I was sad, mad, disappointed, and not sure if I could find a school that I would be truly excited about on Sarah's behalf.

I knew that I didn't want to continue running a full-time Sarah-Rise program. I was running out of energy, and I felt like Sarah was ready to move beyond the Sarah-Rise room. I didn't want to plan a program with more academics. I didn't want to homeschool. I didn't want to figure out ways to make the team stronger or more effective. I wanted to be done.

Was I giving up? Was I a failure of a Son-Rise Program parent? Or was I deciding to be done because it was okay to be finished and it made sense? If I put Sarah in public school in an all-special needs class, then was I giving in to the idea that she would always have special needs? Was I endorsing it or accepting it in a healthy way? Did it matter? I felt like I was lying down on the side of a marathon course, all out of juice. I was done.

My fury ebbed, and soon gratitude began to grow. I was thankful that someone at some point said there must be a place in education for everyone. I was so glad that public schools provided such a place where I knew that Sarah would be welcomed. The public-school doors would always be open to her even though I kept leaning toward them and then backing away. She was always welcome, and that was a relief.

Maybe everything along our school path had worked out perfectly and was continuing perfectly. Sarah had to be evaluated again to see what she qualified for. She seemed ready for the public school's Life Skills class in a way she hadn't been in the past, so I wondered if I should hope that somehow she wouldn't qualify for the Life Skills class because she was now so skilled. *No!* I wanted her to have the small class size and the extra teachers! Would they let her be in first grade as I requested? Or would they put her in third or fourth grade because of her age? If so, I supposed I could humorously brag that she skipped some grades.

I knew that there were skills for which I was an effective leader for our Sarah-Rise team, such as speaking, eye contact, playing games, imagining, reading, potty training, and interaction. Other skills for which I was not the best teacher were reading, writing, and math, never mind subjects such as science and history! Whenever I tried crafting lessons about such subjects, I prepared what I thought might cover thirty minutes, but Sarah and I would look at it for maybe two minutes. I hoped that when we reentered the world of IEPs (Individualized Education Plans) that we used to be in when she was in public preschool, I could maintain the confidence and vision I felt as a Sarah-Rise team leader. I hoped to continue influencing the decisions made regarding Sarah and our goals for her in a school setting. In fact, I hoped we could continue supplementing her schooling with a few Sarah-Rise sessions. Now all I needed to do was to find a perfect fit for her next year.

As forever grateful as I was for Sarah's Sarah-Rise years and the year of kindergarten, I still felt disappointed in myself for not wanting to continue Sarah-Rise. I felt like a failure of a parent. Yet, as often happened when I had sad feelings regarding Sarah or myself with respect to her, Sarah herself was the antidote. She bombarded me with examples of how much she continued to progress and how very awesome she was. Twice in one week, when I was in the throes of disappointment, she requested to play a game with me in the family room. Each time, we proceeded to play an entire game with Amy as a third player. First, we played Quack Quack, and then we played Pengoloo. Sarah asked us questions like "Where is my water bottle?" and "What is this?" and I remembered when the idea of her asking questions was unimaginably far off. She had crazy strong moves around the gymnastics bar, and Carl and I often looked at each other and said, "Remember when she couldn't lift her head?" I know there was a time when all of us couldn't lift our heads, but for Sarah that time lasted a very long time, and we were scared and doubtful new parents in those early days.

Regardless of how I framed everything, no one could take away Sarah's skills or tenacity for learning and for life. Thank goodness she had herself to keep things going even when my energy flagged, because my energy was really flagging after our dream-school rejection. A week after the email, I scheduled a consultation with Megan. I knew I needed help. I was spiraling down into disappointment, worry, and stress, even as I knew there were so many things to be grateful for.

Megan helped me to see how I was holding myself and our Sarah-Rise program to such high standards that I was immobilized by the pressure I was putting on myself. She helped me to see that it was okay that I didn't do much time in the Sarah-Rise room anymore, because one goal of the room was to help Sarah not need the room. So, if our time at this point looked more like playing a game with Amy a few times a week and acknowledging what a big deal that was, then that certainly counted as a Sarah-Rise moment. With these realizations I could breathe again and think a little more freely about how to proceed.

I was ready to contact the Pittsburgh Public Schools system and inquire about our next steps if we wanted Sarah to reenroll with them. I knew she would need to be evaluated so they could recommend a placement suited to her needs, so I emailed someone at PPS to get that ball rolling. Carl reassured me that just because we were making moves to enroll her in the same type of class that she would have been in before we did Sarah-Rise, it didn't mean that Sarah was the same as if we hadn't done the Sarah-Rise program. He stated it like this was obvious, but in my head and heart it hadn't been so clear.

27

An Intestinal Interruption

SARAH AND I WERE clashing more than usual and having a hard time together. Mid-February, we had a rough and rocky five days where tensions ran high. I don't know if Sarah was the canary in the coal mine showing me that I was tense because of other things in my life, or if I was tense because she was having a hard time. Maybe it was both. We could certainly amplify each other's struggles rather than soothe them. Five days into our rocky road, Sarah had a melt-down, crying so inconsolably at school that I had to pick her up early. She had said she didn't want to go to kindergarten that morning, but lately she'd been saying she didn't want to go to kindergarten so often that I didn't acknowledge it as real communication. I should have. On this morning, Sarah had been right—kindergarten wasn't the best thing for her that day. My needing to go pick her up was also helpful, because that allowed all my feelings to surface. Sarah took a nap and then watched a show. I had a huge cry with my mom and then a helpful conversation with Megan, after which I felt much calmer. Sarah seemed calmer, too.

By the time we got to the evening and Sarah was crying about wanting Carl, I was able to see it as a wonderful opportunity to give her the kind of session I had been given in the morning by my mom. I sat on the sofa and held Sarah on my lap, listening to her tell me that school felt hard that day. I was even glad when Carl took longer than usual to come home that night, because that gave us more time to get all of that sadness out of Sarah so she could uncover her sparkly self again, too. And she did. The next morning felt like we were back to normal, and she easily went to school. I didn't have to solve anything. I just had to let our storms rain.

This had me thinking about parenting (again) and about how often and how intensely I judge myself (a lot). I then thought about body image and how for several months I had changed my attitude toward my body. Lately, when I had any little self-critiques about my body, especially regarding what the scale might say, I would look in the mirror and choose to say something like, "There is no truth other than that I look fabulous." I had decided not to allow other thoughts, because other thoughts were ridiculous and only made me feel bad about myself, which sapped my energy and kindness toward others.

What if I could think the same thing about my parenting? I asked myself.

Now, this seemed less straightforward, but it was worth a try. What if I could tell myself something like, "There is no truth other than that I am a wonderful parent." Even when I yelled or got grumpy or cried or didn't get my kids to eat enough vegetables, maybe I was still a wonderful parent.

After our hard week, all seemed well again except, for some unknown reason, Sarah was needing multiple clothing changes per day.

Sarah was almost always on top of her potty use in all ways. But now she wasn't making it in time and would need fresh undies. Now that we'd passed the nine-year mark, not making it to the potty felt like a desperate place to be. Sarah was nine years old! Shouldn't we have figured that out by now? Something was amiss, but I didn't know what.

Could it be okay if Sarah and I spent our whole lives trying to figure out the right food situation for her and if she never got the potty stuff 100 percent? I asked myself on a rather frustrating potty day. Yes, it could. Sarah was at a strong 95 percent, and if she was there for her whole life, then that would really be okay.

It's No Accident by Steve Hodges gave me ideas about what might have been going on in Sarah's body. I had been concerned that it was related to food, and we were going to test her blood regarding a possible allergy or intolerance to wheat and eggs, but after reading this book, I now understood that it is possible to be having daily bowel movements with good output and still be chronically backed up or carrying a backlog of poop. This is very common with kids who hold it or used to hold it in, and Sarah was an expert holder-inner for years. Had her body just reached capacity, and that was why we were dealing with dirty undies again when we hadn't been for many months?

I set up an appointment to discuss things with her doctor and get an X-ray or ultrasound of her bowels to see what was really going on in there. I wish that more professionals understood this possibility of a backlog, also known as impaction, and could have mentioned it to me when I'd described our situation to them. While I didn't know for sure what was going on, this scenario made so much sense to me that even before we had the X-ray results, we started daily MiraLAX plus increased fruits, veggies, and water. I realized that I had been wanting to keep my head in the sand for months because I did not want to give up any food items that I had long ago deemed okay. Clearly, things had not been okay for a while, and so I had to face that and make changes.

On my next grocery run, as I tried avoiding foods that could cause constipation, it took immense effort not to cry in the store. We phased out the rice bread that I had thought was okay. We were not going to have bananas around anymore. No more orange juice, to cut back on the sugars ingested each day. Sarah's food was already so limited. I hated going back to even more limitations, even though Sarah often handled the canceled food with more ease than I did. I had big feelings about it, heartbroken on her behalf, chafing at the restrictions, and wanting to have a tantrum. When I eliminated a food option, it had to be completely out of the house, because it was too hard for me to say no if it the food in question was in the house, and so everyone's eating regimen was affected.

A few days after my grocery trip, we got the X-ray, and I met with Sarah's GI doctor. *Holy shit!* Sarah had a serious backup, up one side of her colon and down the other, with a mass in her pelvis the size of a softball. The doctor explained that with such a mass, it wasn't possible for it to budge on a normal amount of MiraLAX or with dietary changes. We would need to do an intensive cleanse facilitated by medication that would soften the mass enough to liquefy it.

There were times when Carl and I had different opinions about the same situation. This was one of them. I was busy feeling like a failure for Sarah's intestinal problem, but when I told Carl about the X-ray and the treatment plan we were given, he was excited. Now we knew what was going on, and we had a clear plan of how to move forward. Carl thought I was amazing for getting us to this moment. There are times when it is best to listen to one's spouse. I felt a bit better hearing his perspective, and no matter how I was feeling, at least we knew our path forward.

The treatment protocol, only to be used under the guidance of a doctor, was a MiraLAX cleanse. This cleanse was not for the faint of heart. It meant loads of laundry and many, many, many trips to the bathroom. We couldn't leave the house for about a week.

Once Sarah completed the cleanse, she returned to her now-normal daily dose of MiraLAX. Given that her intestines got stretched out of shape by the impaction (a choice word for a backup, because, goodness, what an impact it has on one's life!), we couldn't risk her getting so severely impacted again. We did a follow-up X-ray that showed that Sarah's digestive system was much clearer. Due to the cleanse, she didn't go to school all week except on Friday. Friday was a great day for her, as were the Sarah-Rise sessions she did toward the end of the week. Her volunteers noticed increased connection and spark, a signal that she was feeling better in all ways.

It had been weeks of feeling like something was amiss, weeks of missing Sarah's sparkly self, and weeks of her being less connected to her volunteers and less happy at school. With the potty issues, I had been unsure if she would be able to continue attending school in person to finish kindergarten and for the next year. Finally, she was feeling good physically and was thus clear mentally, which was a huge relief for us all.

"Sarah was on fire today!" wrote Laura after one of her Sarah-Rise sessions. "Really sharp and inquisitive and funny. She really must be feeling so much better and clearer."

I was feeling more playful, too, now that I wasn't weighed down by not knowing how to help Sarah. When Sarah asked for a protein shake one afternoon, I proceeded to get the necessary ingredients while singing a song I made up on the spot: "Boopity boopity doopity do . . . boopity boopity . . . ."

And then Sarah happily chimed in, "Doopity do."

We were both playful and peaceful thanks to Sarah's internal relief.

28

What to Do for School Next Year?

*Sarah enjoyed the school bus that Carl crafted from a large box
gifted to us by a neighbor.*

AFTER KINDERGARTEN ON A Friday in mid-March, I took nine-
year-old Sarah to be evaluated by a public-school evaluator for her
placement in first grade that fall. I liked the person very much and,
even though I wasn't in the room, the snippets I heard suggested Sarah
was in fine form. However, sitting in the office of the public school for
two hours wasn't the best selling point for me. There were countless
bells and buzzers and an overwhelming level of commotion, and I

couldn't help but think of Sarah processing all the sensory demands and what that would do to her attention. I reminded myself that a classroom would be different from the testing room and office space I was currently sitting in, but still, how would such a large school compare to the small classroom she currently attended?

Sarah didn't seem fazed by the testing or the various sounds and commotion around her. She seemed happy and calm as we left the building. So, perhaps I didn't need to worry about the future, but I still did.

Now all we had to do was wait for the results and get our recommendations. We hoped to find a good placement for next year, but if nothing seemed right, then I knew I'd be more at peace continuing her homeschooling. I wanted a classroom and teacher who would love Sarah for who she was, a space that would be small enough for her to focus, and for her to be placed in first grade despite her being nine. That last preference was a big ask of any school and might have been questionable in the long run; however, I felt it was more important that her next step from kindergarten be to the "developmental age" of first grade rather than a leap from kindergarten to the "age-appropriate" third grade.

The following week, Sarah attended kindergarten every day, which was a big deal after having so recently been struggling due to the intestinal impaction and then staying home for the cleanse. Her consistent return was momentous. After a full week back at school, we learned that one issue her teacher was having was that Sarah talked at times when it would be appropriate to be quiet. Sarah liked to describe what she or her teacher was wearing, especially if Ms. Michelle was wearing jeans, and sometimes Sarah made such comments on their outfits during story time or math. Or she would read words she saw around the classroom when someone else was talking.

Her talking was her verbal isming. At first, I was frustrated because Sarah's behavior was making it harder for the teacher to run the classroom for the other kids. But then, I was grateful because Sarah's "too much talking" was incredible. How awesome for a girl who didn't start speaking until she was four and a half! Now Sarah was talking so much it was a problem—the most awesome problem ever! We reminded Sarah to listen to Ms. Michelle and her classmates. We assured her that everyone wanted to hear what she had to say but explained that if she talked when someone else was talking, then it was harder for everyone to be understood. We tried to be more vigilant at home, to watch for when she talked over someone and to remind her to wait her turn.

In addition to her verbosity, there were other details of Sarah's days that we were eager to appreciate—especially regarding Amy. Sarah buttoned Amy's dresses for her! Sarah accompanied Amy in riding on a broom-horse, and both girls used chalk to color on our wooden swing set. Sarah was playing with Amy more than she ever had. In fact, she played with Amy in a way that she didn't play with other kids.

One thing I really loved about The Son-Rise Program was the idea that I could value social connection above and beyond any physical or academic skill. Certainly, we hoped Sarah would learn to tie her shoes or do math, but most important was that she connect with other people. One way to connect with people is through spoken language.

"Amy is ornery!"

This was Sarah's declaration the next day when she joined us for breakfast.

Even if you come late to spoken language or find some words hard to say, it doesn't mean you can't be a word nerd. *Ornery*. I was so proud! I had been using different words when describing Sarah's moods or my own and had recently said Sarah was feeling ornery. She loved it and put it to use immediately. Amy wasn't thrilled about that verbal connection from Sarah, and it actually just made her ornerier in the moment, but Sarah and I happily bonded over her word choice.

We began Easter that year with an egg hunt. I put slips of paper in the eggs as vouchers that the girls could use to get an extra episode of a TV show, an extra book reading, an extra snuggle, an extra chocolate shape, or extra kisses. As with past Easters, Amy was the primary egg finder and Sarah found a few, but I had written their names on the vouchers, so each girl got the same things regardless of who discovered the egg.

I put store-bought applesauce pouches and fruit leathers in their baskets, both of which were consumed immediately. Instead of dyeing Easter eggs, I gave them fruit and veggie materials to create food art. I cut apple slices to be vaguely egg-shaped and gave them mashed avocado to paint with or use as glue. Sarah promptly said she was making an apple bagel with avocado cream cheese, and I was reminded of her flexible creativity and pretending abilities regarding foods she couldn't eat. Amy pretended her apple was toast, and I made a bunny using apple slices, carrots, and raisins, with an avocado tail. Amy made another apple-slice creation that was a self-portrait. It was a success, so much so that we did the activity two days in a row, and while no one really tried new foods because of it, it was still a fun way to interact with food—and I didn't have to store the art!

Sarah had outgrown some of her pants, so as an extra Easter gift, I got the girls leggings. Amy got regular leggings and Sarah got jeggings, jean-like leggings. Sarah loved them as much as the fruit leathers and applesauce pouches! Sarah had loved jeans for ages, but only on other people. She wore her jeggings to school on Monday and had a great day, the best day at school in ages. We didn't know if it was the jeggings contributing to her good day or if it was because I was outside the room the whole time. My presence had been the necessary emotional security blanket to have her agree to go to school that day. While her first week back to school after the cleanse went well, it seemed that the other struggles, such as talking when she shouldn't, were making school harder for her and her teacher. It was harder to convince Sarah to go each day, and her teacher had to work harder to get her to focus and participate in the school activities. Sonia or I had been spending many days sitting outside the classroom, and we figured we'd probably finish the school year in such a fashion.

Despite our presence outside the kindergarten room, and despite the one good jeggings day, Sarah struggled even more at school in the final months. She was distracted; spoke at inappropriate times, often disrupting the flow of the class; and almost always wanted to go home early. One week in May, she had such a hard time on Thursday that we didn't even try Friday.

This was not at all how I'd expected Sarah's school year to go. If anything, I would have expected the reverse—more troubles at the beginning of the year and fewer at the end. Instead, the beginning went smoothly, and at the end we were crawling to the finish line, though I remained grateful for the flexibility to keep trying new things. Sonia and I chose to experiment with having Sonia inside the classroom with Sarah. We thought that might help Sarah reengage and for Sarah and her teacher to have experiences with each other besides frustration. I had a deep understanding of such tensions and much sympathy for the teacher. Trying to teach a group of kids when one of them needed basically full attention cannot have been easy!

Having Sonia in the room worked. Sonia's ability to calmly engage Sarah and enforce some boundaries, such as reminding her to listen to the teacher, helped everyone in kindergarten. The teacher was able to focus more on teaching the class as a whole and giving equal time to the other kids, while Sarah was able to feel surer of herself with Sonia at her side.

During our end-of-the-year kindergarten struggles, Sonia and I (with Sarah and Amy in tow) visited a possible new school. We had heard back from the public-school evaluator that Sarah was deemed a good fit for their Life Skills class, which was what we had expected, and so Carl and I had visited a couple of those classrooms on our own to observe and imagine Sarah in such a setting. Now we had one more school to visit that was not part of the public school system. It was part of the St. Anthony School Program that had designated classrooms within some of the Catholic Schools in the area. The program was specifically for kids with Down syndrome and autism. It had a one-to-three teacher-to-student ratio and did a lot of inclusion with the neurotypical classes, but flexibly, all depending on what each student was ready for. What impressed me most was this school's desire to work with me throughout the process to fit Sarah's needs and strengths. This was the aim in public schools as well, but I was still impressed with the responses to some of my concerns and questions from this private school.

I asked how they responded to a student crying. They would want to talk with the parent to understand the motivation behind the crying (attention, getting out of something, sensory discomfort, etc.) and come up with a plan for responding. And this school had the option of a shorter school day if we felt that would be best. They had a crash pad and a squeeze machine in the Resource Room, the classroom where Sarah would be. Sarah didn't like the squeeze machine, a device designed originally by Temple Grandin to provide deep pressure because some people with autism find that to be calming, but Sarah did like the crash pad, which was basically a large lumpy mattress. She was also intrigued by some of the other sensory-toy options.

When Carl and I had visited our public-school options, it seemed that the classes for kids with disabilities would always join the mainstream classes as a whole, and I really appreciated how this school didn't do that. They would decide whether Sarah was ready on any given day to be part of some or all of the mainstream classes and for how long. I valued such individual attention and decision-making.

The person showing Sonia and me around asked us each what we thought Sarah's greatest strength was. I was out of the room when Sonia gave her answer, so I had no idea what it was. Sonia laughed when I gave my answer, because we both said the same thing: Sarah's greatest strength was "how she connected to grown-ups." I was thrilled, even more so that this was now Sarah's strength, because Sarah was someone who used to have trouble connecting to anyone at all. In terms of her greatest need, we each thought it was connecting to other kids, aside from Amy, with whom she connected relatively well. Academically, her greatest strength was reading, and the area of greatest need was math.

By the time Carl visited the school and found that he liked it as much as we did, we'd learned that they would allow Sarah to enter as a first grader!

I was excited and relieved to have found a place that felt so right for Sarah. She was officially enrolled in the St. Anthony School Program, and she could even receive bus services through the Pittsburgh Public Schools system.

Sarah finished her last week in kindergarten at the end of May, with Sonia as her one-to-one helper for the last couple of weeks. Sarah's class performed a play several times throughout the week. Amy and I saw it on a Tuesday. Evidently Tuesday was not Sarah's most focused performance. She was distracted and needed more prompts from the teacher or Sonia to stay on task. Her words were quiet and mumbled. While I was watching, I felt varying emotions—including disappointment, when I mentally compared her performance to what might have been—but when the play was over, Amy leaped up to give Sarah a huge hug. Of course. All that mattered was that Sarah had been in a play and that we loved Sarah. Nothing else mattered. I was so thankful to Amy for that reminder.

After his session with Sarah on Friday, Gregory wrote:

We dove into Brown Bear, Brown Bear, *moved through the fish-stripes obsession, and ended up singing and laughing quite a bit. Today, Sarah impressed me with her ability to match pitch and*

rhythm as we sang the book to the "Twinkle, Twinkle, Little Star"
melody. She has a very sweet, quiet singing voice full of her person-
ality. As with most things in life, when Sarah decides to do a thing,
she does that thing with all her brain, heart, and soul.

It was interesting to note the difference between Gregory's session with Sarah and her Tuesday performance, when perhaps there were too many stressors and distractions for her to be her sparkly self.

The following week, now that kindergarten was over, Sarah visited her new school for an hour—and it went well! She also went to day care, but on the second day at day care she started crying and asking to go home. It was around 11:00 a.m., which was the same time she used to ask for me and cry during kindergarten, but at day care, caregivers were used to kids crying, and it didn't get in the way of any lessons because there were no lessons. Later, when Sarah was told when I would be there, she asked for Sonia. The lead caregiver said she didn't know where Sonia was. Sarah then digested the information and reached equilibrium. If she continued to want to go to day care, I hoped that it could be a good venue for moving through her moments of upset. At day care there was no agenda that had to be met, and in this environment caregivers expected crying and protesting.

Friday night, after the first week, Sarah started saying she didn't want to go to day care on Monday, but by the time Monday rolled around, she had changed her tune to "I will try." The truth was that whatever she chose was fine. One of the reasons I took her to day care in the first place was because *she* had said she wanted to go. If she wanted to go, then I wanted to support her request, and if she had feelings when she was away from home, day care seemed like a good place to work through such feelings. It was also okay if she didn't want to go because she could stay home with Sonia even if I was working.

I was frequently made aware of the works of art contained within tiny moments of life. Whenever Carl came home from work, he had loving attention for me and the kids regardless of what his day had been like. Sonia could read my mind and take care of something in the house or be with a child before I even spoke a word. And the way my volunteers came every single week and greeted Sarah with such joy and delight never ceased to give me an appreciative pause.

Personally, I judged myself as coming up short in the departments of loving attention, reading minds, and enthusiasm. I started the Sarah-Rise program with loads of loving energy, creativity, and oomph, and I had kept it up many times throughout, but lately the days were feeling long and my measuring stick unkind. I didn't want to keep judging myself so harshly or experiencing such feelings that dragged me into the trenches of blahdom.

To help myself think more clearly, I often reflected on how I approached giving a massage or an Alexander Technique lesson. I could ask myself how to support each fraught parenting moment as I would support a tight muscle. *Press on it? Give support from elsewhere? Give a slight and slow tug? Wait?* It was as though my approach to muscles could be my answer to life, the universe, and everything. Parenting and self-esteem issues felt much more complicated and made bodywork seem comparatively simple. Still, if I felt sad, I tried giving my tears space to fall instead of just reaching for chocolate and pushing on to do whatever I needed to do next. I tried facing my feelings instead of running from them. This helped me be a little clearer. Reflecting calmly and setting intentions was one thing, but when my kids whined and yelled, I would often lose the clarity I thought I had found. Then it was time to again face the feelings, pause, breathe, and maybe cry. These changes seemed to harmonize the household experience.

After four days of more peaceful parenting experiences, on the fifth day I woke up on the wrong side of the bed, which was possibly called "too early in the morning." The harder things got that day, the more upset I got and, the more upset I got, the more frustrated with myself I got. That same night, Carl and I went to a party hosted by some friends. It was a gathering of all their friends and acquaintances from different parts of their lives, and we didn't expect to know anyone besides the hosts. To encourage people to mingle and get acquainted, the hosts suggested that we all think about what we had to celebrate in our lives and share that with everyone.

As we drove to the party, I told Carl that I felt like a big fraud.

"I feel so hypocritical showing up as if I have anything figured out and anything to celebrate," I said. "I know nothing. I have nothing to celebrate."

Carl replied, "I think you know a lot, and just because today was hard, that doesn't change the days that were great. Is there a different way you could look at the situation? What if you were giving an Alexander lesson to a student who had had a week like yours and said all that you just did? What would you tell that student?"

"Oh!" I exclaimed. "I would say it's not about reaching an end point and having it all figured out forever. It is a process of noticing when you aren't how you want to be and then moving into how you want to be. It is something to be renewed repeatedly, and it might feel different each time. It can actually be good when things seem to go wrong because then we can see our habits more clearly."

The party turned out to be fun, and thanks to my realization with Carl in the car, I showed up ready to connect with others and to share my humanness. I could celebrate my moments of parenting clarity and creativity, and I didn't have to beat myself up for not maintaining that clarity and creativity forever. I could notice my habits of tensing various muscles, sometimes in response to stressful thoughts, and gently invite my muscles and thoughts to ease up just the tiniest bit.

Speaking of habits, that summer, Sarah had developed a habit. She would ask if she could have a yogurt, and then—without any help!—she would open the fridge, pick out a homemade yogurt from the shelf on the door, unscrew the lid, get a spoon from the drawer, and go to town. So simple, yet so self-sufficient and so empowered.

Empowerment was the perfect feeling for one going into their final summer before embarking on a new adventure in first grade. That was truly something to celebrate.

29

Trips and Transitions

DURING A SARAH-RISE TEAM meeting in June, we were saying a bittersweet goodbye to Laura, as she was moving to Canada. She had been a loving and steadfast volunteer from the very beginning, and we were going to miss her. Laura had a gentle, quiet way of being that taught me how it was possible to have excitement and enthusiasm in a way that was different from my own higher-energy style.

When it came to all the volunteers, their gifts of time, love, and creativity were priceless. Every time one of them moved on, especially if they had been with us for a while, I felt as sad about their leaving as I was grateful for the time they had spent with us. The beauty of our program was that we continued to have a flow of new volunteers even as others moved on, so our group meetings continued with whomever was currently part of the program.

In this meeting, we talked about how to see ourselves plus Sarah as one entity when we were in the Sarah-Rise room instead of seeing two separate entities. If we wanted to help her be relaxed, we needed to be at ease ourselves. We also discussed how to help Sarah foster connections with other children via our connection with Sarah. This idea was from Gregory and was exciting to contemplate as we hadn't thought of it before. The premise was to make a connection to another child when we were near Sarah and then make a comment that connected to Sarah. This was how we would make a connection from the other child to Sarah. We knew Sarah could connect to us, so now we were taking a baby step toward bridging the gap between Sarah and other kids.

We tempered our expectations. Our goal was to connect to the kid ourselves while being in Sarah's vicinity, and we decided that if Sarah even looked at another kid for a nanosecond, then we could consider ourselves and the moment successful. There was no need to tell Sarah what to say to the other kid and no need to explain anything to the other kid about Sarah.

A few days later, Carl, Sarah, Amy, and I were at a beach, and a little girl wearing polka dots came over to where Sarah was playing.

"Do you want to play with me?" she asked.

"Yes!" Carl answered. "We do want to play with you!"

He talked to the little girl about the dots on her swimsuit. Sarah didn't seem to notice. He asked the girl if she also liked stripes, explaining that Sarah really loved dots and stripes. She did, but Sarah still didn't seem to notice. After a few other failed attempts at finding a common interest between the two girls, Carl observed the girl in the polka dots jump over a wave.

"Sarah!" he exclaimed. "Let's jump over a wave!"

Sarah and Carl jumped over a wave as the other little kid did, too. Success!

The girls jumped over waves together. This was such incredibly wonderful progress for Sarah toward connecting with another kid. I watched the whole thing play out from my position on a towel a few feet away, and I was thrilled with how beautifully Carl put our new idea into practice.

Another topic we discussed at our team meeting was having Amy present for part of each Sarah-Rise session. Sarah C. had been including Amy in many sessions, but now we wanted to do the same with the whole team.

Noah tried it next, and he had a wonderful session directly after the meeting. Their time was filled with fun play and connection, first with both Sarah and Amy and then just with Sarah. For the first half hour, Amy was in the room, and the three all had a riotously good time faking sneezes. Apparently, the girls sneezed so hard they knocked Noah over. When it was just Sarah and Noah, he became a snail in need of a shell. He went to the shell store in the closet, and then Sarah pretended to welcome him to different stores and helped him try on new shells that were made of large plastic steppingstones called River Stones. The creativity of it all filled my heart with joy. I was impressed that Sarah had the energy to connect with Amy and Noah and then continue that connection through her one-on-one time with Noah.

That night, during dinner, I noticed that as Amy was talking, Sarah was looking at her and quietly listening. What shocked me even more was realizing that this might have been happening on a regular basis and that I considered it so normal that I hadn't even noticed it. So many hours with so many volunteers over so many years had helped Sarah grow and advance. Each volunteer had been a part of helping us get to this moment of Sarah regarding Amy calmly and easily as Amy spoke.

Near the end of summer, it was time to meet with our child psychologist to review our homeschooling from the past year, as was required by the state of Pennsylvania. Sarah and I drove the twenty minutes to the psychologist's office, walked up the ramp into the building, and waited a couple of minutes in the waiting room before being welcomed into the office. The windows of the office faced the road where we had parked, a busy thoroughfare with many buses passing.

Sarah was not really connecting to the psychologist with any visual regard. Little of the eye contact she so often gave to volunteers was present because there were buses to watch. And there were interesting toys in the office. The psychologist understood and was still impressed by the details I provided about the ways Sarah had progressed over the past year. It wasn't until the end of the review that Sarah started to get more involved in the conversation. Sarah mentioned Gregory, and I said that they sang together. I asked if she wanted to sing "Brown Bear," and she sang the whole song perfectly—in tune, in rhythm, with good pitch, from start to finish, with sparkly connected eye contact, and with delighted presence. Wow! I wish I had recorded it with my phone; instead I just recorded it with my heart. I relished the clarity of the singing in its own right, but I was also delighted that Sarah chose to show her abilities in front of the psychologist.

I started food preparation for a trip we were all going to take for a large family reunion with Carl's side of the family. It was still a few weeks away, but anything regarding food for Sarah was best with more time. Considering that we were going to fly, meaning bringing my own food in bulk would have been difficult, we had the best possible scenario: Grandma was going to buy or make any food that I requested and bring it all to the reunion site.

As I carried on with my lists, I noticed that I was in full-blown, tighten-all-muscles-in-my-head-as-if-I-am-sucking-my-head-through-a-straw mode. *Ah. Well then. Now what?* I thought.

I clearly needed a good cry. I cried about all the years of doing and planning and worrying around Sarah and food. It was always better to let the tears fall instead of holding it all in, but I didn't always remember that in the moment. I had become very good at all of this organization—especially food organization!—and I had so much support in doing it, but I still got tense and stressed.

After the tears had fallen, I felt more spacious and capable again. Eager to begin to prepare and pack all the foods on my list, I had no problem picking up the phone to talk with Sarah's naturopath about her latest round of tests. The idea behind the tests was to figure out what Sarah's body didn't like and what it needed to thrive. The tests included urine, stool, and blood analysis. The collection of all was fraught and stressful and nearly set us backward with potty training because Sarah hated the collection bucket so much. The blood was used to check for allergies.

The naturopath shared that, apparently, Sarah now had an allergy to mustard. She hardly ever ate mustard, so when I heard this news, I thought, *Okay.* But then I learned that she had a notable sensitivity to cashews, and my mind screamed, *Noooo! No, no, no!* Furthermore, she had a mild sensitivity to almonds. *What? No!* I learned that these sensitivities were probably a result of overdoing these particular foods over the past few years. (But now mustard? She hardly ever had it!) The good news? We were cleared to try wheat and dairy again, and we didn't have to eliminate cashews or almonds, but we did have to cut way back on them and give her more variety overall. Lastly, she had a yeast overgrowth, which she'd never had before. We had no idea from whence it came. *Sigh.* We were going to treat that one with probiotics.

So much for a good cry. I wanted to go sit in a closet and cry for a few more days. As if this food stuff hadn't been hard enough. I worried that I'd never get a break. Now it was going to be even harder. I threw out my lists because now some of the foods on the lists were to be omitted. I cried again and made new lists for Grandma. I wanted to register an official complaint to some Official Complaint Department, but I knew I could still do what I needed to do.

We flew to Wisconsin for the family reunion with Carl's extended family. I loved the people we spent time with very much. The place was beautiful, and we had generally as easy a setup as I could have hoped for. And yet I was still an extremely tight ball of stress and a very grumpy mom on the edge of tears for many moments.

It was hard to be always watching both girls. Despite the presence of a multitude of family members and Carl, I still often felt like it was my responsibility to do so. I wanted to allow Carl the time to have conversations with family members he hadn't seen in a while, taking it upon myself to be on solo-kid duty but then struggling mightily. It was hard when the girls wanted to do different things or when Sarah would change her mind rapidly about the thing that she'd just said she wanted to do or have. For instance, Sarah might ask to go on the elevator and go outside, but as soon as she got downstairs then she didn't want to go outside. She wanted to ride the elevator back upstairs. But Amy wanted to go outside as planned! It was also hard to keep them quiet in the morning when they woke up much earlier than most other people. We usually went out into the common area, and I got each of them something to eat from the small refrigerator there. Then I would attempt to read books together or bounce them on my legs for a quiet ride. But their energy and voices were high, already excited to see their relatives, who were trying to sleep in a bit.

I had many instances of generally feeling good, but my disappointment in myself for the moments when I had a hard time was intense. As I saw it, these wonderful family members saw me at my worst or close to my worst more than anything else. As with many days or weeks, my perception of a day can be skewed by ten minutes of strife that somehow outweigh hours of peace, calm, and creative connection.

On the flight home, I thought about massage. When I was giving a massage, I was glad when I found a spot that hurt or was notably tight because then I could give it some love. The tight or tender spot is often the center of a problem, and if you can get the trigger point to let go or the fascia to release by holding sustained pressure on the area, then the tension will ease. The attention brings new blood into the area, takes out the trash, and sometimes realigns the fibers of the connective tissue that holds everything in place. So I attempted to see the Jenny-stress at this large family gathering as the same sort of good hurt that I could look at with love.

After the family reunion, I promptly left for a visit to see my friend Gretchen in Montana. We had a wonderful visit filled with lots of laughter, and I was able to relax because I didn't have to take care of anyone except myself. In the morning and at night, I only had my own teeth to brush. I could take a shower whenever I wanted. I could curl up on the couch and read or watch a movie with my friend as we ate dinner. We went for walks whenever we wanted to. It was so simple to just grab my shoes and purse and walk out the door. No one needed goading, cajoling, or cheering to get the job done.

I had been away from home for close to a week, and I understood that when one goes on vacation, reentry into regular life is harder upon return. Yet, I was always surprised by the level of difficulty I experienced when reentering the job of my home life. Returning to my paid-work job was always easy. My clients were always appreciative, and my task was straightforward. The first half-day at home was not so bad, mainly because I had very low expectations of myself. The next day, I expected to be back to normal and therefore had higher expectations, which left me grumpy and feeling like Sonia did a better job than I did at mothering my kids. I felt tired and overwhelmed for days, as if I would never get back in the groove of making food and veggie juice and being the kind of mom I wanted to be.

Carl pointed out that in his job, there are people who have different skill sets, and each of them is better than he is at certain things. He said that can be humbling but also really great. He wants smart and capable people helping him get the overall job done. So I had to remind myself that if there were places where I thought Sonia did a better job than I did, then that was wonderful. Right? Wasn't that all the more reason to have such help?

When I was feeling back in the swing of things, Sonia and I took the girls shopping for school uniforms. It felt surreal to be having the girls try on uniform clothes. How were both girls ready for this level of schooling? When did that happen? Despite being present for almost every step of that journey, it still seemed impossible, as if I were living someone else's experience. Sonia and I each took charge of one girl, offering clothing items to try on and sorting what to keep and what didn't fit.

When we got home, Sonia and I put the shopping bags in the laundry room to keep the girls from getting into them before I had time to sort through all the clothing to make sure we wanted to keep *everything*. Then we all took naps because the excursion had been exhausting.

The next morning, Amy came downstairs wearing one of her school jumpers. I went upstairs to investigate and discovered that all the bags had been opened and clothes were strewn all over the laundry-room floor. I found Sarah in her new red gym shorts, which I had known would be her favorite item. I had Amy come back upstairs and made the two of them put the clothes back in the bags, but I let them continue wearing what they had chosen, feeling certain that those items were keepers.

They were so excited for school to start, and so excited to wear their new clothes. I was glad they felt that way, since uniforms would

certainly be a departure from their normal self-expression via clothing choices.

The girls got back-to-school haircuts. They both wanted their hair
to be short like mine was at the time.

"Really?" I asked. "Are you sure? Are you sure you're sure? Are you
really sure you're sure?"

They assured me they were sure.

"Well, okay," I said, and we went for it.

We all loved the cuts.

As we tipped ever closer toward big changes with new schools,
it was as if many things were coming together more than ever. One
evening, as Sarah got a ride up to bed on Carl's back, as she often did,
she started waving to objects that she passed, telling them good night:
"Good night, wooden dog. Good night, piano. Good night, Olivia."

We continued to have beautiful moments in the Sarah-Rise room.
We all knew that the hours in the room were waning, but the room
was still important. On July 22, Gregory wrote:

In the Sarah-Rise room, we bring authenticity and create as natural
an environment as possible. However, it still remains a therapeutic

space. *Does that make sense? In many ways, I see the same things happen with just my presence and certain children. That is, once a relationship is established, just my face can help generate a change in a therapeutic direction. I love seeing Sarah and Amy move through their typical sister stuff . . . the button pushing and button exposing and drama. However, in the room, we've shifted. Amy may snatch a thing, or Sarah might put her chin on Amy's head when Amy is a little stressed and then look at me for a reaction. However, this is diminishing week by week, and they are working out actual challenges while kind of avoiding much of the drama. It's the power of the room, which is really just the power of the relationship and history. It's like the Sarah-Rise room is a sort of chapel, a cathedral . . . of joy, of respect, of relationship, of communication, of human potential.*

One Monday evening I observed Sarah C. in the Sarah-Rise room, and it was wonderful and beautiful. There was a moment, among many great moments, that was an exquisite work of loving artful human interaction. Sarah was upset because she wanted to go outside to join kids playing in a sprinkler. Amy was in the room with Sarah C. and Sarah. Sarah C. scooped Sarah up into her arms while saying, "I love that you can see something you want to do and want to join in the fun . . . now is the time to play in the Sarah-Rise room." It was so lovingly done. Sarah C. then came up with different pretend-sprinkler ideas. The girls didn't go for that, but the art was in the loving response and creative offerings. It really reminded me of how I wanted to be as a parent when I inevitably have to tell my children no.

I read an article called "The One Thing No One Ever Says About Grieving" by Katherine Morgan Schafler. It was about different kinds of grief, acknowledging that there can be grief over things changing. I was nervously excited about the girls being in full-time school, but with that came changes I apparently needed to grieve. We would no longer have Sonia at our house daily during the week. Sonia had been *the most amazing*. I told people that she was the best helper I could ever possibly imagine. I was never exaggerating—it was the honest truth. She was a supportive friend, a thoughtful organizer, a stupendous laundry folder, a creative Sarah-Rise facilitator and curriculum designer, a maker of games and recipes, and a loving and patient aunt. Sonia modeled for me how I could stay calm while enforcing rules. She was a sister, a problem-solver, and an overall assistant extraordinaire. What a gift of herself she gave us for four years.

We were also bidding adieu to most of our volunteers, except for Sarah C. and Gregory. Mary would also continue as Amy's special person when I was with Sarah. With the girls in school, we would not have the hours available that we used to. This was sad, and it was also time. We'd already had many volunteers move on due to changes in their own lives. I, too, was ready for changes even if I had to shed tears.

I took the girls to their last day of day care. The church that ran their day care and Sarah's preschool and kindergarten had been such a wonderful part of our life. I would be grieving this, too. The place and the people always offered me a warm welcome and made sure I knew how the girls were doing in school. It was a place where I knew everyone loved Sarah and appreciated her presence. There had certainly been places we considered for her that were not ready to delight in her. The Second United Presbyterian Church day care was not one of them. They delighted in Sarah and welcomed her with open arms from day one.

When I picked the girls up at the end of the day, I watched them walk through the double glass doors and down the stone steps, and I bid a tearful and thankful farewell to all of the day care staff.

I was sitting at my desk answering an email from a client about scheduling an appointment when Sarah came over and said, "Mom, can I . . . can I . . . ? Yes!"

She didn't even finish her question. When I looked up at her, she just switched to saying the answer she wanted to hear. I loved her complete delight with her assumption that I would say yes.

"Hi, sweetie! What is it that you want?" I asked.

"Mom, can I play in the sandbox?"

"Absolutely!"

I was so glad to be able to answer yes to those shining eyes and happily expectant soul.

What if we could all approach our goals this way? Even if we don't always get what we want, what if we assumed with delight that we could have our dreams? What if we asked our questions to the world and then turned to the world and answered with a smile?

Yes.

Epilogue

Ready for the Sock Hop

SARAH-RISE WAS AN UNMITIGATED success, helping not only Sarah but our whole family and all of those who took part in the program to become our best selves. In the early years, when I wanted a miracle to make everything normal and easy, my mom suggested that the miracle might be a shift in my perspective rather than a shift in Sarah. Sarah-Rise facilitated shifts in both of us. I have a peace and acceptance that is deeper and more solid than ever, and Sarah is flourishing beyond our wildest imaginings, especially compared to the days when we didn't know if she would learn to roll over or eat or speak.

Almost exactly five years after I completed The Son-Rise Start-Up, Sarah started attending full-time school. She was able to focus and participate in ways that had seemed unattainable when I began my training. Except for weekly sessions with Sarah C. and Gregory, our official Sarah-Rise days were over. Our days continued to be filled with wonder and joy, struggle and tears. Sarah and I can excel at clashing with each other, but we also excel at reconnecting and snuggling. And I continue learning how to let go in the face of Sarah's increasing independence. While Sarah-Rise may *officially* be over, it is forever the lens through which we connect and interact helpfully and meaningfully with Sarah.

Sarah's time in the St. Anthony School Program has been a great experience. Her teachers and support staff enjoy her and love her, and that is the most important thing for me. There has also been a level of acceptance from her classmates that touches my heart. The school planned a sock hop, and one parent of a neurotypical kid that I'd never met happened to see a pink 1950s-style costume jacket embroidered with "Sarah." She purchased it and sent it to school for Sarah, and Sarah's classmates sent home nail polish so she could paint her nails and match them for the dance.

Every year until the 2020 pandemic hit, the St. Anthony School Program hosted Inclusive Games, which are like the Special Olympics. Each child in the program gets paired with a neurotypical kid from their class for the day. It is a coveted role to be chosen as the neurotypical companion. When I attended, it was a heart-filling experience to be in a gym full of people cheering for Sarah—and for all the other kids, too.

Sarah participated in the middle school musical two years in a row because any child who wants to participate is encouraged to do so. Sarah's teacher attended every rehearsal with the kids from the

Resource Room, providing hours of additional support so that Sarah and her classmates could be part of such a momentous experience. Sarah absolutely loved it. Seeing her onstage in *Peter Pan Jr.* and *High School Musical Jr.*, smiling and singing, my eyes shone with tears, and my heart burst with love and pride.

Sarah's world and experiences continue expanding. She took swim lessons with the British Swim School, transitioning to private lessons when it made sense given her age. She takes piano lessons with Katie, my friend and fellow Alexander Technique teacher. Sarah took gymnastics until the pandemic happened. For her thirteenth birthday, Carl got her an indoor bike trainer to hold her bike stationary in our living room, and she biked daily on Zwift, watching her virtual self cycle through various cities. In two years, she pedaled three thousand miles! She is learning to ride her bike in our alley, balancing and using the pedals for split seconds at a time.

I remind myself with each area of struggle that everything now attained used to seem impossible. Getting Sarah to take a bath or shower used to be a struggle, one that involved much screaming on her part, especially if she needed to have her hair washed. Now, she takes a shower independently, and she washes her own hair. Maybe someday we will look back on these moments, moments when she pounds on the door when Amy has the audacity to use the bathroom, and laugh with relief that they are in the rear-view mirror. We certainly now laugh with relief as we remember the feeding struggles of her earliest years.

Amy has passed Sarah in terms of height and generally fills the role of older sister—except when there is a physical fight, and then Sarah wins every time. Sarah sometimes enjoys making Amy upset, laughing in her face when Amy is mad or sad. That isn't great, but it also feels like a typical thing for an older sibling to do. What is great is how much they still enjoy each other and play together. Their relations were becoming strained, especially from Amy's perspective, before the pandemic, but the isolation brought increased connection and compatibility between them.

When Amy was developmentally younger than Sarah, we wondered how the transition would work as Amy grew and passed Sarah. It has been the most natural, graceful process. Bit by bit, Amy became the more capable and grown-up of the two without any conversation or explanation needed from anyone. Sarah asks her for assistance, and Amy sometimes steps in to help Sarah through some of her tough emotional moments with thoughtful creativity and kindness. Other times, Amy doesn't have the emotional room to help Sarah because they are both struggling. That is okay, too. I am the same way.

Another person who has come into our lives is Anna. Years ago, when I was Sarah's helper for one of her gymnastics classes, I thought the teacher for her group was particularly good. As I watched them walk across the room, I thought, *I bet someone is going to really love that person*. I just didn't know it would be our family! I asked if they babysat, and they said yes. Occasional babysitting turned into frequent babysitting, which turned into helping guide online schooling during the pandemic and filling our summers with creative play and projects based on weekly themes. Without any Sarah-Rise training from me, Anna already embodies the principles of how to meet Sarah where she is before moving toward any goal or request. While Anna's times at our house have never been labeled as Sarah-Rise sessions, they most certainly are.

I continue feeling the support of our village, even as our needs and lives change. I know I have friends and family I can ask for help at any time. When I am struggling emotionally and write about it in my updates, my readers respond with love and encouragement. I feel like I will be held if I fall, as if there is a net below me, a network of friends, family, and readers who have followed our journey, who love us, and who will remind me of my best self even when I have forgotten my resilience.

When I first signed up for The Son-Rise Start-Up training, I was surprised to learn that I would be the team leader. *What? Me?* I thought. Well, yes. That did make the most sense, and of course that is what I am and have been. But what a team! I could not have gone on this journey without them.

In actuality, Sarah was and is the real team leader. It is she who we support and follow up the mountain of growing into her most capable self. It is she who our extended village has rallied behind. It is she who rose.

In Their Own Words

Sᴀʀᴀʜ-Rɪsᴇ ᴡᴏᴜʟᴅ ɴᴏᴛ ʜᴀᴠᴇ been the powerful program that it was without our wonderful team of volunteers, some of whom have been mentioned by name throughout the book. As you know, it was sometimes hard for me to accept that these wonderful people *wanted* to be a part of our program. Their volunteering was an almost overwhelming gift of love, time, and creativity. As you read in some of the notes from volunteers that I quoted in the book, the gifts of love and learning were mutual. Here are the perspectives of some of our volunteers, as well as Sonia and Carl, as they look back on their time with Sarah-Rise.

Laura

I'd known Jenny since early 2009 (she was my first Alexander Technique teacher), and in the beginning of 2012, I signed on as a volunteer for her Sarah-Rise program. I didn't stop to think if I would be suitable, I just said yes. A decision from the heart rather than a well-thought-out one. If I had thought for minute, I might have realized that I had little experience with children or autism and that I was not really very outgoing by nature, and definitely not effusive. Did I feel a bit lost and out of place? Sometimes. But not for long. Meeting with Jenny after each session helped me work through all my feelings of inadequacy. Did I regret that decision to volunteer? Not once.

For the better part of the first year, I spent four hours at a time with Jenny and the girls, half of the time with Sarah in the Sarah-Rise room, the other half with (then) baby Amy so Jenny could be in the Sarah-Rise room with Sarah.

My hours in the Sarah-Rise room with Sarah were all over the map, to be sure. Thinking in terms of success or failure—either mine or Sarah's—wasn't helpful. The better questions were the ones that Jenny and the program supported: Was I able to stay present with myself? (Not always.) When I wasn't present, what effect did that have on Sarah? On me? How could I better prepare myself for the next visit? I felt we were both learning. Learning to be okay in the room with each other, learning how to interact in a way that felt honest if not always comfortable (me), and learning to trust each other.

One valuable gift of being involved in the program came out of the realization that we are all so different and we all bring something unique and precious to the table, whatever that may be. Being big and effusive in response to eye contact with Sarah, as was encouraged by the program, was uncomfortable and unfamiliar to me. It made me feel like a fraud. So, after trying it and feeling like a failure, I resorted back to my quieter way, witnessing and supporting Sarah by being present with her. We (each volunteer) had our own special relation-ship with Sarah, with each of us offering her examples of interaction uniquely our own.

My time with Sarah in the Sarah-Rise room was precious. Not always easy, but the guidelines of what constituted success—celebrat-ing with Sarah when she noticed me, made eye contact, and amazingly joined in with me—provided their own rewards.

Being involved in Jenny's Sarah-Rise program certainly influenced me at the time and continues to. It was an opportunity to explore "being present" and defining it in a way that had not come up before. It offered me that beautiful/challenging stretch that constitutes personal development. Knowing so little about autism or child development, I had few expectations. The training I received opened a new door on how to really be with someone in a loving, accepting, and ultimately humbling way.

Sarah is amazing. The slow and subtle changes that started happening in the first years of the program fed that spark of hope in Jenny that fed the beautiful energy that fed the program volunteers. Sarah's curious and mischievous nature came out even as I wondered if she would ever notice me. Often, as I see it now, she was waiting for me to catch up.

Adrian

I was lucky enough to meet and hang out with Sarah relatively early on in the development of Sarah-Rise. I had just graduated from Carnegie Mellon School of Drama and received a blanket email from a teacher who knew Jenny through the Alexander Technique community, asking if any students were around for the summer who might be interested in helping with the program. I knew very little about the Son-Rise Program that inspired Jenny in her work with Sarah, but I love working (and playing) with kids and as an avowed eccentric I loved the out-of-the-box approach to working with autistic children.

When I arrived for my first session with Sarah in the Sarah-Rise room, Jenny very carefully explained the guidelines of the technique: from the moment you enter the Sarah-Rise room, you let Sarah guide the activities. If she picks out a board game and starts playing it by a totally different set of rules, it's on you to get hip to those rules. Lead with curiosity and openness; no is not an option. And with that, I went in and played with Sarah for the first time. That summer was a blur so it's difficult to recall exactly what happened in that particular session, but I remember many scenes from the Sarah-Rise room over the following months: playing with the mice from Mouse Match, wielding colorful pieces of toys in ways that I'd never imagined, throwing lots of things up in the air to watch how they'd come back down, going in with my guitar expecting to play a song for her and instead getting a lesson in how to play a guitar by slapping the strings. Oh, and LOTS of giggling. The way Sarah raises her arms and waves her hands when something really excites her—and the sheer amount of things that cause a total rush of exhilaration for her! I came to understand the Sarah-Rise room as a place of possibility and deep presence in each moment, where the strict scripts we tend to follow in our day-to-day lives could be abandoned and I could—or rather, I had to—surrender the categories and appraisals I'd come to rely on in order to participate in the world as we know it . . . sometimes the moments were hard and we'd have breakdowns and tears, but we always rode those waves together in the Sarah-Rise room, and then we'd find ourselves laughing and singing a song about mice at the other end of the session.

I know that there have been challenges big and small over the years—I read about them when I catch up on the Sarah-Rise newsletters—but Jenny has met them with a host of qualities that have made her and the whole Sarah-Rise program unstoppable: humility, humor, dedication, self-compassion, patience, communication, community, and above all love and respect for Sarah and everyone involved. As I've watched Sarah flourish in the years since that summer in Pittsburgh, I've come to marvel at what Jenny has created with Sarah (and of course with the help of Carl and Amy and so many other deeply caring family, friends, and community members) as something of a manifesto that demands a deep sense of respect for us all. Looking back, I don't see Sarah-Rise just as a novel way of getting a person with autism the care they need—it is the embodiment of truly meeting someone where they are, which if you ask me is a basic dignity that should be afforded to everyone. I wholeheartedly believe that there is much more good to be done in our world by meeting people with an openness to engage with them on their own terms and a respect and curiosity for the inevitable differences in how we all experience this weird and wild world we share. We've only got more to learn by broadening our understanding for each other and striving to make spaces that accommodate for us all.

Julia

The other day I realized that what is done in the Sarah-Rise room in terms of watching and waiting for the green light is so applicable to life. I know this is not a groundbreaking revelation, but I realize how in life it is so easy to miss the signs if we are not present and thus miss some opportunity. Being in the Sarah-Rise room really raises this to the forefront, but at the same time provides the assurance that if you miss one it's not the end of the world.

Maiti

Reflecting on my time with Sarah, I realized that while I was trying to get across ideas and lessons to her, she was teaching me at the same time. She taught me the importance of patience, simplicity, compassion, and connection. Patience helps me every day, especially through academics, and will continue to help me as I move through my challenging classes in the fall.

My time with Sarah has taught me that I can conquer what seems to be the impossible. I live a complicated life with all of my jobs, extracurricular activities, and busy family. Sarah taught me that simplicity is necessary. When things get stressful, it's okay to take a step back and give my brain time to relax with no real obligations or responsibilities.

Sarah's compassion and enthusiasm has made me realize that even the smallest of accomplishments matter and make a difference in the long run. When I go through my day with optimism and enthusiasm, I fall asleep at the end of the day happier than I would have been otherwise. With a smile on my face and celebrating my little accomplishments and those of others I find so much joy and fulfillment out of day-to-day life.

I cherish the value of connection that Sarah has taught me. I, as do most people, tend to sometimes withdraw myself and don't always engage in connecting with people. Sarah showed me the reward of connection and how special these moments are.

Sarah B.

Volunteering with Sarah taught me so much about the importance of friendship and open communication. I got involved during the earlier years of Sarah-Rise and it was a new experience for many of us to explore these unique and creative ways to have fun with a young child in such a supportive way. It was funny to see which things I tried brought a happy reaction from Sarah and which things fell flat. Sometimes I felt like we were paired in an elaborate comedy improv sketch and laughing like crazy; other times we just enjoyed looking out the window or quietly drawing shapes. I learned to be a better listener and to be clearer in my requests or explanations. Volunteering with Sarah not only was a lot of fun, but it also taught me better communication skills that helped with other friendships and even with my career.

Noah

When I first met Sarah, I wore corduroy pants, and we instantly became friends. She rushed over to me the moment I entered the room and intensely scrutinized the fabric, bubbling over with joy as she touched the ridged lines. I was so inspired by her overwhelming excitement and found myself almost reflexively joining in, genuinely appreciating the corduroy in a way I hadn't before. I was grateful to be able to immediately connect with her and was surprised it was over something I usually wouldn't give much thought to. This was the first of countless moments I shared with Sarah wherein she taught me to see her world, where so many things we may overlook are made special.

In our Sarah-Rise sessions, I was so lucky to have Sarah's trust as she continued to share her world with me, one filled with patterns, wacky scenes we'd act out, snails, book characters, endless creativity, and joyful play. With this incredibly special opportunity, I did my best to nurture her development and had the privilege of watching her grow into new skills and abilities. She learned to speak, read, and write, becoming more expressive and creative and never losing her enthusiasm and curiosity. Through all of her growth, I noticed myself changing too.

Sarah has been one of the most powerful teachers in my life. She showed me the importance of freely expressing one's inner ideas and creativity, a boundless and precious source everyone possesses. She showed me how to be patient and listen and how to appreciate even simple things like watching leaves fall or drawing patterns in a carpet. Through connecting with Sarah and learning about how she sees the world, my own world became deeply enriched. I learned to slow down and appreciate everything around me. I am so grateful for our time together and it brings me immense joy that Jenny has chosen to share her family's story with the world. I sincerely wish the thoughts and memories contained in her writing may enlighten and uplift your lives as Sarah and her family have mine.

Gregory

I met Sarah when she was three. Jenny and Carl found me through a mutual acquaintance. Sarah had a significant speech and language disorder, and I was, and still am, a speech/language therapist. By the time Sarah's family found Son-Rise and eventually set up what they deemed Sarah-Rise, we had all established a strong relationship. So, although I became a Sarah-Rise-informed clinician, I neither started nor was I sought as such.

In many ways, the very same qualities and recommendations that caused Jenny and Carl to bring me into their lives were the qualities and recommendations that caused them to pursue Son-Rise. So much of absolutely everything in the US is premised upon forcing children and people to assimilate to various standards established and often abusively enforced by families, leaders, policymakers, systems, and an overall white, cis, abled, patriarchal culture. My professional journey has led me to disavow the medical model and shed the indoctrination into Lovaas-inspired Applied Behavior Analysis and what I believe to be a larger cult of compliance and assimilationism.

I found, in Son-Rise, and with Sarah, Carl, Jenny, and all the other volunteers, a community of people who knew the value (and efficacy, mind you . . .) of social and emotional learning, of interpersonal bonds, of building trusting and loving and kind boundaries, and providing children, ourselves, and each other with warmth and a genuine desire for growth, independence, connection, and relationship.

Sarah and her family gave me permission to loosen my grasp on many of the techniques I was trained to use through my early professional life. And through the process, Sarah made progress that no clinician would ever be able to predict. What did Sarah-Rise allow all of us to do? Relax into relating to Sarah and maintaining faith in the journey. The process. Modifying and creating goals and expectations along the way because human behavior and growth is so unpredictable and wonderfully surprising, particularly for the neurodivergent person. Son-Rise allowed all of us to accept ourselves and each other, to love and support ourselves and each other as we supported and loved Sarah. The program points in a very holistic and community-based direction. There is no way to serve a person without doing harm unless we are willing and able to work on ourselves and our adult relationships and ultimately understand that our children are whole people with agency, purpose, worth, and a drive to be independent and loved.

Sarah C.

My time with Sarah has been one of the most profound teachers I've ever had. It taught me that empathy extends beyond sympathizing. If Sarah wanted to take a Play-Doh lid on and off a jar for an hour, sympathy alone wasn't going to help me understand why that was fun. I had to learn to connect with Sarah's joys and sorrows with earnestness and intentionality till I could embody them. I had to allow the rhythmic sounds of the Play-Doh lid to bring me satisfaction and enjoyment. I came to find springs of joy flowing from places that would have otherwise been dry.

It taught me that patience is an act of radical respect. I don't need to force the world around me to bend to my timetable. If Sarah needed to take fifteen seconds to answer my question, that was just fine. The cadence of her speech did not have to match mine for her words to be valuable or her thoughts to be insightful.

It taught me that I didn't need to change myself to be worthy of love. I got to spend hours meeting Sarah where she was and celebrating who she was at that moment. I got to praise her beautifully crooked smile and laugh at her bad jokes. How could I then turn around and beat myself up for how I looked or how I spoke? How could I celebrate and love all of who Sarah was without also loving myself?

It's fitting that we called the nine years I spent at the Briggs Wellington household "Sarah-Rise time." Not only was it a time to uplift Sarah but it was a time that allowed me (Sarah C.) to rise alongside her.

Sonia

I came to Pittsburgh to help my family, have a new experience and, hopefully, teach and support Sarah. I thought I'd learn how to help children with "special needs." I thought I'd learn how to follow the rules and guidance of The Son-Rise Program (which I knew very little about when I agreed to participate as I did). I thought I'd learn how to be a good teacher and caregiver. And yeah, I did learn some of that. But what I learned most of all, in my head, heart, and hands, was to be fully present and fully connected to every single thing you're doing. Don't just love/listen/show up/try/live a little—do it fully with your whole heart and head. Be there, fully, <u>every</u> <u>single</u> <u>time</u>. It is this act of being authentic and fully committed to each moment of your life, and each relationship and interaction you have, that is the basis of The Son-Rise Program, and I find it's also the most fulfilling and magical way to live.

I'll never forget the first time Sarah made eye contact with me in the Sarah-Rise room. It was a regular day. A regular session. Sarah was spinning Play-Doh container lids, and I was joining her. . . . This day seemed no different from any others. Sarah spun her lids and focused on the lids. She barely seemed to know I was there. I spun my lids and tried to be fully present with Sarah. We didn't talk, I didn't touch her, I made no demands upon her at all. I was just there, joining her in what she was doing without forcing any interactions.

Sarah was always a million times better at spinning lids than me. And while I knew there really wasn't anything to be "good" or "bad" at, I did sometimes get distracted from being fully present by noticing how I clearly was not very talented at getting small plastic lids to spin. On this particular day however, I was able to turn off that internal voice (and any other ones). I was spinning my lids. Truly and only spinning my lids. I was there with Sarah but I was there to spin my lids more than anything else. And then, as gentle and quick as a darting bird, Sarah looked at me. She looked right into my eyes with intention and interest. I was shocked! I was elated! I was overjoyed! She'd looked at ME! She noticed my presence! It was just a short moment before we both went back to spinning our lids again, but the connection had occurred. As I reflected on the experience afterward, I couldn't help noticing that this first connection occurred during a time when I was the most present and truly committed to what I was doing. That genuine love and full attention opened the door for Sarah and me to connect in ways we'd never really done before. That experience has stayed with me and continues to touch my life in so many ways.

Learning this lesson was vital for our time in the Sarah-Rise room. True connection and love simply wasn't possible otherwise. But beyond those four walls, this quality has shown itself to be helpful and exciting over and over again in my world outside the Sarah-Rise room.

For example, Jenny and I attended a CPR/first aid training together during our time running the Sarah-Rise program. The class was fine, but fairly stolid edging on boring. It wasn't until we got to the hands-on portion (where you actually practice CPR rescue breathing on the dummy) that Jenny, in all her Sarah-Rise glory, started acting like one would truly act during such a situation. She didn't quietly practice the skills they were teaching us as the rest of us were, she yelled (within reason for the size of the room of course), she was excited, she even seemed to show a little fear! Following her awesome example I did too, and that was truly the most useful CPR class I'd ever attended up until that point.

Years later I was attending another first aid and CPR class. The instructor clearly loved what he did. He was passionate about people having the skills to save lives. The attendees in the class however, per usual to my experience, barely seemed awake. So when the instructor asked me to participate in an example of how to help a choking baby, I channeled that previous experience with Jenny as well as all my time in the Sarah-Rise room.

The instructor gave me the (dummy) baby doll so I could come to him, and he'd be able to show us what to do. I took a deep breath and screamed. "My baby, oh my god, help, help, HELP!" The instructor looked shocked for just a second, then smiled and immediately responded with the alacrity and skill of a highly-trained rescue professional. The class laughed or snickered or both. But as I continued to be 100 percent committed to this experience (I stayed hysterical and got in the way until he calmly but forcefully told me to call 911 for example) I could tell most of the class was also excited, and they were truly paying attention. It was a wonderful experience for me, and I left the training with a much stronger imprint of the information and skills that had been taught.

Being a part of the Sarah-Rise journey not only played a huge part in Sarah's development and quality of life; it has also helped me become so much more true and present and loving to myself and my own journey. I will forever be grateful that I was able to be a part of this experience with Sarah, Jenny, Carl, Amy, and the entire Sarah-Rise team.

Carl

I was scared. Sarah had not been like other kids since fairly early on, but this was different. In preschool she was detaching from her class and the teachers were concerned. I felt like I saw a future where she detached from all of us, and it was terrifying. We had to make a change.

Jenny brought up the idea of doing a Son-Rise Program and I admit being skeptical. But as I read about it, watched videos of Son-Rise sessions, and came to understand it, I liked the idea more and more. I have always felt like there is nothing "wrong" with Sarah—there are all different kinds of people in this world and there is a place for Sarah and her full unique self. And, like any parent, I wanted to help her learn and grow and become successful in her own special way. Son-Rise is built around this deep respect for the person and where they are. I loved the idea of joining. It felt like giving me encouragement and permission to do what deep down felt right.

Taking this on was a big deal, but we were fortunate. We had a ton of support from our family, and especially my sister Sonia, who moved across the country to help us. And Jenny was incredible. I often said that it was like Jenny was running a small nonprofit out of our house with a clientele of one. I have continually been in awe of how complete strangers gave so much of themselves—their creativity, their time, their love—all to help Sarah.

The thoughtfulness and love of the other volunteers really came through in our Sarah-Rise meetings. We would discuss Sarah of course, but invariably we would also discuss ourselves, sometimes explicitly but often implicitly in the way we were interacting with Sarah, the things that came easily and the things that felt hard. I always came out of these meetings with new ideas for working with Sarah, and also new ideas for how to be a better me.

Throughout this process I've also been blown away by Sarah. These sessions can be exhausting, and she put in the work, hour after hour, day after day. Many things don't come easily for Sarah. But within the context of Sarah-Rise, she would practice and practice, and she would get it.

Creating a space for Sarah-Rise, where we remove all the distractions and troubles of our day and focus 100 percent of our attention on one single person, has been one of the most lasting and influential parts of this for me personally. Doing this explicitly pointed out how much of life is not this way. It is actually rare to be 100 percent focused on another person, and it has been humbling to realize how often I am with someone but not there all the way. But it is so powerful. I have tried to create similar experiences with Amy and others in my life—where I am focused on that person and nothing else—and they have been wonderful.

As Sarah progressed, I enjoyed bringing Sarah into the world within a Sarah-Rise context. It was an interesting transition for Sarah and also for me. When we were out in a public space, and she was overwhelmed and things became too much, I would sit down on the floor with her and make a little world between just the two of us. This can be hard. People are looking. I can just want her to stop and be quiet. But I quickly learned this powerful lesson that others take their cues from me. If I get upset, not only will Sarah get more upset, but others will be uncomfortable with the situation as well. If I am calm and loving and know deep down that Sarah is doing her best and this is okay, then others generally think it's okay, too. This can be challenging, and many times I have tried things that turned out not to work well. But I found it empowering to be able to bring the techniques from Sarah-Rise out beyond the walls of the room and see Sarah take on the world.

These days, sometimes Sarah will come over and talk to me while I am distracted on my phone. She doesn't tell me explicitly to put my phone away, but she makes it clear that I need to pay more attention to her. She will position herself in my view and look me directly in the eye. Turning the tables on how we used to work with her, she is making herself the most interesting part of the room. And she is.

I am so proud of Sarah. I can't wait to see what she does next.

Thank You

THERE IS A BOOK by Mo Willems called *The Thank You Book*. In the book, Gerald the elephant is concerned that Piggie will forget to thank someone if she attempts to thank everyone. I share Gerald's concern here that I might forget to thank someone or will not thank people deeply enough.

When my gratitude has no bounds, how do I put it into a few concise words? If you read this and know you were a part of our lives, but I forgot to thank you, know that I do remember you in my heart and I thank you! If you read this and think, *How did I only get a few words or an honorable mention?* know that I could write a page or two just for you.

Thank you, early readers: Janet Mather, Jack Briggs, and Elizabeth Fein. Elizabeth, you were my book midwife in the early days, taking my dreams seriously and asking insightful questions that helped me believe this could be a reality before I even knew how to make it so. Our conversations help me feel smart and remember some other part of who I am.

Thank you to my editors Janna Hockenjos and Carl Wellington. Thank you to everyone at She Writes Press. I could not have done this without you.

Thank you, John and Jane Mather, for your generous financial support. You made it possible to go for our dreams, and that is priceless.

Thank you to the schools, businesses, and institutions that helped us along the way: the Autism Treatment Center of America, Gymkhana

Gymnastics, British Swim School, The Children's Institute, Second United Presbyterian Church, Family First, Evergreen Integration, ASD Climber, the Institutes for the Achievement of Human Potential (How to Teach Your Baby to Read), the St. Anthony School Program, St. Therese, and the Facebook group for Sarah's diagnosis.

Thank you, Bears, Samahria, and Raun Kaufman, for creating The Son-Rise Program and sharing your love and wisdom. Thank you, Bryn and William Hogan, and Kate Wilde, for sharing your expertise. Thank you, fellow Son-Rise parents, for inspiring me with your journeys and celebrating ours.

Thank you, Emma Rosenthal and Jess Moritz, for the creativity and enthusiasm you brought when you provided childcare. Thank you, Caitlin Walker, for being a sitter for us since Amy was in utero until she was eleven and always helping keep my kitchen clean. Thank you, Rachel, Henry, and Nora Schlosser, for the playdates. Thank you, Janeen Meyers, for cleaning my house with care and love. Thank you, Monika Wilkinson, for helping Sarah's hands. Thank you, Kara, for Reiki and food. Thank you, Miles Harbor, for helping with the big picture. Thank you, Janine Bartholomew and David Bradley, for thinking we might be interested in How to Teach Your Baby to Read. Thank you, Jenny-Rise bodywork team, for your care of me: Priscilla Brown, Carolyn Johnston, Sheri Sable, Joel Bruening, and Timothy Kocher-Hillmer.

Thank you, Sarah's teachers and helpers: Laura Donaldson, Sarah Hultgren-Lund, Kathy O'Neil, Mary Kliwinsnki, Becky Blake, Michelle Fishell, Colleen MacDowell, Ms. Barb, Cat, Lynn, Jodi Smith, Brad Reed, Kathy Gagetta, Mrs. Z., Maryellen Begley, Kayla P., Diana G., and Katie Palumbo. Thank you to those of you who helped me find volunteers: ASD Climber, The Friendship Circle, Sabina Dietrick, Priscilla Brown, Noah Freedman, Adrian Enscoe, Janet Feindel, Tommy Costello, Joanna Winograd, and Ilyssa Ringold.

Thank you to my wonderful team of Amy volunteers: Diane Rudov, Laura Scott, Jennifer Tober, Mayalena Maher, Cara and Zoe

Costello, Adam Coleman, and Mary Lenox. Thank you to my amazing team of Sarah volunteers: Julia Roberson, Laura Scott, Adrian Enscoe, Sarah Belousov, Marilyn Carpenter, Maiti Keen, Noah Freedman, Shephaly Soni, Katya Stepanov, Jason Corvia, Michelle Gonoude, Zoya Demashnev, Abby Cryan, Maddy Ruder, Sheri Sable, Kelley Kallon, and Amanda Schmidt. Thank you, Megan Simpson, for the outreaches and inspiration.

Thank you, Anna Rosati. You bring so much light and wonder and mental well-being to our whole family that it is hard to imagine life without you, especially during the pandemic. Thank you, Sarah Ceurvorst (aka Sarah C.), for bringing an incredible amount of love, joy, and creativity to our lives for so many years. You are an absolute blessing. Thank you for the multitude of drawings. Thank you, Gregory Del Duca, for helping Sarah amplify her voice from the moment you met her, when she had hardly any spoken language. Still, you heard her. You told her you heard her. That first moment is forever cemented in my heart.

Thank you, Erika and Gretchen Troutman, for being my best friends and soul sisters for this lifetime and however many others we have shared. When we first met, I thought, *Oh, finally!* even though I was only four. I knew you were the friends I had been waiting for. Thank you for your support through everything.

Thank you, Nancy Wellington, for your incredible sewing and making so many clothing dreams come true. Thank you, David Wellington, for letting Sarah play in your minivan for hours. Thank you both for the various weeks of care allowing Carl and me to travel just the two of us. Thank you, Dad/Jack Briggs, for always having an ear if I need it and for sending pictures of the chain mail you made, porcupine quill art, and pavement maps that you painted whenever I ask. Thank you for the week you came to Pittsburgh as my support person. Thank you, Cinda Crane, for your Grammy magic, and for knowing when to use it. Thank you for asking me what I need for me and for the playful energy you bring wherever you go. Thank you, Brian Briggs, for the memes and calls. Thank you, Ralph Purvis, for your frequent email support of my updates, for letting Sarah help you make pancakes, and for teaching her about the specific parts of cars that I don't know the name for.

Thank you, Mom/Janet Mather, for all the phone calls that helped me keep my head above water. Thank you for your unwavering, enthusiastic, persistent unconditional love. Thank you for coming with me to take care of Sarah when I did some of my Alexander Technique training. Thank you for coming with me to take care of Amy when I did the Son-Rise Program training weeks. Thank you for coming to take care of me after I had my hip replaced! Thank you for enthusiastically replying to or commenting on every single Sarah-Rise Update and for reading many versions of this book.

Thank you, Sonia Wellington, for helping after Amy was born, helping with Sarah when I did my Son-Rise Program training, and uprooting your life in Seattle to come be my person. "Assistant" doesn't feel like an adequate term. I cannot imagine a better helper and companion for those intense days of Sarah-Rise and GAPS and parenting life in general.

Thank you, Carl, for being by my side through *everything*. For loving me even when I am at my worst and my lowest. For tickling my brain with your sense of humor and for enjoying how riotously funny I find it when certain grammar or spelling rules go awry. Thank you for your thoughtful editing and feedback regarding this book—that was a brave and loving thing to do. Thank you for being a work of art as a human being and a parent. It is an honor to parent by your side.

Thank you, Amy, for being the most amazing sister for Sarah that I could have dreamed possible. Thank you for your creativity and the warm sun of your being.

Thank you, Sarah, for your sparkle and your perseverance.

Thank you for showing us all how much is possible.

Resources and Recommended Reading

Resources

Anat Baniel Method: https://www.anatbanielmethod.com

Autism Treatment Center of America: https://www.autismtreatment-center.org

Evergreen Integration: http://www.evergreenintegration.com

Megan Simpson: https://www.pathfinderneuro.com

Sarah-Rise Updates: https://www.watchingsarahrise.com

Recommended Reading

Autism Breakthrough: The Groundbreaking Method That Has Helped Families All Over the World by Raun Kaufman

Autistic Logistics: A Parent's Guide to Tackling Bedtime, Toilet Training, Tantrums, Hitting, and Other Everyday Challenges by Kate Wilde

How to Teach Your Baby to Read by Glenn Doman and Janet Doman

Listening Effectively to Children by Patty Wipfler

Miracle in Slow Motion: From Autism Diagnosis to an Exciting Future by Sally Wagter

Son-Rise: The Miracle Continues by Barry Neil Kaufman

Special Children, Challenged Parents: The Struggles and Rewards of Raising a Child with a Disability by Robert Naseef

What You Can Do Right Now to Help Your Child with Autism by Jonathan Levy

About the Author

JENNY BRIGGS has a BA in English Literature from Swarthmore College. She lives in Pittsburgh, PA with her husband and two daughters.

Looking for your next great read?

We can help!

Visit www.shewritespress.com/next-read
or scan the QR code below for a list
of our recommended titles.

She Writes Press is an award-winning
independent publishing company founded to
serve women writers everywhere.